Vaughan Williams

Read March 2011

THE SAXON SHORE

A Handbook

A dry read but an invaluable source book full of references

A shame is that the author uses Latin terms without translation or explanation

COMES LITORIS SAXON PER BRITANIAM.

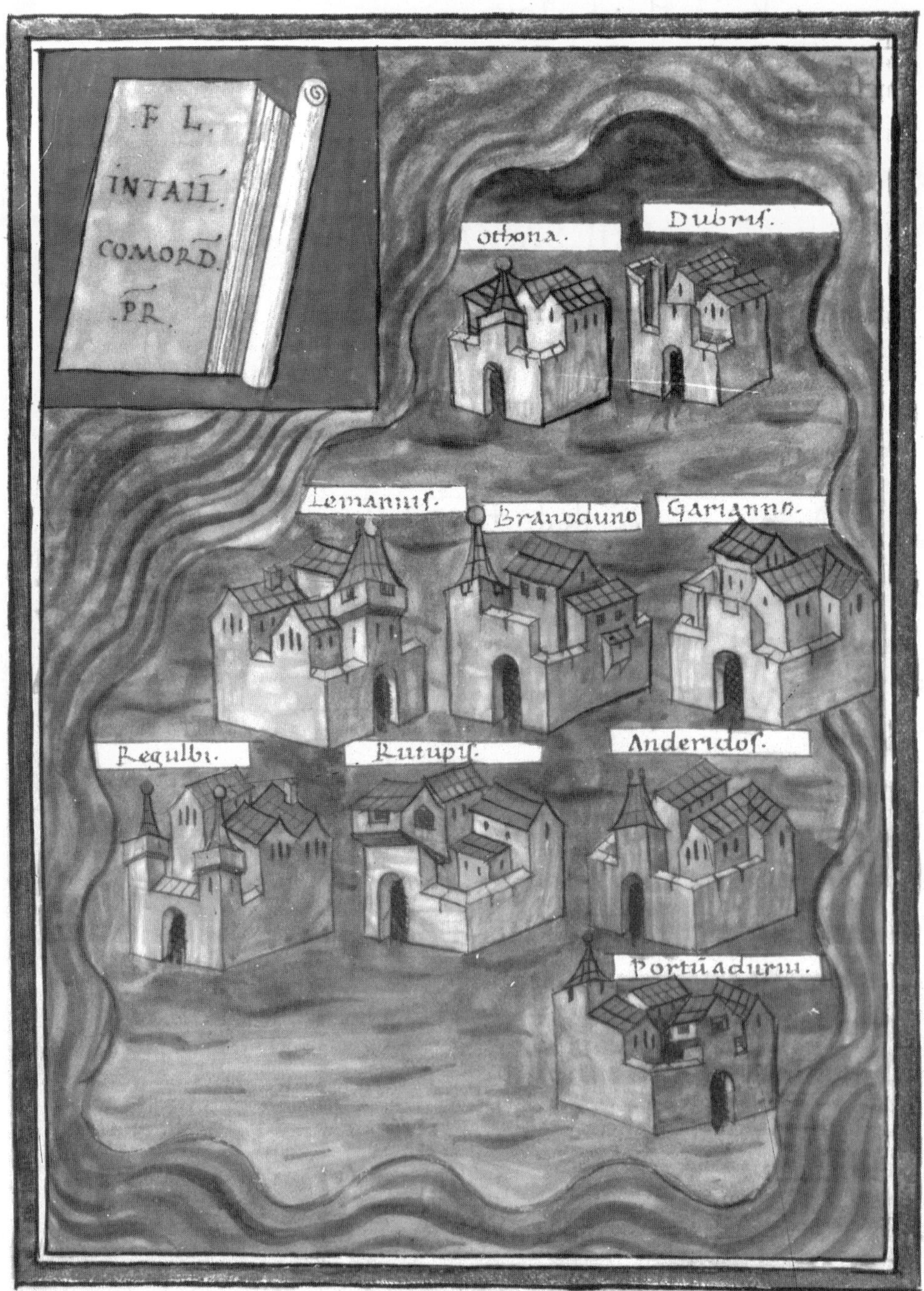

THE SAXON SHORE

A Handbook

Edited by
Valerie A. Maxfield

Contributors
P. Bennett, T. Blagg, R. Brulet, P. Burnham,
H. Chapman, H. Cleere, S.C. Hawkes, S. Johnson,
J.C. Mann, J. Munby, R. Reece, A.D. Saunders

EXETER STUDIES IN HISTORY No. 25

Produced on the occasion of the 15th International Congress of Roman Frontier Studies, held at Canterbury, 2-10 September 1989

First published by the University of Exeter 1989

EXETER STUDIES IN HISTORY

ISBN 0 85989 330 8
ISSN 0260 8626

Frontispiece: the Insignia of the Count of the Saxon Shore (Bodleian Ms. Canon Misc. 378, fol. 153 verso).

Contents

Foreword

More than a decade has elapsed since the appearance of the last major publication devoted exclusively to the subject of the Saxon Shore and its problems (Johnston ed. 1977). These have been years of considerable archaeological activity, with the survey, excavation and publication of reports on several of the individual fort sites, as well as research into various of the associated problems, geographical and historical. This handbook is designed to present an up-to-date survey of the Saxon Shore and its setting in time and place. A series of essays first sets the scene, discussing the nature and development of the Saxon Shore itself, its geographical setting, its forts and its command, cross-Channel parallels and post-Roman history. There follows a gazetteer of sites, summarising (with plans) the current state of knowledge about each of the individual shore forts as well as the two adjacent cities of London and Canterbury.

The authors and publisher would like to thank the following institutions and individuals for providing and permitting the reproduction of illustrations (copyright reserved to these institutions and individuals in all cases): Bodleian Library, frontispiece, figs 9 and 16; Cambridge Committee for Aerial Photography, front cover photograph; English Heritage, figs 1, 32, 45, 46, 47 and 48; Kent Archives Office fig. 34; Norfolk Archaeological Unit of the Norfolk Museums Service, fig. 42 (illustrator / surveyor Derek A. Edwards); Society of Antiquaries of London & Prof. Barry Cunliffe, figs 54, 55, and 56; Society for the Promotion of Roman Studies, figs 59 and 60. Fig. 35 is Crown Copyright material housed in the Public Record Office, document ref. MR1342. It is reproduced by permission of the Controller HMSO.

Thanks are due to Stephen Johnson for general assistance with the preparation of the volume, to Paul Wright for translating the article by Raymond Brulet, to Jennifer Warren for help with typing and to Tracey Croft and Karen Guffogg for help with the production of illustrations. Mike Rouillard and Mike Dobson played a very major part in the production, working on the graphics and computer typesetting respectively. The cover design is by Mike Rouillard.

This volume has been produced on the occasion of the 15th International Congress of Roman Frontier Studies which takes place from 2-10 September 1989 in the University of Kent at Canterbury and whose members will make visits to several of the Saxon Shore forts, as well as to museums and monuments in London, provincial capital in the Roman period, and Canterbury, administrative centre of the *civitas* of the Cantiaci.

Notes on Contributors

MR PAUL BENNETT is Director of the Canterbury Archaeological Trust.

DR T. BLAGG is Staff Tutor in Archaeology in the Department of Continuing Education, University of Kent.

PROFESSOR RAYMOND BRULET is Researcher at the Centre de Recherches d'Archéologie Nationale, in the University of Louvain.

DR C.PAUL BURNHAM is Senior Lecturer in Land Resources Science at Wye College, University of London.

DR HUGH CHAPMAN is General Secretary of the Society of Antiquaries of London.

DR HENRY CLEERE is Director of the Council for British Archaeology.

DR SONIA CHADWICK HAWKES is Lecturer in European Archaeology, Institute of Archaeology, University of Oxford.

DR J.S. JOHNSON is a Principal Inspector of Ancient Monuments, Academic Editor, English Heritage.

PROFESSOR J.C. MANN is Emeritus Professor of the History and Archaeology of Roman Britain in the University of Durham.

DR VALERIE A. MAXFIELD is Senior Lecturer in Archaeology in the University of Exeter.

MR JULIAN MUNBY is an architectural historian who has been working on medieval Portchester and the history of antiquarianism.

DR RICHARD REECE is Senior Lecturer in Archaeology in the Institute of Archaeology, University College, London.

MR A.D. SAUNDERS is Chief Inspector of Ancient Monuments and Historic Buildings, English Heritage.

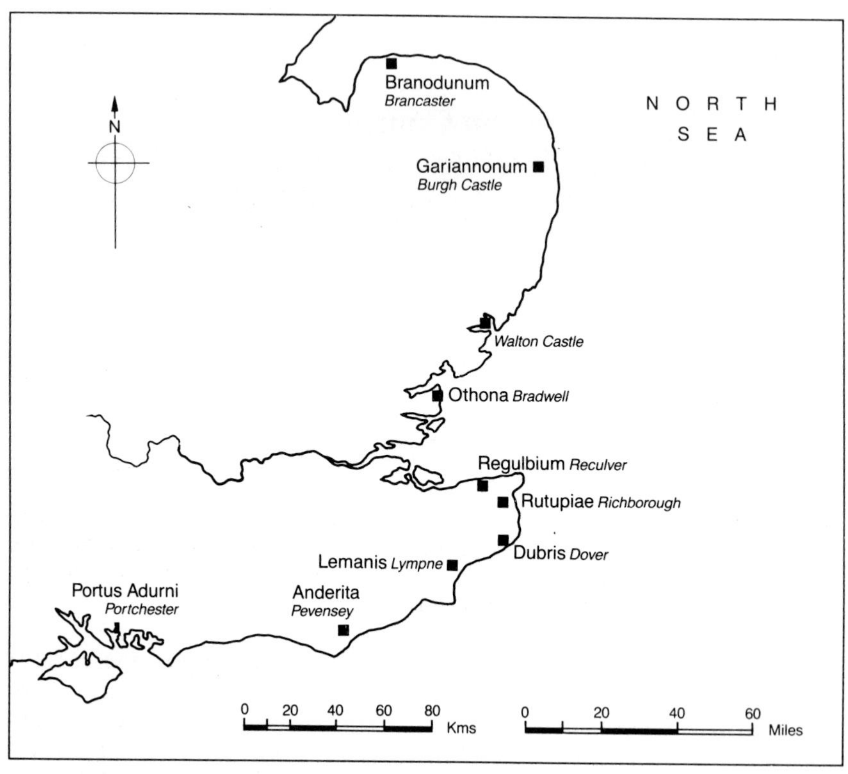

Fig. 1 Map of the Saxon Shore forts.

1

THE HISTORICAL DEVELOPMENT OF THE SAXON SHORE

The name 'Saxon Shore' appears only in the *Notitia Dignitatum*, a document drawn up about AD 408. The Saxon Shore is, in that document, primarily a list of army units stationed at sites in south-eastern Britain. But both the Notitia Dignitatum and the Saxon Shore must be handled with great care.

The existence of the Notitia Dignitatum has resulted in the emergence of a number of mistaken ideas. In the chapters of the frontier commands, each unit is accompanied by a fort name. This has been interpreted too readily to mean that, at all periods, there was one unit, no more and no less, in each fort, a notion which has obstructed recognition of the fact that the normal situation for any unit, in any period of history, is that it is fragmented, and distributed in several different places. (For example, a new document from Vindolanda shows that, *c.* AD 90/100, of the 761 men of *cohors I Tungrorum*, at least 336 were at another fort, probably Corbridge.) If a unit in any official list is assigned to any particular place, in all probability that place will merely be the location of unit HQ, nothing more. Some elements are quite likely to be elsewhere.

Another idea that has inevitably emerged from the study of the Notitia Dignitatum is that in some sense the Saxon Shore was an entirely new creation of the fourth century. This view is reinforced by the fact that under its commander are listed nine units, seven of which are totally new to the army of Britain as known in the Principate. This view is reinforced even further by the appearance of the Saxon Shore forts themselves, mostly built in a style totally foreign to that of the military structures of the northern British frontier, even northern structures of fourth century date. The army of the *dux Britanniarum* in the north remained excessively conservative in this respect, eschewing particularly the robust projecting bastions which characterise most of the Saxon Shore forts (and most fourth century forts on the continent of Europe), except on the river-front (and only the river-front) of the legionary fortress of York, where indeed this looks more like the *dux*, ensconced in the legionary fortress, putting up an impressive facade to outface the *praeses* of the York province, established in the *colonia* across the river.

But the view is of course supported most of all by the fact that nowhere else does the name Saxon Shore appear, much less the title Count of the Saxon Shore. But a closer look, possible now in view of the new evidence that is becoming available, indicates increasingly that the situation is primarily one of continuity: continuity between the *classis Britannica* and the dispositions discernible in the late Empire.

It is all too easy to see the emergence of piracy in the late empire as a totally new phenomenon. But the maritime activity in the Channel, not least that of the Veneti which Caesar noted (*de Bello Gallico* 3, 8-16) was no doubt paralleled in the North Sea, and as with the later Vikings or the modern boogiemen of Indonesian waters, it is often difficult to tell where merchant ends and pirate begins. It is probably fair to think that piracy did not exist in the Channel or the North Sea during the Principate precisely because the *classis Britannica* did exist.

Some indications of the role and importance of the British fleet have been given in the past, albeit mainly in relation to Britain, and especially to military operations in Britain. There is as yet no evidence that it was felt necessary to provide a fleet on the north coast of Gaul before the time of Claudius, but the building of a lighthouse at Boulogne by Gaius presages increased official involvement, culminating in the invasion of Britain in AD 43. That a ship's captain who was a freedman of either Claudius or Nero was buried at Boulogne (CIL XIII 3542) is clear evidence of the early establishment of a fleet base there, although the name *classis Britannica* is not known before the Flavian period (Digest 36.1.48). The fleet's involvement in the operations of Agricola and Septimius Severus needs no reiteration, although these operations are only known to us in some small detail because they attracted the attention of Tacitus, Dio and Herodian. Yet the fleet must have been employed also in the operations of Ulpius Marcellus, and probably those of Lollius Urbicus. Its role in transport and supply in time of war is well established, although the inscription recording a steersman (*gubernator*) of VI Victrix at York (RIB 653) reminds us that ships may well have been operated by many other units.

Members of the British fleet appear in other roles. A vexillation was concerned in the construction of a building (probably a granary) in the original Hadrianic fort at Benwell on Hadrian's Wall (RIB 1340), while, probably at a later date, other men from the fleet were involved in building work along the Wall further to the west (RIB 1944-5, and perhaps 1394). The general employment of men from the fleets in road-building is well established ([Ps. Hyginus] *de Munitionibus Castrorum* 24), and although not yet attested, it is possible that some roads in Britain were built by men from the *classis Britannica*. Members of the fleets could be chosen for such specialised work as building an aqueduct (CIL VIII 2728 = ILS 5795). The two Italian fleets had their own camps in

Rome, to house the men who operated the awnings of the capital's amphitheatres (SHA *Commodus* 15.6). For the *classis Britannica* we have further the large body of evidence for its involvement with iron-working in the Weald.

Men from the fleets could be released for such useful employment because they had few strictly naval duties to perform. But this does not mean that the fleets were surplus to requirements. Without fleets to patrol the sea, the Mediterranean had been a happy hunting ground for pirates in the first century BC. The menace had been removed by Pompey after vigorous action, only to reappear during the Civil Wars. It was totally repressed by Augustus, but it is significant that of the fleets which he established, those of Ravenna and Misenum as well as those of Syria and Egypt (the latter with a detachment in Mauretania Caesariensis) remained in existence throughout the Principate: only that based at Forum Julii in Narbonensis was disbanded. The mere presence of these fleets was enough to prevent the resurgence of piracy, at least before the great military and economic collapse of the third century.

They could not however have done this if they had not been maintained as effective fighting forces. In particular, the fact that men from the Misene, Ravenna and British fleets were employed along with cavalry from Africa and Mauretania in scouting operations in Pannonia during the Danube Wars of Marcus (AE 1956, 124) reminds us that no military force can operate effectively, whether in peace or in war, without an efficient system of intelligence-gathering, whether by uniformed scouts or by agents in plain clothes, an aspect of Roman military operations which has been grossly and mistakenly neglected. We need not assume that the naval scouting vessels operating off the British coasts, described by Vegetius (IV.37) - hulls, sails and rigging camouflaged sea-green, as also the men's uniforms - were a new invention of the fourth century. Only such vigilant operations will have kept down North Sea and Channel piracy before the third century crisis. Conversely, because the sea was thus efficiently secured, other men of the British fleet could be released for construction and other work. However it must be emphasized that for the fleet, construction, as well as transport and supply, were secondary to its prime military function.

Archaeology is gradually revealing that there was much more to the *classis Britannica* than its depot, presumably its headquarters, at Boulogne. Structurally, we now have the magnificent *classis Britannica* fort at Dover. At Lympne, a dedication of *c.* AD 135/145 by a prefect of the fleet (RIB 66) combines with stamped tiles to argue for a fort or depot of the second century, yet to be identified on the ground. At Portchester and Pevensey, *classis Britannica* tiles also suggest depots still to be located, while at Reculver there are suggestions of a first century fortlet. There is an absence of tiles of the fleet north of the Thames, but this does not necessarily mean that the fleet had no bases there. At Boulogne, tombstones of members of the fleet who can be assigned to the first century (CIL XIII 3541-4) are followed by others of second (3540) and third century date (3545-6). The latest reference to the *classis Britannica* by name appears in a tombstone of the reign of Philip (AD 244-9) from Arles (CIL XII 686 = ILS 2911).

Whether the *classis Britannica* needed significant reinforcement before the crisis of the mid-third century is debateable. Unfortunately, something of a red herring was introduced by early attempts to date the military building inscription from Reculver (Richmond 1961). A suggested date in the second decade of the third century led to the assumption that the Saxon threat to the east and south coasts, known later in the third century, had in fact appeared shortly after AD 210. But the inscription cannot be so closely dated (Mann 1977b). The governor named (his cognomen was Rufinus), with the title *consularis*, will earlier (like most senators in the emperor's service) almost certainly have held not an ordinary consulship but a suffect consulship, and must thus be almost impossible to identify (Degrassi 1952). The term *consularis* dates the inscription to anywhere between the early years of Marcus and the reign of Diocletian, the period precisely for which the names of hardly any suffect consuls are known.

If the Reculver inscription dates before the middle of the third century, then it could represent simple construction of a fort for the British fleet, similar to that at Dover, and illustrate that that organization was flourishing and on top of its job. What is interesting and important is of course that Reculver has produced tiles of *cohors I Baetasiorum*, a unit well known in the north, last heard of at Maryport in the later second century. (The unit survived at Reculver, to appear there in the Notitia Dignitatum.) It is interesting and important because the known and excavated fort at Reculver conforms to the regular plan of auxiliary forts as found on the northern frontier. It has narrow stone defensive walls backed by an earth rampart, rounded corners with internal corner towers, and an internal plan of headquarters building, barracks and so on, of the expected form. The only other Saxon Shore fort known to conform to this plan (so far as it has been excavated) is Brancaster. This has now produced tiles of *cohors I Aquitanorum*, another unit drafted in from the northern frontier. Because these two forts have plans similar to those of forts on Hadrian's Wall, it could be argued that they are earlier in date than the other Saxon Shore forts, which show all the characteristics of late Roman military architecture - very high and thick walls with no internal rampart, massive external towers, mostly rounded in plan, and few, if any, substantial internal buildings.

This could be true. Reculver and Brancaster could have been built in the late second or early third century to house units called from the northern frontier to assist the *classis Britannica* in its task of securing the North Sea. However, the architecture of these two forts is not in fact any proof of early date. Given the architectural conservatism of the army on the northern frontier, the form of Reculver and Brancaster could merely indicate that *cohors I Baetasiorum* and *cohors I Aquitanorum*, on moving south, simply brought with them the familiar building styles that they were used to. This could have been as late as the later third century, contemporary with the construction of other forts in the 'late Roman' style by units brought in from the continent.

What is most important in the whole of this subject is the great decline that the Roman world in general suffered in the 50 years between the end of the Severan dynasty and the accession of Diocletian. From this time, all the frontiers of the empire came under pressure, pressure such as they had never known before. The empire, 1000 years after the foundation of Rome, was, at last, no longer the confident, expansive force that it had been. The peoples who lived around its borders now took the initiative and began to press in on its frontiers.

As far as the North Sea is concerned, a hint of increased naval activity is contained in the coins of Postumus with the legends *Neptuno Comiti* and *Neptuno Reduci*, suggesting successful operations in the North Sea (RIC Postumus 30, 76, 214). If so, then the *classis Britannica* will certainly have been involved. Similarly with Carinus (AD 283-4), *bella sub Arcto* sound like naval operations (Nemesianus *Cynegetica* 69-70).

Because of his later bid for the throne, the sources make a great song and dance over Carausius, given command against Saxon raiders some time in the 280s. There is however no absolute certainty that he was not already in office before the accession of Diocletian. Even more important, there is no certainty that he was the first commander whose task it was to deal with Frankish and Saxon raids *per tractum Belgicae et Armoricae*, in the words of Eutropius (9.21). What is clear is that his headquarters were at Boulogne. He was surely prefect of the *classis Britannica*, whether that command yet had a new name or not.

Last heard of in the 240s, the *classis Britannica* had been strengthened to deal with the Frankish-Saxon threat, whenever precisely it was that it became serious. The coins which Carausius produced show that by the 280s, if not earlier, he (or a predecessor) had had his command strengthened by a large force of legionary detachments, at least nine in all (RIC Carausius, passim). From Britannia Superior came paired detachments of II Augusta and XX VV; from Germania Inferior, I Minervia and XXX Ulpia; from Germania Superior, VIII Augusta and XXII Primigenia; from Moesia Superior, IV Flavia and VII Claudia; a single detachment came from the 'central reserve' legion, II Parthica. If these were detachments of the normal size (two cohorts or about 1000 men from each legion), this would add 9000 infantry to the forces at the disposal of the commander of the British fleet - a formidable force, whose size may well have encouraged Carausius to make his bid for the throne. (For two-cohort detachments: CIL VIII 8440=ILS 4195; 1000 men from each legion: CIL X 5829=ILS 2726).

Whatever the date at which effective measures against the Franks and Saxons began to be urgently needed, successive prefects of the *classis Britannica* reinforced their command with new forts. In the absence of precise literary evidence and of inscriptions giving a close date for the construction or rebuilding of individual forts, it is difficult to describe exactly the progress of this reinforcement. Construction of the known forts at Richborough and Lympne probably began before the time of Carausius, judging by the coin evidence. Others, such as Portchester, may have been added by Carausius himself. Only in the case of Pevensey does the construction of the visible fort seem to have occurred at a later date. Archaeology does not allow of greater precision as yet. Equally, however, the incomplete archaeological evidence that we possess may be misleading us: the nine known forts can be seen as a coherent group (as discussed below), whose unity could logically require construction of all of them to a single plan, in a single building programme.

The history of the rebellion of Carausius and Allectus does not need to be retold. Clearly, once the area under the control of Carausius was reduced to the island of Britain only, the unity of the command of the *classis Britannica* was broken. Certainly Carausius and Allectus may well have hoped to employ and reinforce forts standing on the shore of Britain as a means of defence against the re-establishment of control by Diocletian and his colleagues. If they did so, we really have no way of proving it.

Only after the invasion of Britain by Constantius I in 297 can the command have been reunified. That it was so re-united in or after 297 is by no means certain. A continental command based on Boulogne may have been re-established, while it is perfectly possible that the forts in Britain simply came for a time under the control of the *praesides* of the provinces in which they lay. The process of separation of military command (under *duces*) from civilian control (remaining under the *praesides*), although begun by Diocletian, took a long time to cover the whole empire, being virtually complete only by the end of the reign of Constantine (Mann 1977a, 11-12). As far as concerns the date of the creation of a new military command in south-east Britain, much depends on how soon the fear of Frankish and Saxon raiding returned. Nevertheless, it seems improbable that lesser endeavours were now made, than had been the case in the Principate, to secure the North Sea and the Channel. Perhaps the *classis Britannica* was simply re-formed, based on Boulogne and operating as before on both sides of the Channel, and occupying some or all of the newly-built forts. Whether the command was still known by the same name is another matter.

Until recently a survey such as this would have simply continued chronologically up to the events supposed to have taken place in 367, more precisely an attack by the Saxons in that year (see now Bartholomew 1984). But it may well be that no such attack took place then and that what Ammianus is referring to (26.4.5; 27.8.5) are the campaigns against the Saxons around the mouth of the Rhine in AD 370 (28.5.8.; cf. 30.7.8). There is no absolutely certain evidence of a Saxon attack on Britain in the mid-fourth century.

This being so, the most profitable course at this stage will probably be to start with the relevant chapters of the Notitia Dignitatum and work backwards. In that document the Saxon Shore is actually mentioned in three places. In addition to the chapter of the Count with his nine units in Britain, there appears, under the control of the *dux tractus Armoricani* (Not. Dig. Oc. 37.14):

> *tribunus cohortis primae novae Armoric(an)ae, Grannona in litore Saxonico*

Similarly, under the *dux Belgicae secundae* (Not. Dig. Oc. 38.7):

> *equites Dalmatae, Marcis in litore Saxonico*

It is worth remembering that the Notitia Dignitatum is not an operational handbook, listing units in Order of Battle. It is an administrative handbook, primarily concerned with the peacetime organization of units as it relates to pay, supply and similar matters. The *cohors I Armoricana* and the *equites Dalmatae* listed above clearly came under the administrative control of the *duces* concerned. But the definition *in litore Saxonico* could well mean that they came under the operational control of the Count of the Saxon Shore. These entries are not necessarily evidence that the Saxon Shore had once formally covered both shores of the Channel and had been later confined to the island. We may note in passing that earlier the *classis Britannica*, while clearly in whole or in part subject operationally to the governor of Britain, if its headquarters were at Boulogne then administratively it will have come under the control of the governor of Gallia Belgica. Thus, for example, diplomas for men of the British fleet will have been issued through him and not through the governor of Britain.

These two commands which appear in the Notitia Dignitatum alongside the Saxon Shore seem, like the latter, to appear for the first time. It is important to note that both are orientated towards the sea. Under the *dux* of Belgica Secunda are listed only three units: the *equites Dalmatae*, already mentioned, stationed 'in the Saxon Shore'; a fleet based on the Somme; and a unit of Nervii, based on a harbour, Portus Epatiaci. The forces of Belgica Secunda, although so near the Rhine, are in no sense a reinforcement of the German frontier.They are clearly intended as a defence of the Belgian coast. Similarly with the *dux* of the Tractus Armoricanum: he is credited with responsibility for five provinces, Aquitania I and II and Lugdunensis II, III and IV (Not. Dig. Oc. 37.24-29). Of these, Aquitania II and Lugdunensis II and III have long coastlines, while Aquitania I and Lugdunensis IV (Senonia), lie immediately inland from them. The ten bases which are assigned to him can be identified as places on the north or west coasts of Gaul, or (in the case of Osismi, Carhaix) at no great distance from the sea. But it is worth looking more closely at the words of the Notitia Dignitatum (37.24, cf. 13):

> *extenditur tamen tractus Armoricani et Nervicani limitis per provincias quinque.*

This fuller title reminds us at once of the words of Eutropius (9.21) in describing the command assigned to Carausius:

> *cum apud Bononiam per tractum Belgicae et Armoricae pacandum mare accepisset, quod Franci et Saxones infestabant.*

It looks as though the command which had been the sphere of the *classis Britannica* was simply transformed, in the later third century, into that of a *dux tractus Belgicae et Armoricae*, an echo of which survives in the Notitia's words (Oc. 37.24), *tractus Armoricani et Nervicani limitis*. But by the time when the Notitia as we have it was composed, this command had been divided into two, the more vulnerable coast of Belgica Secunda now having its own *dux*. A clear case seems to be presented for this straightforward history.

The problem is, of course, how the command we know as the Saxon Shore fits in with this sequence. The command of the *classis Britannica* had manifestly extended to the north side of the Channel. Perhaps the sphere of operations of Carausius and other commanders *per tractum Belgicae et Armoricae* also extended north of the Channel, although these words do not suggest it. More probably, it may be thought, the 'Saxon Shore' was hived off at an early stage, as a command covering the south and east coasts of Britain, and under a separate *dux*.

Admittedly, what we know of the title *dux* raises a question. Where the title *dux* appears before the time of Diocletian, as with the *dux ripae* on the Euphrates or the *dux per Africam*, the command did not survive beyond his reign. (P. Dura 97, lines 21, 23 and 24; cf. Gilliam 1941, 158 (AD 245-8) for the *dux ripae* on the Euphrates: it did not survive the fall of Dura in AD 253; CIL VIII 12296=ILS 2774 for the *dux per Africam*: date in 250s given by CIL VIII 21000 + AE 1900, 125 + Libyca I, 1953, 181ff. IRT 97 records a short-lived third century ducal command on the Tripolitanian frontier.) Under Diocletian, military command on the frontiers apparently everywhere reverted to the *praesides* of the frontier provinces. Then new ducates began to be formed, then and only then on a permanent basis, but only very gradually: no more than three can be shown to have come into existence before Diocletian's abdication (CIL VIII 764 = ILS 4103, cf. CIL III 14450; CIL III 10981; *Acta SS Sergii et Bacchi*, *Annalecta Bollandiana* XIV, 1895, 375ff; perhaps a fourth in CIL XIII 3672). This being so, it may well be that under Diocletian previous developments in the Channel were swept away, and a new start made with totally new commands.

This is a wholly unsatisfactory state of affairs for the historian, but this is where he is placed by the character of the evidence as it is at present known. However, so far as the Saxon Shore is concerned, there is one ray of light, which applies to the situation in 367. Whether or not an invasion by the Picts and their allies took place in that year, and whether or not the Franks and Saxons attacked the Gallic shore, or the British coast, what Ammianus says on two points is crystal clear (27.8.1-10). Firstly, it was in Britain in that year that some serious crisis developed, and it was to Britain that Theodosius was sent to deal with that crisis. Secondly, in the course of that crisis in Britain the *comes maritimi tractus* was killed. There cannot then be any serious doubt that the *maritimum tractus* lay in Britain: the name is either a 'polite' literary form of the uncouth and uneuphonius *litus Saxonicum* or, less probably, it is an earlier name for the same command.

The fact that in 367 Nectaridus was *comes* and not *dux* does not necessarily represent any great problem. That the threat from the Franks and the Saxons had been growing in the 360s seems clear from the way in which Ammianus mentions the fact as early as 364 (26.4.5). In this survey of the state of affairs at the beginning of the reign of Valentinian, he is drawing attention to one of the great problems which that emperor faced, and looks forward to its great resolution in 369/70. Whatever the precise significance of the title Francicus in 369 (CIL VI 1175 = ILS 771), the defeat of the Saxons recorded in 370 (28.5.8), however dubious the means employed, was to be hailed as one of the prime achievements of Valentinian's reign, in the summary which Ammianus supplies after his death in 375 (30.7.8). It is significant therefore that, in the face of this threat, the two ducates of upper and lower Germany were in 365 combined under the control of Charietto, *per utramque Germaniam comes* (27.1.2), an arrangement apparently repeated, or perpetuated, in 370 when, just before the climactic battle against the Saxons, command of the same ducates was assigned to the *comes* Nannienus (28.5.1). In the face of pressure from Franks and Saxons, it would hardly be surprising if in 367 the command of a ducate on the coast of Britain were entrusted to a *comes rei militaris*. As with the German commands (which reverted to ordinary ducal commands after the crisis was over) this may have been a temporary situation: Nectaridus could well have been *comes et dux*. This is also suggested by the fact that Theodosius had a *dux*, Dulcitius, brought in from the continent in 367/8: surely he was to replace the dead *comes maritimi tractus*? Admittedly, Ammianus may be here merely using *dux* to mean 'general' in an informal sense, and it is true that the seniority accorded to the *comes litoris Saxonici* in the lists in the Notitia Dignitatum suggests that the post could have been of full comitival rank in 367 (Mann 1976, 6).

However this may be, Saxon pressure seems to have subsided after 370. Only at the very end of the fourth century, if we may believe Claudian (*de laudibus Stilichonis* 2.247-55), do the Saxons seem to have re-emerged to threaten Britain. But the threat mounted, to culminate in the attacks of the 'barbarians from across the Rhine' (Zosimus 6.5.2-3) which paralleled the end of Roman rule in Britain in 410 (Chronicler of 452, s.a. 410; cf. Procopius *Vandal War* 1.2.37). The Notitia Dignitatum lists what the bureaucrats of Ravenna believed to be the situation in Britain in 408. This represents the latest stage in the effort to maintain Britain as part of the empire. The chapter of the Count of the Saxon Shore no doubt represents theory rather than the practice of AD 408, so far as details are concerned. For example, archaeological evidence suggests that both Lympne and Portchester had by then ceased to hold the military garrison credited to them by the Notitia. Carelessness, or corrupt practice, could equally account for their names still appearing on the list.

In contrast, men from Pevensey seem to appear elsewhere - a *classis Anderetianorum* at Paris (Not. Dig. Oc. 42.23), a field army unit in Gaul (*Anderetiani*: Not. Dig. Oc. 7.100), a frontier unit in Upper Germany (*milites Anderetiani*: Not. Dig. Oc. 41.17). Even if all these units derive from Pevensey (Anderita), it does not follow that the site must have been deserted when the Notitia lists were compiled. Even after the departure of detachments carrying with them the name of the fort (cf. the Petuerienses at Derventio: Not. Dig. Oc. 40.31) the Abulci could well have survived, and been reinforced, at Pevensey. Alternatively, of course, the Abulci could have replaced an earlier unit as the garrison of Pevensey.

Two final aspects require discussion. First the question whether 'Saxon Shore' means 'the coast subject to attack by the Saxons' or 'the coast settled by Saxons'. This string of forts, even if it had been built for some other purpose - which seems hardly likely - was clearly employed during the fourth century, and whether efficiently or not, in some defensive fashion, against attack from the sea: such attack can only have come from

Saxons, with or without Frankish allies. The Saxon Shore was threatened with attack by Saxons. Surely then the name 'Saxon Shore' means 'the shore threatened with attack by Saxons', and this is true whether or not it was also settled by other Saxons, or other Germans.

Second, study of the sequence of units and forts as listed in the Count's chapter in the Notitia suggests that at some stage at least an attempt was made to create a coherent practical organisation. If for the moment we leave out of account the first fort on the surviving list, Othona, we have the following sequence of places (if we accept that Richborough and Pevensey are correctly restored, transferring the names from the insignia, and that Portchester is Portus Adurni):

14. Dover	18. Reculver
15. Lympne	19. Richborough
16. Brancaster	20. Pevensey
17. Burgh Castle	21. Portchester

Grouping these places in pairs (as first observed by Stevens 1941a, 138 note 2), and noting whether each is in a harbour or is merely a place where ships could be hauled ashore on a shelving but open beach, we have:

14. Dover	harbour
15. Lympne	beach
16. Brancaster	beach
17. Burgh Castle	harbour
18. Reculver	beach
19. Richborough	harbour
20. Pevensey	beach
21. Portchester	harbour

If we then add the lost fort at Walton Castle to the head of the list we have a further pair:

Walton Castle	beach
13. Bradwell	harbour

Archaeologically, there is virtually no evidence of roads connecting any one of the forts with its neighbours and, indeed, with the 40-oared scouting ships that Vegetius describes (4.37); communication by sea could have been almost as fast as by land. The limitation of the format of the Notitia prevents us from seeing exactly how much the Saxon Shore was a naval command, and although the significance, in operational terms, of the harbour-beach pairing noted above is not immediately obvious, operations by sea were clearly central to the whole functioning of the Saxon Shore. Furthermore, to intercept raiders who managed to penetrate inland, men may have been stationed elsewhere than in the named forts - presumably inland. They could have been billeted in various towns or even villages, although it must be admitted that the road system, at least as it is known to us at present, does not really support that suggestion: hardly any roads are known running to the forts from inland.

Attacks from across the North Sea seem not to have been frequent in the fourth century. Pressure elsewhere, particularly on the Rhine, was clearly much more serious. Nevertheless, the mobile army of the *comes Britanniae* - a creation very probably only of the last few years of the fourth century - may have been billeted similarly in towns which would give it rapid access as much to the Saxon Shore as to the northern frontier (Mann 1976, 4-6; 1977a, 13-14; 1979, 182). Were units of the *comes Britanniae* stationed in towns such as Lincoln or Leicester? The *comes* had only nine units. Did he nevertheless have sufficient men to garrison (however briefly, as it turned out) Caistor by Norwich, or Colchester or even London?

APPENDIX

The Command of the Count of the Saxon Shore

Sub dispositione viri spectabilis Comitis Litoris Saxonici per Britanniam
Praepositus numeri Fortensium, Othonae
Praepositus militum Tungrecanorum, Dubris
Praepositus numeri Turnacensium, Lemanis
Praepositus equitum Dalmatarum Branodunensium, Branoduno
Praepositus equitum Stablesianorum Gariannonensium, Gariannonor
Tribunus cohortis primae Baetasiorum, Regulbio
Praepositus legionis secundae Augustae, Rutupis
Praepositus numeri Abulcorum, Anderidos
Praepositus numeri exploratorum, Portum Adurni

(Not. Dig. Oc. 28)

J.C.MANN

THE COAST OF SOUTH-EAST ENGLAND IN ROMAN TIMES

Sea Level Change

All landscapes change over time, but changes near the coast are made noticeable by the fine balance between land and sea. Major climatic changes have made the last 12,000 years especially eventful. Twelve thousand years ago, at the end of the Devensian glaciation, sea level was about 60 m below present (West 1972), and the southern North Sea basin was land to considerably north of the Dogger Bank. The lower courses of the rivers of south-east England had cut down appropriately, and at Grain the Thames joined the Medway at a level of 30 m below present sea level. Sea level rose rapidly, and around 7,600 BC the sea advanced through the Straits of Dover to reoccupy the outer Thames estuary at about 23 m below present sea level (Devoy 1980; D'Olier 1972). Just before 6,600 BC further rapid rise overwhelmed the Dogger Bank isthmus, and Britain became an island (Jelgersma 1961). The lower parts of the river valleys were drowned, creating the tidal inlets which remained an important feature in Roman times.

Since 4,000 BC sea level rise has slowed asymptotically, totalling about 8 or 9 m (Akeroyd 1972). From Roman times the rate has been so slow that it is difficult to measure. Everard (1980) estimates the present rate at 20 cm, Akeroyd at 10 cm, per century, in any case small enough for changes in tidal regime from embankment of estuaries or ground subsidence from drainage of marshes to affect considerably the interpretation of archaeological evidence. Akeroyd and Devoy agree that Roman high tide levels vary in different places from about 0.4 to about 3.0 m below those of today.

Postglacial sea level rise around the coasts of south-east England has not been uniform over time, but has been mainly concentrated into five episodes, called transgressions, when the sea has advanced to leave marine alluvium on top of fresh water deposits such as peat (Devoy 1979). Devoy (1980) dates the most recent transgression in the Thames estuary to the Roman period, and Akeroyd (1972) notes that transgressions occur in the Solent, Arun valley and Norfolk Broads areas at about the same time. In both the Broads and Thames estuary mean sea level rose from 1.8 to 3.0 m below that of today, to 0 to 0.6 m below. Tooley and Switsur (1988) concluded that there was also a relatively high sea level in Romney Marsh between AD 0 and 400. Applebaum (1972) supposed that this sea level rise caused the abandonment of potteries at Upchurch during the third century, and Akeroyd (1966) noted a resulting need to protect occupation areas from flooding. Conversely, inlets, harbours and estuaries would have become easier to navigate during the third and fourth centuries AD, as the otherwise inexorable siltation was offset. After this, relative sea level fell back: as much as 1.3 m by AD 600 in the Broads (Lambert & Jennings 1960), the 'Saxo-Norman Regression'.

Overall, however, variations in sea level have been small, and so other factors must have provoked the very large post-Roman changes in the position and character of the coast, evidenced by finding many harbours and forts for coastal defence either far inland or destroyed in part or whole by marine erosion. The forts of the Saxon Shore all seem to have been built on the coast near to good anchorages in the third and fourth centuries AD, and are thus good reference points for the assessment of these changes.

Siltation of estuaries

Soil erosion from forested areas is very slight, and so in pre-Neolithic times the sediment load of the rivers of lowland Britain would have been small. However, during the last Glaciation, much of East Anglia, Kent and Sussex was mantled with a thin layer of incompact windblown silt, known as loess (Catt 1978; Burrin 1981). Early forest clearance, whether for arable cropping or relatively intensive grazing, was concentrated on such well drained silty soils, the most fertile but also the most likely to erode.

By Roman times exploitation for timber and perhaps grazing was doubtless increasing erosion in less fertile areas such as the Weald. In the High Weald, soils on the fine sandstones of the Ashdown and Tunbridge Wells formations are particularly vulnerable to erosion. During the third century the climate became wetter, which would have increased erosion, especially since great efforts were made to maintain cereal production, even at the cost of widespread kiln drying of grain (Applebaum 1972).

It is therefore no surprise that the deep tidal estuaries that were such a feature of the early postglacial coastline rapidly silted up from Neolithic times (Burrin 1988). It is noteworthy that the tidal inlets between Pagham and Gosport constitute an exception because they are not fed by any considerable streams. So Portchester retains its seaside environment. Powerful tidal scour can maintain channels which are open at both ends, such as the Solent and Spithead. The fate of the similar channel between Thanet and the mainland, which had enabled Richborough to be a 'Roman Portsmouth', was put in jeopardy by the shingle spit at Stonar, and sealed when the causeway known as the Sarre Wall was built.

As a result of sedimentation several 'Shore' Forts are now a considerable distance from the sea. Brancaster is almost 2 km from the coast, but, as Edwards and Green (1977) noted, there is a tidal creek which would have been deeper and nearer in Roman times. Funnell and Pearson (1984) have investigated sedimentation near Brancaster, and observed that it had more than kept pace with a rise of sea level of 3.0 m since 800 BC. They found that, in Roman times, channels about 4 m deep with sandy bottoms crossed areas of intertidal mud.

Burgh Castle fort, now 6 km inland, originally stood on the sea shore, facing an embayment fully 10 km across. On an island in this bay stood the walled town of Venta Icenorum, now Caistor. However, by AD 600 there had been considerable regression of the sea, with a relative fall in sea level of at least 1.3 m (Green & Hutchinson 1965). Then a shingle spit grew from the north to link Caistor with the mainland, and extended in the twelfth and thirteenth centuries to form the promontory, almost blocking the entrance to the bay that forms the site of Yarmouth (Lambert & Jennings 1960). Extensive siltation took place so that the present Breydon Water occupies only a fraction of the original embayment. The creek to the south of Burgh Castle, which presumably formed its inner harbour, is now Belton Fen.

The mouth of the Kentish Stour originally took a northward course beside Reculver (Coleman 1952), but when the postglacial rise in sea level flooded the lower part of the valley it also drowned low ground occupying the soft Tertiary core of a syncline running to the east, so completing the Wantsum Channel and making Thanet an island. The channel, originally more than 2 km wide, surrounded near its southern shore a small islet of Tertiary rocks on which Richborough developed (Hawkes 1968), but it was never very deep, for the total depth of the alluvium to Thanet Sand at the nearby Weatherlease railway bridge is only 12 m (Hardman & Stebbing 1940). Moreover, White (1928) and Robinson and Cloet (1953) considered that the eastern entrance was already partly blocked by the Stonar shingle spit in Roman times. By the time of Bede the Wantsum was only three furlongs (600 m) wide, although even the branch towards Reculver continued to be navigable until the seventeenth century. River traffic up the Stour to Fordwich, the port of Canterbury, where a Roman jetty was found during gravel working, continued to the nineteenth century (Goodsall 1981). A more confined Stour flowed more powerfully, and undercut Richborough fort so that landsliding destroyed the eastern wall.

The mouth of the little river Dour at Dover was also flooded in early Post-glacial times, but because it was small and largely fed by springs its alluvial fill is not extensive. Nevertheless the Roman harbour near which the two successive forts stood, did silt up, despite a rise in high tide level since Roman times of about 1.2 m (Rahtz 1958).

Portus Lemanis, now Lympne, has seen greater post-Roman changes in its environment than any other shore fort. It stood at the mouth of the Rother, which has now moved more than 24 km to the south-west. Fortunately, the history of Romney Marsh has recently been reviewed (Eddison & Green 1988), and specific attention given to the

Roman period (Cunliffe 1980a; 1988). Soil mapping (Green 1968; Allen *et al.* 1983) enables a tentative reconstruction of its Roman geography (Fig. 2). From Portus Lemanis the Rother was navigable to a river port at Bodiam (Lemmon & Hill 1966) and possibly another nearby (Lebon 1984), linked with the Wealden iron industry on the basis of *classis Britannica* tiles found at Beauport Park, Bardown and Cranbrook (Cleere 1975; 1977).

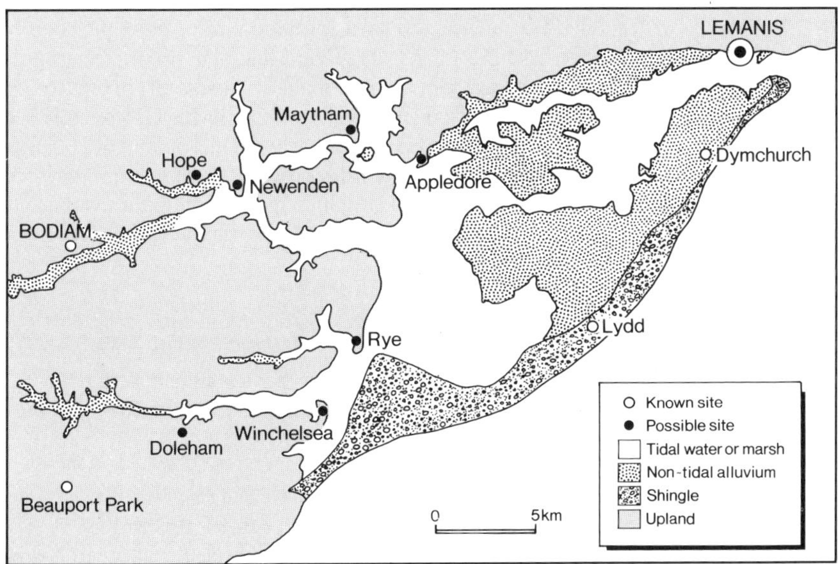

Fig. 2 Reconstruction of the Roman geography of Romney Marsh on the basis of soil maps.

Pevensey Fort stood, almost surrounded by the sea, at the end of a narrow peninsula (Mill Hill) running 7 km into a large bay now occupied by Pevensey Levels. The bay was still largely tidal until Norman times (Robinson & Williams 1983), although the history of the area has been much less intensively studied than Romney Marsh. The main inflowing stream, the Ash Bourne, was navigable to the ironworking area around Ashburnham (Ennever & Tebbutt 1977). The Roman harbour would have been to the north of the peninsula. To the south of it is a shingle spit (The Crumbles) with a history of change (Robinson & Williams 1983); but, unlike Dungeness, it was not important in Roman times (Jones 1981).

Coastal erosion

Consideration of the rate of recent erosion of unprotected coasts indicates that considerable tracts of land present in Roman times must have disappeared. Chalk cliffs in Sussex are retreating at rates which range from 0.3 to 1.3 m per year (Robinson &

Williams 1983), representing the loss of a strip of land ranging from about 0.5 to 2.0 km in width. Typical figures from Kent are 0.2 to 0.8 m per year (May 1966), but locally the rate of loss can be much higher (So 1965). The rate of retreat of Hastings Beds sandstone cliffs is about the same as of chalk, and a Roman settlement near Hastings which would have been a logical terminus of the road from Rochester through Cranbrook and Bodiam may well have been destroyed by coast erosion.

When clays are interbedded or underlie the hard formation, as at Fairlight Glen or Folkestone Warren, erosion is more rapid. Large landslips may occur, creating an undercliff. The Folkestone Warren landslips have probably removed part of the Roman road from Dover to Lympne which is shown in the Peutinger Table (Detsicas 1983). Nearer to Folkestone, a Roman villa linked by the discovery of tiles stamped CL BR to the coastal defence system has been partly lost to coast erosion. Also lost is a 500 m wide strip presumed by Rigold (1972) to contain a substantial settlement on the evidence of an aqueduct. A cliff with clay at the base may remain subject to slips when abandoned by the sea, as Lympne Fort shows (Hutchinson 1988).

Soft formations erode more rapidly. Parts of the west Sussex coast, such as the east side of Selsey Bill, have retreated at a rate of 4.5 to 6.0 m per year when unprotected (Robinson & Williams 1983). If this astonishing rate has been maintained, much of the Roman West Sussex coastal plain, then an important cereal producing area (Applebaum 1972), must now have disappeared.

Much of the eastern coast of England is made of soft formations, which have been subject to rapid erosion during the last five hundred years (Clayton & Straw 1979). The view that this can be extrapolated back to Roman times has been challenged on the ground that in the Saxon and Norman periods sea level was a little lower than today (Green 1961). The forts at Reculver, Bradwell and Walton (Felixstowe) were all built over London Clay. No doubt the figure of 3.0 m per year quoted by Steers (1964) for the erosion of London Clay at Warden Point on the Isle of Sheppey is exceptional. On the other hand the rate of 0.69 m per year for Reculver during the last 79 years (May 1966) will be affected by coast defence works, and So (1966) estimated a higher figure for unprotected coast, which, in conjunction with consideration of features now offshore, suggested between 4 and 5 km of erosion since Roman times (So 1971). He discounted the arguments of Green on the ground that the dominant role of landslipping makes coastal erosion of London Clay insensitive to small changes in sea level. Detsicas (1983) suggests that Reculver Fort was originally 1.25 km inland. He is extrapolating the rate observed between 1600 and 1784, during which period 165 m was lost. Although the fort would have been near to the Wantsum, one feels it would also have been built quite near to the open sea, certainly not more than 1.25 km away.

Similar considerations apply to Bradwell, which has also been partly lost to coast erosion. This fort was obviously built to command the entrance to the Blackwater estuary, an extensive sheltered anchorage. Walton Castle has been entirely lost; its site is nearly

200m off shore. From nearby a shingle spit about 1 km long runs part way across the mouth of the Deben. If this spit and the alluvium behind it was absent, the position of the fort becomes exactly analogous to most of the others. For Reculver, Bradwell and Walton, coast erosion of 0.5 to 1.0 km leads to the most plausible geographical reconstruction.

C.P. BURNHAM

THE CLASSIS BRITANNICA

Introduction

By comparison with the army, the role, organization and tactics of the Roman provincial fleets are only dimly understood. Starr (1960) devotes most of his magisterial treatise to the two great praetorian fleets of the Mediterranean, based at Misenum and Ravenna, and can give no more than tantalizing glimpses of the provincial fleets created during the early years of the Empire to operate on the long imperial frontiers. These included the *classes Pannonica* (founded around 25 BC), *Moesica* (20 BC), *Germanica* (12 BC), *Africana* (AD 40) and *Pontica* (AD 64). With the exception of the last-named, which was created from the Royal Pontic Fleet, these fleets were all initially established to meet the needs of a specific military campaign, and presumably survived to fulfill a support function for the garrisons in the new provinces. In his excellent survey Kienast (1966) analyses the same corpus of data, together with some more recent epigraphic material.

In this context, therefore, it would seem self-evident that the *classis Britannica* was created to transport and supply the army that invaded Britain in AD 43, although it may have come into being at the time of the abortive expedition during the reign of Gaius three years earlier (Atkinson 1933; Cleere 1977). During the invasion and for the campaigns of Agricola in north Britain forty years later, and the expedition against the rebellion of Julius Civilis (Tacitus *Histories* 4.79), the fleet would have operated in the first of its two major roles, namely, in close support of an active military operation, providing transportation and landing craft for the army, keeping the army supplied with provisions and military matériel, and on occasion assuming the primary responsibility for tactical operations. Tacitus is explicit in his reference to Agricola's use of the fleet as a raiding force: *igitur praemissa classe, quae pluribus locis praedata magnum et incertum terrorem faceret* (Tacitus *Agricola* 10, 12, 38).

The second role of the British fleet (and doubtless of all the provincial fleets) was a logistic one. In periods of peace it would have been the responsibility of the *classis Britannica* to ensure the regular distribution of military matériel and imported luxury goods to the frontier garrisons in the north and west, and also, no doubt, to provide transport for reinforcements and soldiers going on leave or into retirement.

The organization of the classis Britannica

Epigraphic evidence demonstrates that the command of provincial fleets was reserved for members of the equestrian order. Birley (1981, 305-309) is the best source of information on the prefects of the British fleet. An unidentified knight of the 2nd century (CIL VI 1634) began his *cursus* in the equestrian *militiae* before going on to a procuratorial career as sub-prefect of one of the praetorian fleets and then *praefectus* of the Pannonian, Moesian, German and British fleets - successively, according to Starr (1960, 161, fn 58), or jointly for the purposes of the campaign of Severus in Britain (Kienast 1966, 44). Another commander of the British fleet (CIL XIV 5341) had previously served as a procurator in Armenia and Cappadocia, and went on to command the praetorian fleet based at Ravenna. Of especial interest is the career of M. Maenius Agrippa L. Tusidius Campester (CIL XI 5632 = ILS 2735; Pflaum 1960-61, No 120; Birley 1981, 292-4), who, in the reign of Antoninus Pius was successively *praefectus classis Britannicae* (a somewhat unusual entry into the procuratorial career, as Pflaum points out, in a centenary post) and *procurator provinciae Britanniae*, a ducenary appointment. This progression is of importance when considering the relationship of the fleet with the iron industry of the eastern Weald.

The only prefect of the British fleet who is recorded on an inscription from Britain itself is Aufidius Pantera, whose name appears on a barnacle-encrusted altar built into the east gate of the later Saxon Shore fort at Lympne. The inscription (CIL VII 18 = RIB 66) is dated to AD 140. The only other inscription from Britain relating to the *classis Britannica* is a building slab found in the portico of the granaries at Benwell fort on Hadrian's Wall (RIB 1340), recording construction work by a detachment of the fleet.

Little more is known about the internal organization of the fleet. The crew of every vessel constituted a military *centuria*, irrespective of its actual size, and there was apparently a separate and parallel command structure for fighting as opposed to nautical purposes, under the command of a centurion, which co-existed alongside that needed for working the ship, which came under the command of a *trierarch*. The archaeological evidence from Dover (Philp 1981, 108-9) and Boulogne (Seillier 1986, 172-3: see below, II. Sites: Boulogne)) confirms the existence of military-style barrack blocks in these major fleet installations, though there are discrepancies in size which make it difficult to be dogmatic about the exact size of the basic fleet unit. It may be that barrack size is directly related to the size of the crew needed to work vessels of varying sizes.

It is equally difficult to make an accurate estimate of the full establishment of the *classis*

Britannica. It was clearly a large force, since only this and the German fleet qualified as centenary commands, the others being sexagenary (Domaszewski 1908, 153, 160ff). Philp (1981, 101-2) calculated that the garrison at Dover (*Dubris*) was in the range 600-700, and the Boulogne (*Bononia/Gesoriacum*) fort may have housed at least five times that number. Cleere (1976, 244) has calculated that 500-700 men must have been involved in iron production at the six major sites in the eastern Weald known to have been associated with the fleet. The establishment must have been in excess of 5000 men (*i.e.* comparable in strength with a legion), although the exact number is impossible to derive without more information about other military installations associated with the fleet.

Classis Britannica bases

Excavations in the past two decades have confirmed that two major forts of the *classis Britannica* existed, one on either side of the Channel.There were two phases present at the Dover fort, the second and principal of which enclosed an area of 1.05 ha (Philp 1981). The Boulogne installations was much larger, the fortifications enclosing 12 ha (Seillier 1986, 172-3), and so its claim to be the headquarters of the fleet seems unassailable.

On present evidence Dover has no challenger as the main fleet base on the British side of the channel. It faces Boulogne across the short sea crossing and is linked with London by major Roman roads. It was clearly well sited to act as the distribution point for supplies travelling in both directions.

Apart from the installations associated with ironmaking in the eastern Weald and the adjacent forts at Lympne and Reculver, Dover is the only coastal military installation in Britain that has produced evidence in the form of stamped tiles of housing a garrison of the *classis Britannica*. Cunliffe (1968, 255-6) makes out a case for there having been small ports at harbours such as Fishbourne, Fingringhoe, Hamworthy, Sea Mills and Topsham in the first century, to supply the field armies during the invasion, but these would have been no more than temporary. It has been suggested by the excavator that the port at Brough-on Humber was 'a base for a naval detachment' during the later second century (Wacher 1969) but the evidence is slender, and no CL BR stamped tiles were found. In the north-west, Maryport has been proposed as 'a naval base against deep sea invaders from Ireland and west Scotland ... [where] the supply-base advantages also become relevant (Jarrett 1976, 83), but here, once again, there is no direct evidence of fleet occupation in the form of stamped tiles. Similarly, the South Shields fort, the indisputable supply-base for the garrison on the eastern sector of Hadrian's Wall, is equally devoid of evidence of this kind (Dore & Gillam 1979).

The inscription from York relating to a *gubernator* or river pilot of legion VI Victrix (RIB 653) seems to indicate that military ports of this kind were in fact the responsibility of the army proper. Cargo vessels of the fleet would almost certainly have used them to bring supplies, but there seem to have been no permanent naval garrisons apart, perhaps, from the crews of a handful of fast patrol boats of the type described by Vegetius (*De re militari* 4.37).

Returning to the south-east corner of the province, Reculver and Lympne require some comment. The former, best known for its garrison of the *cohors I Baetasiorum* (Philp 1970), also yielded stamped tiles of the *classis Britannica*, as did the much-damaged Saxon Shore fort at Lympne (Roach Smith 1850, 258). The latter might be explicable as a small intermediate port between the ironworks of the eastern Weald and Dover, but the presence of tiles at Reculver is more difficult to interpret. The reason for fleet involvement at a port so close to its main British base at Dover is not immediately apparent. It is possible that this was a specialized detachment, perhaps of faster warships, designed to cover the approaches to the Channel and the Thames estuary.

Finally, it is necessary to look at the group of sites associated with ironmaking. Stamped tiles are known from three ironmaking sites - Bardown (Cleere 1970), Beauport Park (Brodribb & Cleere 1988) and Little Farningham Farm, Cranbrook (Cleere 1975, 195-6) - and from the estuarine port at Bodiam (Lemmon & Hill 1966). In addition there are several other ironworks very similar in size and layout and in close proximity to Bardown and Beauport Park which were in all probability operated by the same group. There is a non-standard slag-metalled road system in the area which links all these sites.

It has been postulated (Cleere 1975) that the Weald was designated as an imperial estate shortly after the conquest, following normal imperial practice in respect of metal-producing regions, and was administered by an imperial procurator. The western half of the estate was leased to *conductores* but the eastern half was exploited directly by the provincial procurator, perhaps through a *procurator ferrarium* of the type known from other parts of the empire (*e.g.* Dalmatia: Wilkes 1969, 267-8). What is not clear is whether the technological processes of iron production were carried out by the fleet, or whether its role was merely to transport the material to Dover for distribution to garrisons in Britain, and perhaps also on the Rhine frontier, from Boulogne. The presence of a timber-framed barrack-block of standard pattern at Bardown (Cleere unpublished) seems to indicate that the military control was all-pervasive, and military proficiency in technological processes is widely attested.

The history of the classis Britannica

It seems likely that the original base of the fleet in Britain was Richborough, which has produced examples of stamped tiles (Cunliffe 1969). In the early years of the first century - around AD 117 according to the excavator's interpretation (Philp 1981, 910-9) - work began on a new headquarters at Dover. This was left uncompleted, the garrison being withdrawn to assist the army in quelling the northern revolt and subsequently to work on the construction of Hadrian's Wall; work did not begin on the construction of the new fort, on a different alignment, until around 130. The fort was then occupied, with short periods of disuse when the fleet was in close support of military operations in 150-155,

180-190 and 196-200, until 210 at the latest, when it withdrew permanently. It is suggested that the fleet was then involved in the construction and garrisoning of the first of the chain of Saxon Shore forts and was also redeployed to counter threats in the north of the province (Philp 1981, 118).

The evidence from Bardown and Beauport Park is somewhat at variance with this terminal date. Severan coins on both sites suggest that they were in use well into the first half of the third century, and perhaps even as late as the middle of the century (Cleere 1970; Brodribb & Cleere 1988). It may be that another coastal establishment - perhaps Lympne - superseded Dover as the trans-shipment point for Wealden iron. The Boulogne fort was occupied throughout the third century (Seillier 1986, 174), whilst a funerary inscription from Arles (CIL XII 686) suggests that the fleet itself was still in being in the 240s.

It seems likely that there was a major reorganization of the Roman army some time in the mid-third century which resulted in the disbandment of the *classis Britannica* (and, indeed, of other provincial fleets, none of which is recorded after that date). It is possible that the support and supply roles were fulfilled by attaching ships and sailors directly to army units, which already had experience in this field, as shown by the *gubernator* inscription from York. The tactical thinking behind the Saxon Shore forts would lead to the creation of new types of military unit, with capabilities for fighting both on land and at sea.

During its two centuries of existence the *classis Britannica* must have been a large, versatile and efficient component of the Roman imperial military machine. It is to be hoped that continuing research will throw more light on its operations and its organization in the years to come.

HENRY CLEERE

THE STUDY OF THE SAXON SHORE

The surviving monuments of the Saxon Shore are perhaps the most remarkable Roman antiquities in Britain, despite the extra hazard of seawater that has added to the actions of men and time in destroying or damaging them. Their prominence in a prosperous and much frequented part of England has ensured that they have always been known and visited. Their study effectively begins with John Leland, Tudor propagandist, Renaissance scholar and topographer, who in the course of his itineraries during the 1530s made a tour of Kent and visited Richborough, Reculver and Lympne. At Reculver he made much of the Anglo-Saxon cross and other antiquities of the church, hardly noticing the Roman fort, beyond 'much Roman money found about Reculver' (Leland 1907, 60). Richborough is rather more comprehensively described:

> ... the main sea came to the very foot of the castle. The main sea is now off of it a mile by reason of wose, that hath there swollen up. The site of the old town or castle is wonderful fair upon an hill. The walls the which remain there yet be in compass almost as much as the Tower of London. They have been very high, thick, strong and well embattled. The matter of them is flint, marvellous and long bricks both white and red after the Britons fashion. The cement was made of sea sand and small pebble. There is a great likelihood that the goodly hill about the castle, and especially to Sandwich ward hath been well inhabited. Corn groweth on the hill in marvellous plenty, and in going to plough there hath out of mind found and now is more antiquities of Roman money than in any place else of England. Surely reason speaketh that this should be Rutupinum.... There is, a good flight shot off from Richborough towards Sandwich, a great dike cast in a round compass, as it had been for fens [*i.e.* defence] of men of war. The compass of the ground within is not much

above an acre, and it is very hollow by casting up the earth. They call the place there Lytleborough. Within the castle is a little parish church of St. Augustine, and an hermitage. I had antiquities of the hermit the which is an industrious man. Not far from the hermitage is a cave where men have sought and digged for treasure. I saw it by candle within and there were conies. It was so straight [*i.e.* narrow] that I had no mind to creep far in. In the north side of the castle is a head in the wall, now sore defaced with weather. They call it Queen Bertha head. Near to that place hard by the wall was a pot of Roman money found.' (Leland 1907, 61-22)

At Lympne

> 'was sometime a famous haven, and good for ships that might come to the foot of the hill.... There remaineth at this day the ruins of a strong fortress of the Britons hanging on the hill, and coming down to the very foot. The compass of the fortress seemeth to be 10 acres, and be likelihood it had some wall beside that stretched up to the very top of the hill.. The old walls .. made of Britons bricks, very large and great flint set together, almost indissolubly with mortars made of small pebble. The walls be very thick, and in the west end of the castle appeareth the base of an old tower. About this castle in time of mind were found antiquities of money of the Romans.' (Leland 1907, 65)

Of the other forts there is scarcely a mention, most being off the routes of his journeys, though for Burgh Castle Leland reports 'Great ruins of the walls of this castle yet appear', without mentioning their Roman origin. He was aware of the Roman past, and place-names, yet does not refer to the Saxon Shore. But he established a model of topographical discourse that was the basis of the English antiquarian tradition.

A scholarly account of the Saxon Shore, as with Roman Britain in general, first appeared with the publication of William Camden's *Britannia* in 1586. First published in Latin, it was translated in 1610, and reprinted with additions in 1695 and 1789. One of Camden's aims in his topographical account of the British Isles was the rediscovery of Roman Britain, and the collection of local evidence to illustrate the accounts provided by ancient authors (Piggott 1976, 33ff). An introductory account of the 'Romans in Britain' provides the first full-length history of the province, and describes the government of Britain as recorded in the Notitia (later comparing the Saxon Shore with the medieval institution of the Cinque Ports):

> 'the Sea coast which they termed Littus Saxonicum, that is, *The Saxon shore*, like as the opposite shore unto it, from the River Rhene to Xantoigne in France, had a ruler over it from Dioclesians time, whom Marcellinus calleth, *Tractus maritimi Comitem*, that is, The Count, or Lieftenant of the Maritime tract: the *booke of Notices*, stileth him: The honorable, Earle or Lieftenant of the Saxon Shore along Britaine, whose office was garisons set upon the shore in places convenient, to represse

> the depredations, and robberies of Barbarians, but of Saxons especially, who grievously infested Britaine.' (Camden 1610, 76, 325: 1695, lxxvii, 186-7)

Camden's use of the Notitia allowed him to identify most of the Saxon Shore forts except Pevensey and Portchester, and he described the surviving remains at several of the sites. His account of Richborough clearly derives in part from Leland, but contains the earliest description of a cropmark:

> 'This City seemed to have beene seated on the descent of an hill, the Castle there stood overlooking from an higher place the Ocean which is now so farre excluded by reason of sandy residence inbealched with the tides, that it comes hardly within a mile of it. Right famous and of great name was this City while the Romans ruled here. From hence was the usual passing out of Britain to France & the Neatherlands, at it the Roman fleets arrived ....' [there follow references to Rhutupiae in ancient sources]. 'Now hath time razed out all the footings and tractes thereof, and to teach us that Cities as well as men have their fatall periods, it is a verie field at this daie, wherin when the corne is come uppe a man may see the draughts of streets crossing one another; (For, wheresoever the streetes went, there the corne is thinne) which the common people terme Saint Augustine's Crosse. And there remaine onelie certaine walles of a Castle of rough flinte, and long Britan brickes in forme of a quadrant and the same cemented with lime, and a most stiffe binding sand, mightily strengthened by tract of time, so that the cement is as hard as the stone.... Moreover, the plot whereon the Citie stood, being now plowghed up, doth oftentimes discovered peeces of Romane coines as well gold silver, evident tokens of the antiquity thereof.' (Camden 1610, 341-2: 1695, 202)

At the time Camden wrote, archaeological discoveries were few, or scarcely recognised as such, but with the rise of scientific investigation in the course of the seventeenth century antiquities took their place in the growing body of publications on topographical and natural history. Information collected in the last decades of the century was collected by John Aubrey in his general text-book of British Antiquity, the *Monumenta Britannica*, which was not published, though it was freely made available to scholars, and much information from it found its way into Edmund Gibson's enlarged edition of Camden in 1695 (Munby 1977, 421-4). However, the Saxon Shore was outside Aubrey's main area of work, and consequently he did not include much information on the Shore forts, though Sir Thomas Browne informed him about Brancaster and Archdeacon Battely gave him coins from Reculver (Aubrey 1980, 364-5, 1016-7).

The last years of the century saw an increasing interest in Roman Britain, with a number of publications as separate monographs and as papers in the *Transactions of the Royal Society*. Somner's treatise on the *Ports and Forts of Kent* was published by Gibson in 1693, where Pevensey was identified as *Anderida*, whilst another postumous publication was Archdeacon Batteley's *Antiquitates Rutupinae* in 1711, which discussed and illustrated several discoveries at Reculver, including a bronze strigil, now in Cambridge, which had been triumphantly identified by Aubrey as a golden druidic sickle for cutting mistletoe (Battely 1711, 77). These discoveries found their way into the additions in the 1695 edition of Camden's *Britannia*. In 1709 an edition of the Antonine Itinerary was published by Thomas and Roger Gale, both illustrious products of this age of scholarship.

The Society of Antiquaries of London was founded in 1717, and its first Secretary, William Stukeley, was engaged in the 1720s on serious fieldwork in Roman Britain, published as a series of illustrated itineraries in search of Roman antiquities. In the autumn of 1722, shortly after the establishment of the 'Society of Roman Knights', dedicated to the study of Roman Britain, Stukeley set out on the lengthy *Iter Romanum*, a tour of Roman sites conducted almost exclusively on Roman roads (Piggott 1985, 53, 64, 162). In October he travelled to Kent, visiting Richborough, Dover and Lympne. At Richborough he described the topography of river and marsh, discussing the site of the Roman port and city.

> 'Richborough Castle, as now called, was the fort, as it were to this city, and station of the garrison, which was to watch and defend the port and sea-coast hereabout; or rather one of those castles built upon the *littus Saxonicum*, in the time of Theodosius.... It is a most noble remnant of Roman antiquity, where in later times of their empire the *Legio II Aug.* was quartered: the walls on three sides are pretty intire, and in some places still about twenty-five or thirty foot high, without any ditch: the side next the sea being on a kind of cliff, the top of the wall is but level with the ground .... it was a square CV. paces one way, CL. the other; according to the Roman method of making camps, a third part longer than their breadth'.

He describes the gate, the foundations of the monument, and discusses the formation and ruination of the walls, and paused to draw the amphitheatre:

> 'In the way thither, upon an eminence is the carcass of a castrensian amphitheatre made of turf; I suppose, for the exercise and diversion of the garrison: the soil of it is gravel and sand, and has been long ploughed over, that we need not wonder it is so level'. (Stukeley 1776, i, 124-5, Pl. 97; ii, Pls 35-7)

At Dover he carefully drew the remains of the lighthouse, and made a remarkable reconstruction of the topography of the Roman port (Stukeley 1776, i, Pls 46-7; ii, Pls 38-40). Then he visited Lympne:

> 'This fine remnant of Roman work, and which was the garrison of the Turnacensian band, hangs as it were upon the side of the hill; for it is pretty steep in descent: the walls include about twelve acres of ground, in

> form somewhat squarish, without any ditch .... The circuit of this wall is manifest enough on three sides, but that southward is levelled to the ground: every where else, where not standing, it lies sideways, flat, close by, in prodigious parcels; or where standing, cracked through the whole solid thickness, as if Time was in a merry humour, and ruined it in sport.' (Stukeley 1776, i, 132, Pl.99)

As at Richborough, he describes the composition of the walls, and compares them with those at Burgh Castle, which he illustrates with a view supplied by a friend (Stukeley 1776, i, Pl. 58; Piggott 1985, 126ff).

Stukeley's early fieldwork was later overtaken by fantastic ideas, largely affecting his study of prehistory. But his respectable work on Roman place-names was marred by his following the spurious text of Richard of Cirencester, though by good fortune the hoax was played on him too late (1747) for it to affect his fieldwork (Stukeley 1776, ii, 79-168).

The culmination of this generation of activity was the publication of the scholarly account in John Horsley's *Britannia Romana* of 1732. This included not only a history of the province and a collection of inscriptions, but a full discussion and publication of all the ancient texts dealing with the places of Roman Britain, and numerous maps of the province. It was described by Haverfield in 1907 as 'till quite lately the best and most scholarly account of any Roman province that had been written anywhere in Europe' (Haverfield 1924, 75). Horsley's discussion of the Saxon Shore is chiefly concerned with the identification of the stations mentioned in the Notitia, and he fixes on Portchester for *Portus Adurni,* but fails to identify *Anderida* with Pevensey (Horsley 1732, 487-9).

After Horsley, the study of Roman Britain was to advance little for several decades, for despite the growth of classical studies, attention to discoveries in Greece and Rome does not seem to have been matched by similar interest in provincial antiquities. There were outstanding individual contributions, such as the publication of William Roy's *Military Antiquities of the Romans in North Britain* in 1793, and Lyson's illustrations of Roman mosaics, but in many ways the exacting scholarship of Horsley and his predecessors was not equalled until the twentieth century, and attention to field monuments was devoted more to the exploration of the medieval past. Symptomatic of this phase was the demolition of the walls at Brancaster in 1770s, situated as it was but a few miles from the great house at Holkham with its collection of classical statuary. Nonetheless, the first explorations at Richborough were begun in 1792.

It was only with the great expansion in public works in the early nineteenth century, and with the discovery of so many Roman finds in the building of railways, canals and in the course of urban development (especially in London), that Roman archaeology again came to the fore. The growing thirst for specialised knowledge by the early Victorian public led to the formation of the British Archaeological Association (1843) in the wake of the very successful British Association for the Advancement of Science in 1831. It was an exciting age, when the middle classes (of both sexes) could associate with aristocrats in pursuit of antiquity, and learn at first hand of the latest discoveries. On the model of the B.A.A.S., the B.A.A. initiated archaeological congresses, and the first was held at Canterbury in 1844. 'Primeval antiquities' (including Roman) was but one of the four branches of archaeological science represented at Canterbury, and in between barrow-digging, unravelling of Egyptian mummies and learned tours of Canterbury Cathedral, the remains of Roman Kent were prominent. Mr Rolfe of Sandwich exhibited materials from his collections, Lord Alfred Conyngham entertained and fed the archaeologists at his mansion, where his collection was inspected - undoubtedly the social high-point of the meeting. An entire day was devoted to a trip to Richborough (stopping also on the way to visit Wingham Church), where a description of the latest discoveries was provided by the excavator. A geologist in the party commented on the variety of limestones present in the walls, and in a discussion of the collapse of the walls 'Dr Buckland pointed out to the archaeologists the corrosive effects of the common snail, and succeeded in spoiling the riband of a lady's bonnet in illustration' (Wright 1845, 15). On the return journey, some of the party went to view Mr. Rolfe's museum at Sandwich, a collection that was later to be sold to Joseph Mayer (Gibson & Wright 1988, 12).

Fig. 3 The east gate of Lympne fort: Roach Smith 1852.

The archaeologist of the 1840s (a term matching the newly-coined 'scientist') was by no means necessarily associated with archaeological investigation by excavation, which was to develop as a technique during the course of the nineteenth century; the study of the architecture of Canterbury Cathedral was seen as equally 'archaeological' by the Congress. The exploration of Richborough by Rolfe in 1843, as that of William Boys in 1792, was primarily architectural, uncovering the buried portions of the stonework and investigating the foundations of the monument, but Roach Smith, in publishing their discoveries, also gives much space to illustrating the pottery and finds from the excavations, an aspect of the work in which he set new standards. He also reported the later discoveries when the railway was made below the castle in 1846, and a careful investigation of the amphitheatre in 1849 (Roach Smith 1850).

Roach Smith undertook excavations of his own at Lympne, paid for by subscription, an appeal to the Treasury and the Society of Antiquaries having been unsuccessful. The campaign in 1850 was able to recover the outline of the walls, and reveal the collapsed and disjointed remains of the gate (Fig. 3) and some internal buildings; it was promptly and very adequately published (Roach Smith 1852). A subsequent season in 1852, at Pevensey, was also undertaken by subscription (this time with the benefit of free railway travel) and identified the extent of the Roman fortifications (Roach Smith (1858).

The excavations of the southern forts were as good as any undertaken in the era before Pitt Rivers transformed the science of excavation, and were not matched by work on other forts, though Burgh Castle was investigated in the 1850s and Bradwell in the 1860s. The short campaign at Pevensey conducted by L.F. Salzman early in the twentieth century was little better, recovering the original dimensions of the plan, and the timber sub-structure of the bastions, but was marred by the planting of forged tiles stamped HON AUG ANDRIA (Johnson 1976, 37-41, 43, 57-60).

The modern excavations will not be given detailed treatment here, as relevant details are provided elsewhere. The long series of excavation by Bushe-Fox at Richborough (1922-38) were better than many of their period, and were at least published (Cunliffe 1968). But the explorations at Burgh Castle in 1958-61, and a long series of rescue and research excavations at Reculver between 1952 and 1970 have not yet been published. An extensive research campaign on Portchester between 1961 and 1972 has been reported in exemplary form (Cunliffe 1975), though the major discoveries since 1970 in the course of rescue work at Dover have only partially been printed. Most recently, a successful short campaign on Lympne Castle finally established the true plan of the fort and the extraordinary transformation of that site caused by subsidence (Cunliffe 1980b). Given the extensive literature on Roman Britain, general scholarly accounts of the Saxon Shore were surprisingly long in appearing, the first in 1961 (White), and then two in close succession (Johnson 1976 and Johnston ed. 1977, the Proceedings of a conference held in 1975).

JULIAN MUNBY

THE ARCHITECTURE OF THE SAXON SHORE FORTS

The appearance, round the southern and eastern shores of Britain, of a series of strongly walled enclosures, dated to a variety of periods in the late second to early fourth centuries, is a phenomenon which requires explanation (Fig. 4). Although from our evidence in the Notitia Dignitatum, several of these fortifications were occupied by garrisons of *limitanei* who were in some way co-ordinated under the command of the Count of the Saxon Shore, there is room for substantial debate both about when (if ever) this series of installations was first seen as a co-ordinated command, and when, and by what stages, it grew.

One of the ways of approaching this is through the study of the archaeological occupation of the sites themselves: but this is fraught with difficulties because of the limited nature of either excavation or publication of some of the sites which have been examined, or the fact that such work carried out earlier in this century may not now admit of any close definition of foundation or occupation date for the walled enclosures. Walls or defences, however, are exceptionally difficult to date in themselves by stratigraphic means, unless one can be certain of a well defined sequence within which they come, itself carefully held in place by (preferably) relatively abundant evidence for dating. A mere *terminus post quem*, often seized on as a clear indication of close dating, will not do. It should be useful, therefore, to seek to use other methods - those of typological progression - to attempt to define both what is peculiar and novel within the architecture of these sites, and to attempt to isolate aspects of these fortifications which may provide clues as to sequence, tactical or strategic parallels, or even dating. It cannot automatically be assumed either that any of the forts was built at the same time as any other, or that they formed a 'system' from the word go.

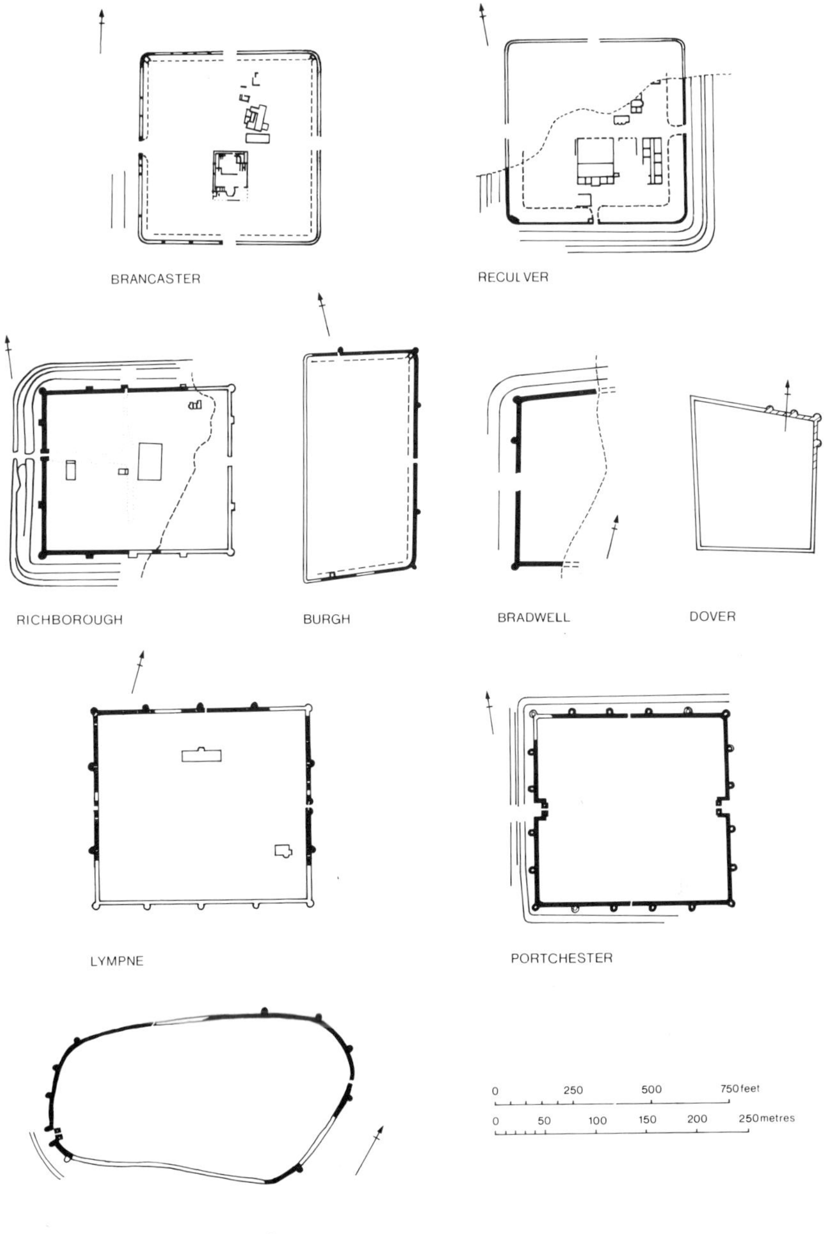

Fig. 4 Saxon Shore forts: comparative site plans.

Certain elements of the points of comparison between these sites can be presented as tables. These attempt to show the range of significant variation in widths of the defensive walls, the constructional detail, the presence, shape, size and spacing of towers, all of which present immediate and obvious points of comparison. It is not easy, however, to be certain what are the most significant differences or similarities between the sites, and for that reason various points of discussion and description are outlined in the following sections under three headings, the walls themselves, the towers, and the gates.

Ditches and walls (Fig. 5)
It is likely that most of the fortifications were surrounded by ditches, and their presence has been established archaeologically in most cases. Double lines of ditches have been established at Reculver, Richborough and Portchester, and may yet be found to have existed elsewhere.

In almost all cases where their construction techniques have been examined, the walls were found to be set in a trench, with foundations composed of locally available material - clay and cobbles, crushed chalk, or flint and chalk rubble. At Pevensey, vertical piles or stakes have also been recorded, pinning this layer to the underlying clays, while at Pevensey, Richborough and Portchester a framework of criss-cross timber beams has also been identified at or slightly above foundation level, apparently intended to make the walls and projecting towers (at Pevensey and Portchester at least) more of a cohesive unit. Tie beams of this kind, as well as vertical timber piles, can be paralleled at a growing number of sites assigned to the late Roman phases of the Rhine frontier: for example Strasbourg, Altrip and Breisach.

Above foundation level the walls of the majority of the forts were completed in a facing of small blockwork round a core of layered rubble capped with strong cement. There are indications at a number of places that different mixes of cement were used for the core and for the pointing of the facing stones. Facing material was normally locally available materials - flint, septaria or ragstone - interspersed with double or triple courses of tiles. There are in places variations on this pattern: at Portchester and Pevensey, for example, courses of thin stone seem to be used rather than tiles for bonding, and re-used material is occasionally found within the composition of the fort walls, most commonly in the use of *tegulae* for the tile bonding courses rather than the more normal *lateres*. The proportion of stone to tile varies - perhaps according to the local availability of stone: in the East Anglian sites there are triple courses of tiles to every four or so of flint; at Pevensey, Lympne and Richborough, the ragstone or greensand forms a much greater proportion of the facing material, so much so that for portions of the walls of Pevensey there are virtually no tiles used at all. There is no evidence for tile courses at Reculver or Brancaster.

The wall superstructure did not necessarily retain the same thickness all the way up, nor were internal and external faces treated in the same way. Offsets on the external face are

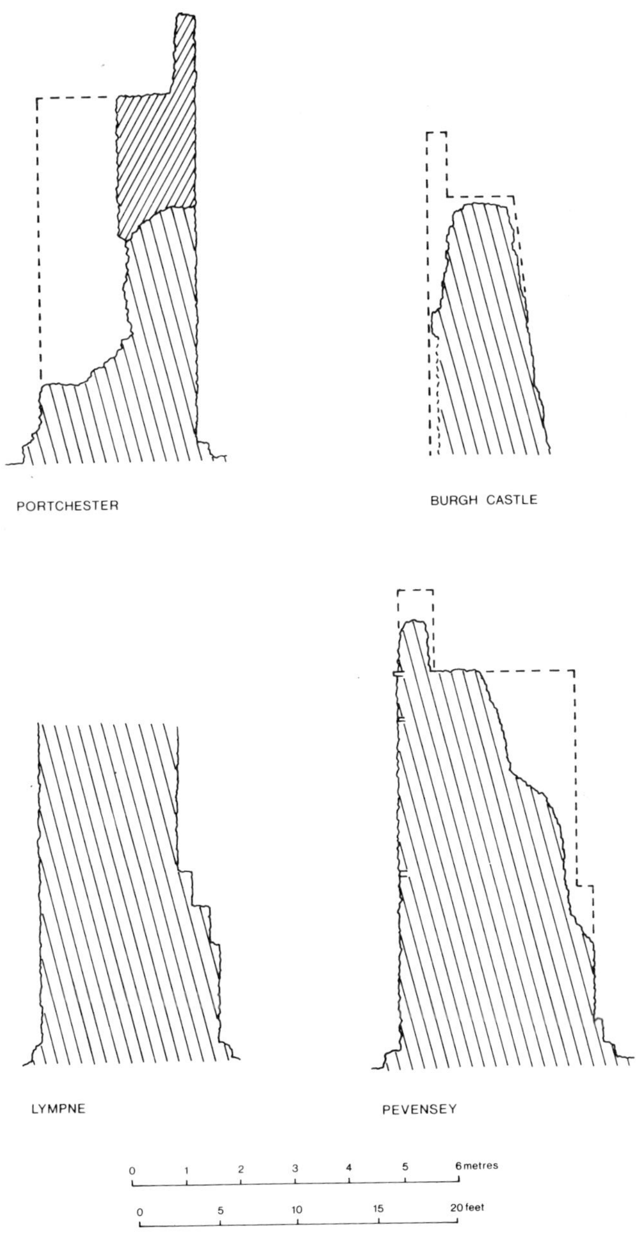

Fig. 5 Saxon Shore forts: wall profiles.

uncommon, but are to be found at Burgh Castle and at Bradwell, where the ground level tile course acted as a plinth, and at Portchester where there was a similar faced offset. Otherwise, all the evidence points to the external face of the fortifications being vertical. Internally, there is evidence for internal offsets at Lympne, Pevensey and Portchester, and for walls which gradually taper towards the top at Burgh Castle. Earth ramparts backing the walls are attested at Brancaster, Reculver and at Dover, and there is a suggestion that a similar rampart may have existed at Burgh Castle before it was removed and buildings placed against the internal face of the wall. In virtually all cases, the internal face of the walls is less carefully finished than the external - less well worked blocks, fewer, and more irregular tile-courses. This all suggests that the external faces of the walls as visible at present were meant to be seen as they are, and not whitewashed or rendered as has been claimed for other defences.

The height of the walls and how they were finished is another problem. The walls of Burgh Castle stand about 4.6 m high at present, those of Richborough about 7.3 m, and those of Pevensey around 7.5 m to wall-walk height. Assessment of the elevation of the east gate at Lympne has suggested that the walls there were at least 5.45 m high to parapet level, and those at Portchester - though the upper stages are clearly a medieval rebuild - are currently 6.75 m high. It is clear that at Burgh Castle, the walls' present height is virtually their size in the Roman period: holes in the tops of the projecting towers, including the fallen one, suggest that this was the level at which additional structures, probably of wood, were keyed in. The taper of the walls makes it difficult to sustain the view that there was anything other than a very narrow wall-walk round the Burgh Castle wall-tops, though if the walls were originally backed by an earth rampart, there would have been room and support for a more ample provision. Equally, the presence at Pevensey of an external string-course at 7.5 m height suggests that the Roman wall walk, as the medieval one, was at this level where portions of the Roman breastwork also appear to survive. It is less easy to be certain what was the original height of the walls at Richborough: in places the topmost courses of the walls at present appear to be built in a far smaller module of stonework than the rest of the walls, suggesting that they, too, may have been a breastwork. Conversely, however, although the towers were floored with wooden beams, there is no trace of doorways into them at present wall-height, thus suggesting that the walls may in fact have been higher.

At Richborough and Lympne there are traces of slots in the walls for wooden beams at higher levels. Above the arch of the north postern gate at Richborough, there are the signs that there was once a substantial beam: similarly at Lympne, the presence of a similar beam spanning one of the postern gates has been identified.

The towers (Fig. 6)

Three of the sites have, or are claimed to have had, internal towers at their angles and elsewhere. Brancaster fort had an angle turret in its north-west rounded corner, and Reculver has similar towers at both south and east gates, as well as a thickening of the

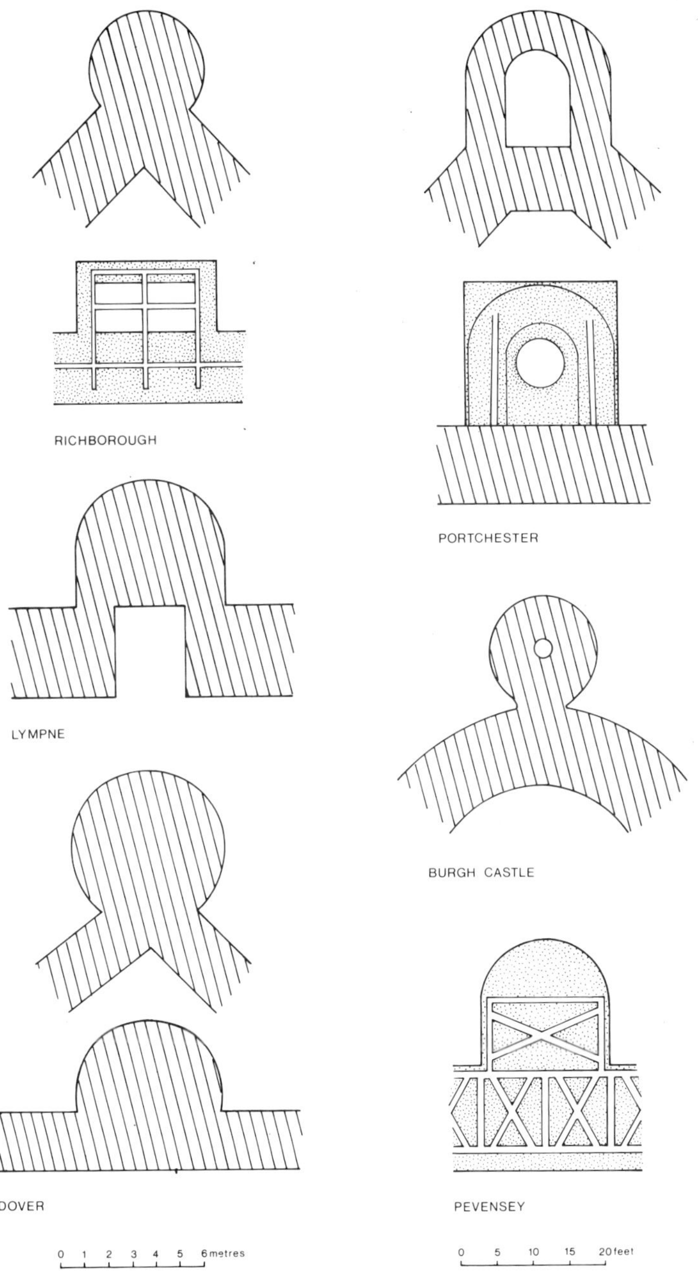

Fig. 6 Saxon Shore forts: towers.

defensive walls at the south-west corner. The evidence for an internal turret at the north-east angle of Burgh Castle is probably to be discounted, though its existence seems to be at odds with the presence of buildings against the internal face of the fort wall nearby. More positive was the discovery against the south wall of the fort of a rectangular foundation, though this has external dimensions of around 7 m square, and therefore seems more likely to have been a separate room belonging to a complex of structures ranged along the south wall, than intended as an internal turret.

Of these three sites, only Burgh Castle also has externally projecting towers. These are solid, and of exactly the same build as the walls but apparently added to them later than at least the initial stages of construction. What is more, because of the curvature of the fort walls at the angle, the towers set at the corners fail to project sufficiently to give any cover to the stretches of fort wall either side of them. Bradwell appears also to have curved angles with towers added at the point of curvature: plans and sketches of Walton Castle suggest that although it was very similar in aspect to Burgh Castle its projecting corner towers sprang from right-angled corners.

Added towers also make an appearance at Richborough, where the south-west corner tower was an addition to the corner, and is the only added tower on the surviving circuit, and at Dover where certain of the towers - for example the corner ones - are integral, but others were in a different style of masonry and added to the walls. At Richborough are to be found the only rectangular projecting towers within these fortifications: some of these are hollow, others solid up to a certain level, and all were tied at their upper levels into the main fort wall by large beams, the holes for which can still be clearly seen. One of the towers has a chute, formed of tiles - probably a latrine - at its foot. At its surviving corners, Richborough has three-quarters round towers, a feature also to be seen at Dover and, if its corners were indeed rectangular, at Lympne. The internal towers at Lympne appear unusual in that they contain open-backed hollow chambers: those at Dover appear to have been solid.

Both Portchester and Pevensey have projecting towers of U-shape rather than semicircular. The spacing of them at Portchester is regular: at Pevensey it is far less so, but there the towers are placed at points where the fort walls, normally in short straight stretches, change angle. Apart from at Pevensey, the general principle which governs the spacing of the towers seems to be to subdivide evenly the distances between angles and main gates on the wall-circuits: this is certainly the case at Burgh Castle, Bradwell, Richborough, and probably Dover.

There is little evidence for the original heights of the towers. Only at Pevensey does any of them survive above rampart walk height, and here there was originally at least one large round headed window at this level, confirming that there was a chamber in the tower at wall-walk level. Similar arrangements can be expected to have been made at Richborough, where the rectangular towers were hollow, but there is no trace of any arrangements for access either to the topmost surviving storeys or to the lower levels: the presence of the latrine chute in one of the towers however, confirms their functional use and the fact that occupation of the upper storeys was expected.

Gates (Figs 7 & 8)
Three classes of gates are found within these fortifications: those flanked by a pair of towers, those which are close to or emerge through a single tower, and those apparently unrelated to towers at all. All the gates so far known are single-portalled, though those at Reculver and Brancaster have not been published or examined in any detail.

Gates flanked by double towers are known from Richborough, Lympne and Pevensey, while two of the gates at Portchester are flanked by guard towers within an inturned entrance (Fig. 7). It seems likely that the gates at Richborough and Pevensey were intended to be the main entrances, since they lay astride the normal and obvious land-route into the respective forts: Lympne's east gate may well have been the same, though it is not certain precisely what its landward approaches were.

The gates at Richborough and Lympne make use of substantial quantities of large stone blocks, probably re-used from earlier buildings on the two sites. Although little of it survives, the west gate at Richborough appears to be built of large squared blocks: it takes the form of a passageway between rectangular towers which project externally and internally, and probably supported a large nearly square tower astride the fort walls above the gate. The gate at Lympne stood on a stepped platform of large stone blocks, presumably buried when the gate was actually in operation, or it would have been of no use at all for wheeled traffic. Above this platform were flanking semi-circular towers of small blockwork and tile bonding courses: guard chambers were provided on both sides of the entrance passage. At Pevensey the main gate is on a more massive scale: its flanking U-shaped projecting towers are set wider apart and form the sides of a small courtyard in front of the gate: the gate itself is a single passageway between rectangular guard chambers set at the innermost side of the courtyard.

The only other 'main' gates identified and published are the land and water gates at Portchester. Here the principle is similar to the gate at Pevensey, but without the flanking towers. The same effect, of producing a small courtyard in front of the gate, is achieved by setting the gate passage itself and its flanking towers at the inner edge of a short inturn of the fort walls.

Gates flanked by single towers are found at several sites. At Reculver both the south and the east gates are of this type - a single carriageway flanked by a single guard turret. At the west gate at Portchester, too, a simple opening in the fort walls between two of the normal equally spaced projecting towers, was flanked on its interior by a single post-built guard chamber. At other sites, Lympne and Burgh Castle, the gate passage was flanked by a projecting external tower (Fig. 8). At Richborough the north postern emerges

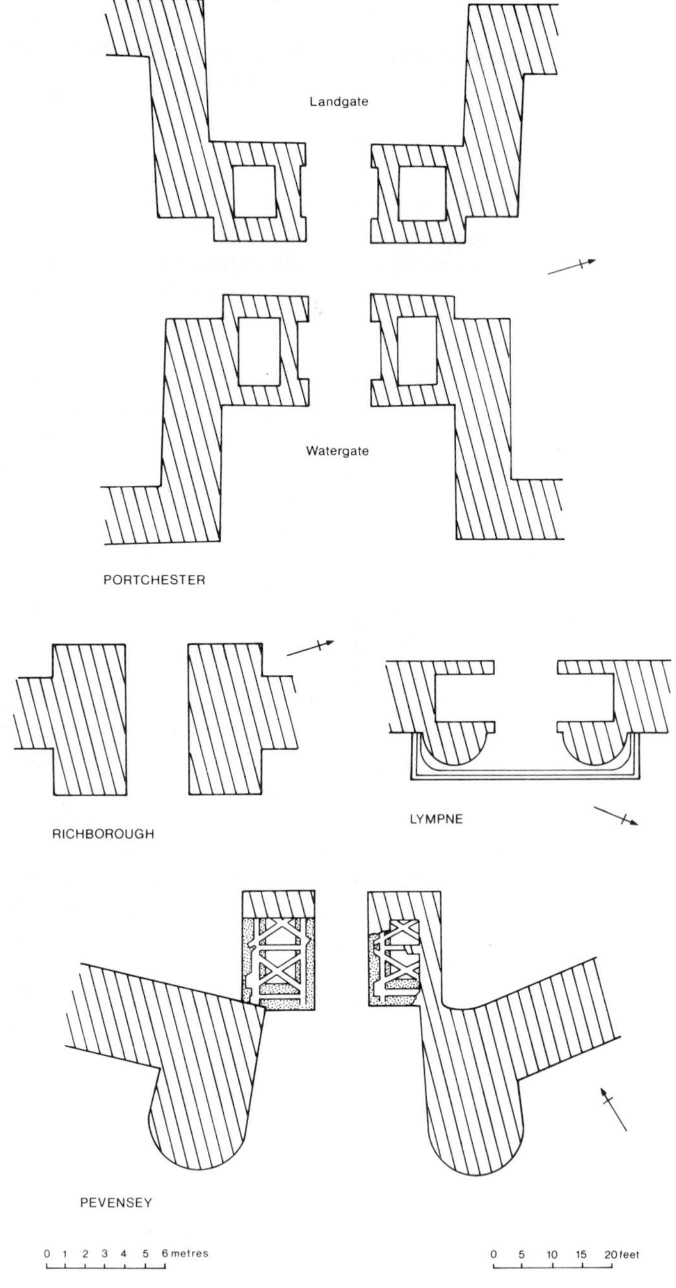

Fig. 7 Saxon Shore forts: main gates.

through a rectangular tower in the north wall, and it is possible that a south gate also did the same.

Only at Pevensey is there evidence of gate passages which appear to be sited in positions unrelated to the placing of the towers. One of these, at the eastern extremity of the site, was equidistant between two of the normal projecting towers: another, in the north wall, took an S-shaped curve through the wall.

General considerations (Fig. 4)
The comparison of the defensive architecture of these ten sites presents considerable difficulties. Viewed against a typological progression of Roman fort architecture, certain features are distinctive of what is generally assumed to be an earlier date, while others are regarded as signs typical of a later date. 'Early' features are the rounded corners, rectangular plan, internal towers at angles or intervals, the presence of an earthen rampart: later features are the thicker freestanding walls, projecting towers, and adaptation of plan to the land's contours. If the development of Roman fortification, therefore, is seen as a steady progress from one end of this spectrum to the other, it might be relatively easy to arrange each site typologically in a sequence running from Brancaster or Reculver at one end and Pevensey at the other.

Certain features of the sites, however, suggest that they occupy a more formative stage in the evolutionary changes of Roman fortification than this. External towers project from the rounded angles at Bradwell and Burgh Castle, in a position that renders them on the face of it virtually useless for enfilading the curtain wall in either direction - if that was their intended function. There are clear signs that certain of the towers at Richborough and Dover, and all of those known at Burgh Castle were additional to the original structure, though they may have been planned from the beginning. Dover's fortifications in particular are a curious hybrid: they are remarkably narrow, and backed by an earth rampart, yet were planned from the first with some projecting towers. Many of the forts have an essentially quadrilateral shape, even though their walls fail to describe neatly rectangular shapes, a feature that suggests the adherence to a traditional form of castrametation rather than immediately embracing a new style of adapting the fortification to the available terrain.

It is hard to point to any Roman fortifications within the province of Britannia which might have formed a precedent for the newer elements of the 'Shore fort' series. Establishment of firm dates for particular urban defences is here crucial, and is, as always, remarkably difficult. It is clear, however, that while walls backed by earthen ramparts were relatively common by the middle of the third century in Britain, there is little evidence that projecting towers yet formed part of the defensive repertoire: they may by then have existed at Canterbury or at St Albans, but the evidence for their date at either of these sites is not decisive.

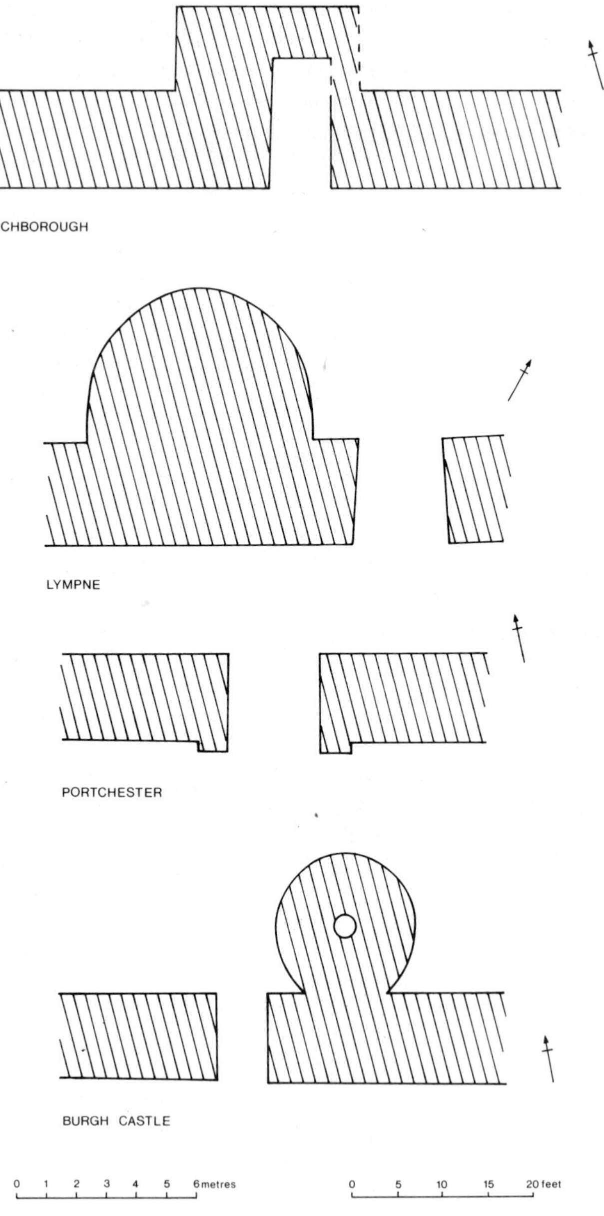

Fig. 8 Saxon Shore forts: postern gates.

The sites which appear to have the majority of early features are Reculver and Brancaster. The building inscription found at Reculver, dating its *principia* can reasonably be taken as an indicator of date for the whole site; its mention of a consular official called Rufinus, however, does not allow a date any more precise than somewhere between the late second and the late third century to be assigned to it. For comparative purposes, there are few military establishments built afresh in the rest of Britain within this period: only those associated with the Severan campaigns in Scotland in 208-9 for example, but even here, use was normally made of pre-existing forts which may have acted as a constraint upon the builders.

It is therefore difficult to determine merely by their architecture, whereabouts on this timespan of a century or so these two sites, apparently occupying virgin sites, might belong. The width of the walls, the plan of the gates and the internal towers all suggest some change in design from the standard pattern of fortifications of Hadrianic or Antonine days. What can be seen of the internal layout, however, suggests that traditional forms were still adhered to - there was still an earthern rampart, an intervallum road and a central headquarters building of what seems to be the traditional design. There is no sign that the traditional rectangular shape with rounded corners had yet been abandoned in favour of a type of fort which instead was adapted to the terrain: conversely, however, neither at Reculver nor Brancaster was the chosen site one that was ill-adapted to a rectangular installation. It may well be that troop units which were confined to Britain - and there are indications that the builders of Brancaster and Reculver may have been their first garrisons, the *cohors I Aquitanorum* and the *cohors I Baetasiorum* respectively, both of which were stationed in northern Britain in the Antonine period - were uninfluenced by new ideas about fortification which were creeping into the Roman defensive repertoire during the course of the third century.

In their different ways, Burgh Castle and Dover both seem to be transitional between the older style of fortifications and the newer. All the indications are that the fully-fledged style of fortifications, with freestanding, thick walls, provided with well-protected gates flanked by double towers, and with projecting external towers, was being introduced in the West in the new defences erected round towns and forts from the last quarter of the third century onwards. None of the externally projecting towers which feature on the walls of British towns and cities can at present be dated substantially before this and the majority of them date from a great deal later. What is more, the general design of the defences round the south-east coastline of Britain have a great deal in common with not only town walls being built in Gaul and other western provinces of the time, but also with new fortifications now appearing on other frontiers: these, too, are difficult to date, but many of the features to be seen in the coastline forts of Britain can be paralleled at places on the Danube - Iller - Rhine frontier, at Kellmünz, Isny and Goldberg.

On these grounds, and in accordance with the archaeological arguments advanced for the date of Richborough (Johnson 1970), it seems most likely that the construction of the main series of these installations was taking place in the 270s and 280s, at a time when, to all appearances, Roman ideas about fortifications were undergoing a substantial change, first instanced in the West by the walls built round Rome itself between 270 and around 280.

This argument would see most of the East Anglian series of forts - Burgh Castle, Bradwell and probably Walton Castle - and the Kentish sites of Richborough, Dover and Lympne as belonging to this phase. It must be said that this view of the East Anglian forts is still unsubstantiated by hard evidence: at Burgh Castle the overwhelming evidence for occupation is in the Constantinian period, though in the publication (Johnson 1983b) it was suggested that this could be explained by the excavated areas lying mainly close to the inner face of the walls, in a position which seems more regularly to have been used in the Constantinian period than any other. Apart from the general spread of coin finds from the site, which reaches back into the third century, there is little to confirm the suggested dating to the late third century apart from the rather hybrid architectural style of the defences.

With Dover, we are perhaps on surer ground. Here the corner of the later Roman installation overlaps a corner of the earlier *classis Britannica* fort. This at any rate gives a *terminus post quem* later than about AD 210 from material discovered in association with occupation of the earlier fort (Philp 1981, 946). Other spot-dates for material buried within the rampart of the later fort have so far not been published, but may give firmer definition to its construction date. There is little prospect, however, of archaeologically sensitive dating at Lympne, where the layers have been so comprehensively muddled by landslips that not even the original plan of the fort can be established with absolute certainty.

Two sites have yet to be fitted into this pattern: both Portchester and Pevensey are usually seen as belonging to a slightly later phase of coastal defence than the 270-280s. The walls and projecting towers are integral: Pevensey at least is naturally adapted in plan to the promontory which it occupies, and the two sites share an unusual design in gateways, hard to parallel elsewhere in the later Roman period.

The dating evidence for Portchester rests on excavated contexts, which have provided a coin of Gallienus (260-8) in a quarry-scoop sealed by upcast from the digging of foundation trenches for the fort wall, and thus immediately pre-dating the construction of the defences, and coins of Tetricus I and Carausius within what are interpreted as primary layers against the fort wall piled around the scaffold posts used to construct the walls (Cunliffe 1975, 40-1; 42). A date for the construction of Portchester after 286-7 therefore is assured. Examination of the coin finds also indicated a burst in activity at the fort in the late 280s with a recession within the succeeding decade, suggesting that the fort was the hive of limited activity, soon abandoned, and only renewed in the early fourth century. The date for Pevensey, too, rests on the evidence of a single coin, located well underneath one of the integral bastions in one of the hollow beam holes. This coin, of the house of Constantine (330-335), if it was deposited in position at the time of building must date the construction of Pevensey to after the 330s or 340s and make it one of the last forts to be added to the coastal sequence (Bushe-Fox 1932b, 67).

Neither of these dates, imparted by archaeological contexts, is inherently implausible when viewed against the architecture of the two forts concerned. Portchester's defences retain a regularity which aligns them with earlier sites, and the use of the projecting towers is at once more assured and integral to the design. The treatment of two of the gates in a way which is totally different from the others is odd, and at present inexplicable, for if defensive considerations were paramount, all four gates are equally vulnerable and deserve a parallel measure of protection. Overall, however, the site now exhibits a confidence in the planning which acts as a forerunner for a standard rectangular fort of the late Roman period, later also seen at such places at Deutz, Pachten, Alzey and elsewhere.

Usually because of its plan, Pevensey is often seen as the total 'odd man out' as regards the British coastal forts. With the irregular oval layout, its massive walls, which seem to have been perhaps 25% higher than those of Richborough and maybe 50% higher than Burgh Castle, it can be seen typologically as yet another stage removed. Yet it does have much in common with the rest of the coastal forts - the use of timber beams to strengthen its walls, the projecting towers, not so dissimilar from those at Portchester, the internal offsets which reduce the wall thickness, and the similar curious double treatment of main and subsidiary gates which suggest that it need not be so far removed in time from the rest of the series as all that. Proper analysis, as at Portchester, of the build-up of layers in associations with the construction phases of the walls may reveal much more telling detail both about the construction date and about periods of initial occupation within the walls. The shape of the fort alone, and the massive bulk of its architectural style, do not immediately discount the possibility of contemporaneity with Portchester. It may be special pleading, but a site which had fake tiles planted on it to substantiate a date in the reign of Honorius (Peacock 1973), might also have been tampered with in other ways. An open beam-hole at the wall's foot, clearly visible today, could easily have a coin pushed into it from outside.

Apart from Portchester and Pevensey, therefore, where the style of defensive architecture had now become far better rationalised and all essential components integrated, the individual sites display such a range of formative ideas, an amalgam created from the established repertoire of Roman defences coupled with new features now arriving in the western empire, that despite their apparent differences, they can deservedly be called a 'group'. If not actually planned together, they show all the hallmarks of different sets of military architects and surveyors shown an original blueprint and told to go off and apply the new methods to what was built. On this argument, the lack of standardisation must bespeak contemporaneity, for if there had been an obvious model to work to, there would have been less room for divergent interpretations of such features as how external towers worked, whether there should or should not be an earthen rampart, and so on. It could even be claimed that the defences of Brancaster and Reculver, which have an earlier 'feel' about them are actually steps on the road towards the new style of fortification, and thus not so far removed in time from the others.

As far as their architecture is concerned, therefore, all these coastal defences could have been built between AD 250 and 300; though it would be more comfortable to place Brancaster and Reculver earlier than this. The main group of sites (Burgh Castle, Bradwell and Walton Castle in East Anglia, Richborough, Dover and Lympne in Kent) should fall within the decade 275-285, with Portchester and even Pevensey following in reasonably close sequence. Whether this suggestion, made at present from considerations of the defences above all else, is actually borne out by more detailed work on the occupation dates of the installations, is another question.

STEPHEN JOHNSON

THE CONTINENTAL LITUS SAXONICUM

Since the last overall reviews of the *litus Saxonicum* by various authors (Johnston 1977; Johnson 1976 & 1983a) a certain amount of research has been conducted on the Continent. The latest excavations and contributions are particularly concerned with the sites of Alet, Avranches, Coutances, Cherbourg, Boulogne-sur-Mer, Oudenburg, Aardenburg and Brittenburg. This account is devoted to this new research, taking up also the list of previously known sites and tackling the main problems of identification of military sites along the coast.

THE AREA OF INFLUENCE OF THE DUX TRACTUS ARMORICANI ET NERVICANI

According to the Notitia Dignitatum, the command of the duke of the *tractus Armoricani et Nervicani* extended, at a late period at least, over five continental provinces: *Extenditur tamen Tractus Armoricani et Nervicani limitis per provincias quinque: per Aquitanicam Primam et Secundam, Lugdunensem Senoniam, Secundam Lugdunensem et Tertiam* (Fig. 9).

Problems of identification

Most of the fortified sites given in the list of the Notitia Dignitatum have been identified, but some of them have not yet been satisfactorily explored (Fig. 10).

BLABIA corresponds to Blaye, a site marked as *Blavia* in the Peutinger Table, on the Bordeaux-Saintes road, nine leagues from Bordeaux. The proposal to locate *Blabia* at Blavet in the Morbihan is not really held any more.

DVX TRACTVS ARMONICANI
Blabia.
Benetis.
Mannatias.
Aleto.
Rotomago.
Constantia.
Abrincatis.
Granono.
COMORD
PR.

MANNATIAS can be identified with the main town of the *civitas Nammetum*, Nantes. The wall of the *castrum* is known. Its identification with Le Jandet (Côtes-du-Nord) is no longer held.

BENETIS is Vannes, the main town of the *civitas Venetum* in the Morbihan, where town fortifications have been identified.

OSISMIS, which must have been situated in the territory of the Osismi, cannot bear any relation to Carhaix, the unwalled former capital of the *civitas*. It must refer to the site of the castle at Brest, an impressive *castellum*, at the very least, in the 4th century, or even a civil centre.

ALETUM is the peninsula of Alet, which played a not inconsiderable role in the later Empire as the main town of the *civitas Coriosolitum*, as a fortress and as a port.

ROTOMAGO can be identified with Rouen, walled capital of the *Rotomagensium*.

ABRINCATIS is Avranches, the main town of the *civitas Abrincatum*, where traces of an enclosure have been discovered. Attempts to restrict the late Roman fortified site to a small *castellum* measuring 26 by 30 m are wrong, even if one is tempted to resort to the camp of the Grand Dick de Vains, a poorly dated earthwork nearby, as a possible alternative.

CONSTANTIA is probably Coutances in the Cotentin peninsula, the main town of a *civitas* according to a reference in the Notitia Galliarum. Because of the lack of archaeological proof of the existence of an enclosure wall at Coutances, it has been suggested (as in the case of *Abrincatis*) that the military site be identified with the Camp du César, a pre-existing fortified site at the mouth of the Sienne. It is worth mentioning that a massage of Ammianus Marcellinus locates the *castra Constantia* at the mouth of the Seine.

The location of GRANNONA IN LITORE SAXONICO and of GRANNONA continue to present problems. It was after comparisons had been made with the ditched sites of Vains and the Camp du César at Coutances, that a connection was made between these fortifications and the Camp de Carteret, a promontory fort 8 km north of Portbail, and the proposal made that *Grannonum* be located there. Other older identifications continue to be considered; those of Granville (*Grannonum*), of Port-en-Bessin in Calvados, of Le Havre (*Grannona*) and that of Benouville, near Caen, where the Câtillon, at the mouth of the Orne, has produced some Roman foundations (baths) and a 5th century Saxon brooch. However none of these have been confirmed. A new proposal for *Grannonum* is Cherbourg, where traces of fortifications dating to the late 4th century have been identified. In the context of this hypothesis, *Grannona* would then be the little fort on the Isle of Alderney, the closeness of the two names indicating their geographical proximity. The small area of the site on Alderney would have been suited to accommodating a single cohort.

Fig. 9 (opposite) The insignia of the dux Tractus Armoricani (Bodleian Ms. Canon 378 fol. 163 recto).

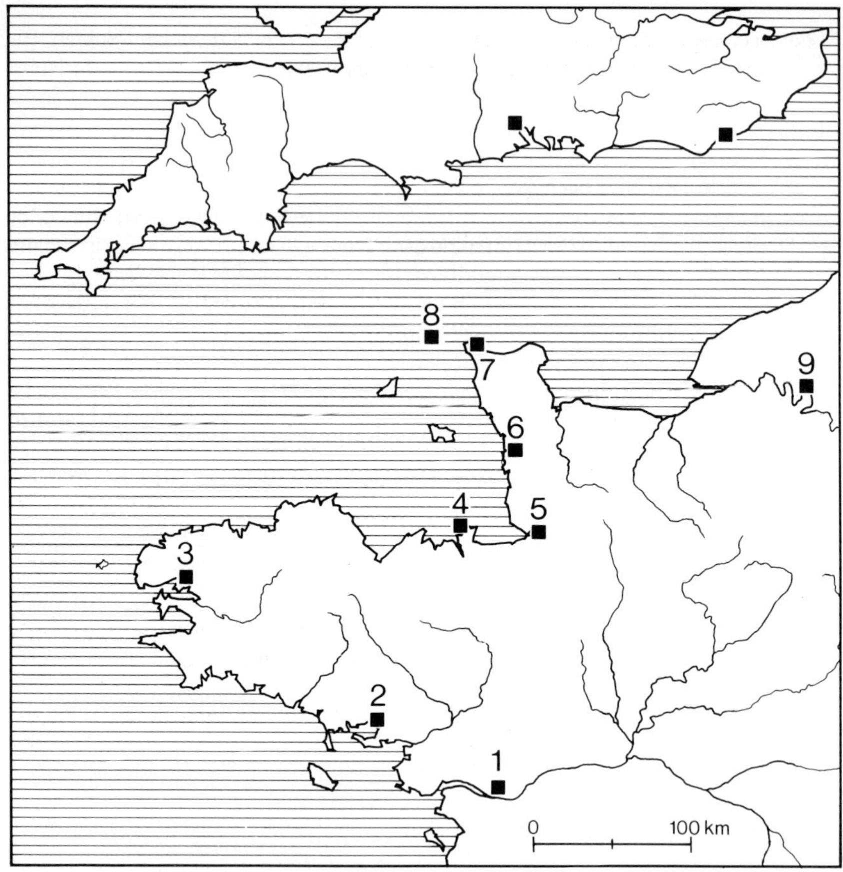

*Fig. 10 Continental fortifications sited in the area of influence of the dux tractus Armoricani et Nervicani at the end of the Late Empire (after Langouët). 1-Nantes (*Mannatias*), 2-Vannes (*Benetis*), 3-Brest (*Osismis*), 4-Alet (*Aletum*), 5-Avranches (*Abricantis*), 6-Coutances (*Constantia?*), 7-Cherbourg, 8-Ile d'Alderney, 9-Rouen (*Rotomago*).*

The known sites

BLAYE: *praefectus militum Carronensium, Blabia*

The commune of Blavet has wrongly been considered as having a connection with the *Blabia* of the Notitia. In fact the Peutinger Table gives a site called *Blavia*, 9 leagues from Bordeaux.

Blavia can be located at Blaye on the Garonne estuary, on the site of a 17th-century fort to the north-west of the small modern town. Some Gallo-Roman material and the topographical position of the plateau seem to point to this.

Literature
Johnson 1976, 76-77.

NANTES: *praefectus militum Superventorum, Mannatias*
Mannatias is a mistaken reading of *Namnetum*. The city of Nantes had a very large walled area for the late Empire, covering some 16 to 18 hectares. Topographically, the site is protected naturally on three sides by the channels of the Loire and the Erdre. The city plan developed as an irregular quadrilateral, its six-sided layout having a perimeter of 1,665 metres. The line of the walls has had to be largely restored, except on the eastern side, south of the cathedral. A few sections of wall enable us to pick up part of the circuit on three sides of the 'quadrilateral', at the south-east corner of the *castrum*.

The wall foundations are made of large reused architectural fragments. The superstructure is of small stones with a triple tile-course visible on the outer face. The wall is narrower on the Loire side where it does not exceed 3.8 m, compared with 4.3 m on the eastern sides. A circular tower marks the south-east corner of the fortifications, while four known semi-circular towers, 30 m apart, strengthened the curtain wall. These towers are hollow and have a diameter of 7.50 m, projecting 4.20 m from the wall.

Several gates and posterns, in rue Dubois and rue du Port-Maillard, made for ease of access. The best preserved is that of Porte Saint-Pierre, a small (single portal) carriage gate 2.55 m wide and 8.70 m long.

Two milestones reused in the lower part of the wall give a *terminus post quem* of 275-6 for its erection. One dates to the reign of Tetricus II, the other to that of Tacitus. The construction work must have been finished under Constantius Chlorus (292-306) to whom an inscription inside the *castrum* is dedicated.

Literature
Johnson 1976, 77-78; Galliou 1980, 246; Sanquer 1978, 1-44.

VANNES: *praefectus militum Maurorum Benetorum, Benetis.*
The fortified site of Vannes occupies a promontory overlooking the sea, at the foot of which may have lain a Roman harbour. The medieval walls partly reused the late Roman fortifications, being built hard up against them. The *castrum* had a semi-oval plan, covering an area of 5 hectares.

The Gallo-Roman curtain wall is known at least towards the east. Its foundations are made of large blocks with smaller stones in the gaps to accommodate the slope of the land. The superstructure has triple tile-courses alternating with fifteen rows of small blocks, except at the north-east corner of the wall where there are only single tile-courses. The known wall is 4 m wide and has put-log holes spaced 1.5 m apart vertically, and 1.35 m horizontally. The medieval towers seem to have Roman foundations projecting from the rampart.

Literature
Johnson 1976, 78; Galliou 1980, 245

BREST: *praefectus militum Maurorum Osismiacorum, Osismis*
The proposed identification of Carhaix, capital of the Osismi in the early Empire, as the location of the fortress of *Osismis* is no longer held today, because the town of Carhaix was not enclosed by a wall in the late Roman period, and the territory of the Osismi seems to have been divided into three units corresponding to Léon, Trégor and Cornouaille.

The existence of an important late Roman *castellum* at Brest is only a recent discovery, even though the presence of ancient towers in the facade of the castle had already been recorded in the 17th century. The site extends over a tongue of land overlooking the sea.

A single stretch of the Roman fortifications has been the object of recent survey, the rest probably having been obliterated by the present-day fort. Nevertheless, in view of the topography of the plateau, the general shape of the ancient fortress could have been roughly trapezoidal. The sections of wall which have been located extend over a length of 185 m to the south of the site; there must originally have been about 10 towers, 6 m in diameter and 21 m apart. These towers were naturally destroyed on several occasions, notably in the 16th and 17th centuries, but their positions can be deduced from the interruptions that can still be seen in the Roman facing. Those ancient towers which strengthened the front of the later castle were, moreover, visible until the end of the 17th century.

The wall resting on the rock is constructed of layers of stone and tile; the tile-courses, in a double row, 400 mm deep by 40 mm thick, are separated by six or seven courses of small stonework. In places this alternating pattern is repeated two or three times, giving a surviving wall height of 2 m on the south face, 7 m to the north.

One of these towers, on re-examination, has a circular plan, with an external diameter of 6.7 m, a quarter of which is embedded in the thickness of the rampart. At the foot of the central tower of the southern curtain can be seen a postern gate, fitted into the wall which is 4.05 m thick.

Other sections of the Roman wall are naturally hidden by the corner towers and the medieval gateway. In 1832 the base of a round tower was discovered within the line of the castle foundations but without any connection with them; as in 1837, there is mention elsewhere of the existence of a tower of Roman type, evidence which proves the extent of the site.

The available evidence does not allow us to conclude whether there existed at Brest a purely military *castellum* or an urban site to which a military contingent was attached.

Literature
Gallia 25, 1967, 225; Galliou 1980, 244-5; Johnson 1976, 79-80; Pape 1978, 75; Sanguer 1972, 43-53: 1977, 45-50.

ROUEN: *praefectus militum Ursariensium, Rotomago*
The angular shape of the modern city betrays the pattern of the ancient one. A 5 m section of the circuit wall has been revealed below the Hôtel des Finances. A triple tile-course alternates with small stonework.

Two sections of wall, totalling about 20 m, have been seen in the rue des Fossés Louis VII. The underlying occupation deposit has produced a collection of 600 coins of the second half of the 3rd century, the most recent bearing the image of Carausius. A demolition deposit created by the collapse of the walls of the early imperial period, and a thick layer of levelling material, provides a terminus to the occupation of the earlier buildings and a chronological starting point for the construction of the late Roman enclosure wall. The wall here has foundations 2.55 m wide. The superstructure, which survived up to 3 or 4 metres high, rested on a bed of large blocks, which are sometimes cut. The inner facing was not uniform in structure.

Many hypotheses have been put forward, notably about the four gates giving access into the town and the square and circular plans of the towers attached to the walls.

On the evidence of recent discoveries made south of the cathedral, the city extended over an area of between 8 and 12 hectares.

Literature
Gallia 40, 1982, 302-5; Johnson 1976, 82-3.

ALDERNEY
The isle of Alderney could have served as a base for a small naval detachment. The small fort is to be found on the north-east tip of the island. It has sides 40 m long, with semi-circular angle-towers and rectangular projections into the interior. The walls are 1.80 m thick.

Literature
Johnston 1977, 31-4; Johnson 1976, 81.

New Research

ALET: *praefectus militum Martensium, Aleto*
The town of Alet which belongs to the old commune of Saint-Servan, today forms part of the town of Saint-Malo. It is a large rocky promontory, 14 hectares in area, which dominates the mouth of the Rance and faces Saint-Malo in the form of a peninsula (Fig. 11). High cliffs surround three sides of its perimeter which is almost 2 kilometres long. The peninsula of Alet, as well as offering natural fortifications, provides a good maritime shelter, thanks to the bay of Saint-Malo and to the fact that it controlled navigation on the Rance.

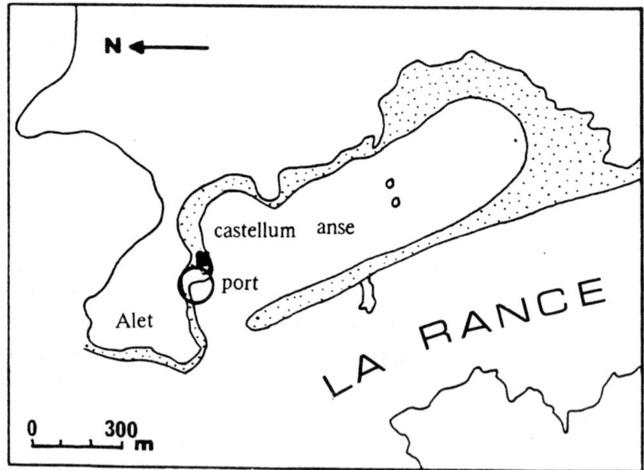

Fig. 11 The peninsula of Alet, the harbour in the shelter of the bay and at the mouth of the Rance, and the castellum of Solidor in the Late Empire (after Langouët).

Between the allusion to Alet in the Roman period (in the Notitia Dignitatum) and the modern name, other references are known from the 8th to the 12th centuries, in the form *civitas Aletis, Aleta* or *Aletensis*. The special military role of Alet in the late Empire enables us to explain the moving of the boundary of the *civitas Coriosolitum* towards the east; the maritime part of the *civitas Riedonum* was transferred to the *civitas Coriosolitum* perhaps so as to concentrate military power at Alet.

The important excavations which took place at Alet between 1972 and 1978, and which have been recently published, have increased our knowledge of the ancient town but also of one of the most important sites of the *litus Saxonicum*. They have focussed on various aspects of the occupation of these places: the town walls, the area around the cathedral, the *castellum* and the installations in the bay of Solidor.

The plateau of Alet corresponds to that type of pre-Roman fortification described by Caesar in Armorica. It consists of a promontory with the characteristics of a closed-off spur. Urban expansion covering at least 3 hectares is well attested there, to the advantage of the Coriosolites, at the end of the La Tène period. The abandonment of the Alet promontory and the destruction of the Gallic settlement around AD 15-25 (as has been observed also at Carhaix and Quimper), must undoubtedly be linked with the consequences of the Gallic revolt of AD 21 (Galliou 1980). Even if the site of Alet was then abandoned in favour of Corseul, some traces of occupation survive for the first three centuries AD.

The strategic qualities of the site were, however, to give rise to renewed occupation of Alet, as both refuge and habitation, from the end of the 3rd century, as is attested by the large proportion of coins of Tetricus. In the 4th century the capital of the *civitas* was transferred again from Corseul to Alet, which became the main town of the region. Its new status was confirmed by the establishment of an ecclesiastical see. This definitely dates back to the end of the 8th century, but its creation is certainly earlier.

THE TOWN

The rampart

The reconstruction of the line of the walls is confirmed by surviving remains which lie above the cove of Bas-Sablons, above the natural harbour at Solidor and at the inner end of the cove Saint-Père which may be correlated with the evidence of 17th century documents and of early accounts. The enclosure walls extend over 1,400 m, following the cliffs which give them a very irregular line (Fig. 12). The wall, built in small stonework, is between 1.50 and 1.90 m thick (as can still be seen in sections that have been conserved). The walls were provided with at least ten square-shaped towers or bastions, set on the outside of the rampart, and two gates. The main gate is situated at the end of the isthmus; it is flanked by two square bastions. The other, to the south, opens onto the harbour; it is flanked by two circular towers. Some coins of Tetricus discovered in the masonry provide a *terminus post quem* for its erection.

The interior

The inside of the town was laid out around two orthogonal axes. The early imperial buildings have a different orientation to those of the late Empire, which clearly shows that this period was decisive for the town of Alet. Moreover the east-west axis was set out in relation to the main gateway of the town. The nature of the buildings discovered and the associated archaeological material favour civilian occupation. 3rd and 4th century coins are very abundant, and the samian with roller-stamped decoration includes a large representation of Hübener's types II, III and V. The excavations took place mainly in the cathedral area of Alet.

The principia

During the excavations conducted between 1972 and 1978 in the area around the cathedral, a large building at the crossing of the two thoroughfares was investigated (Fig. 13). It is a rectangular structure, 62 m long and of unknown width. It consists of a gallery, 4.50 m wide, surrounding a courtyard 40 m long. To the south, a large rectangular space with gallery and concrete floor, runs the width of the courtyard. This large room which was about 10 m wide and at least 35 m long, was provided with a paved platform which rested against the west wall of the building. Regular interior buttresses within this space, probably served to break up the internal area. The floor was covered with brick slabs. Some fragments of painted wall-plaster came from the gallery, and a red-brown plinth ran along the bottom of the wall of the north gallery. To judge from the archaeological material the building does not date any earlier than 365/375. It was an important public building, but its appearance and its date led the excavators to interpret it as a *principia*.

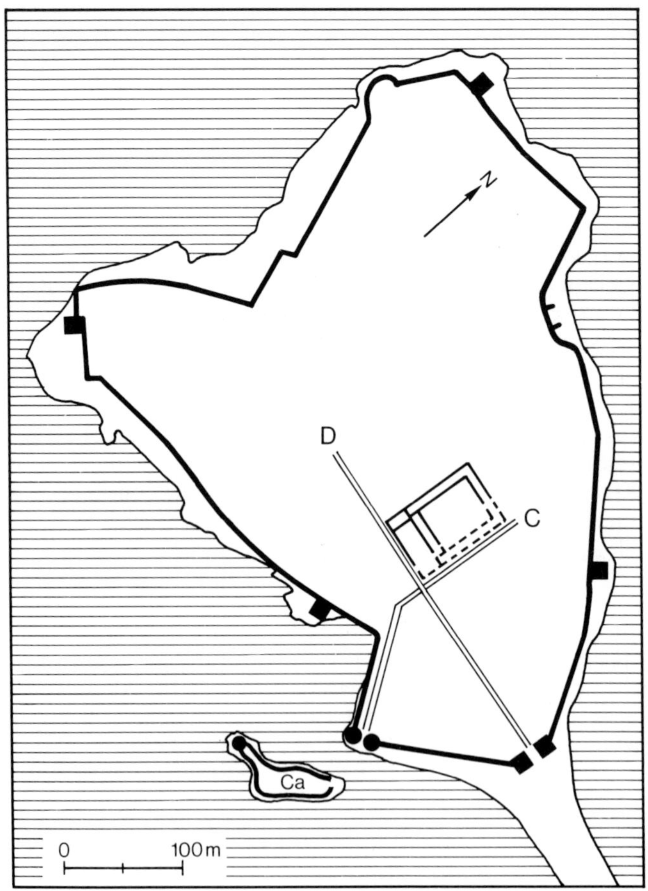

Fig. 12 The Late Roman town of Alet and the site of the castellum of Solidor, (Ca) (after Langouët).

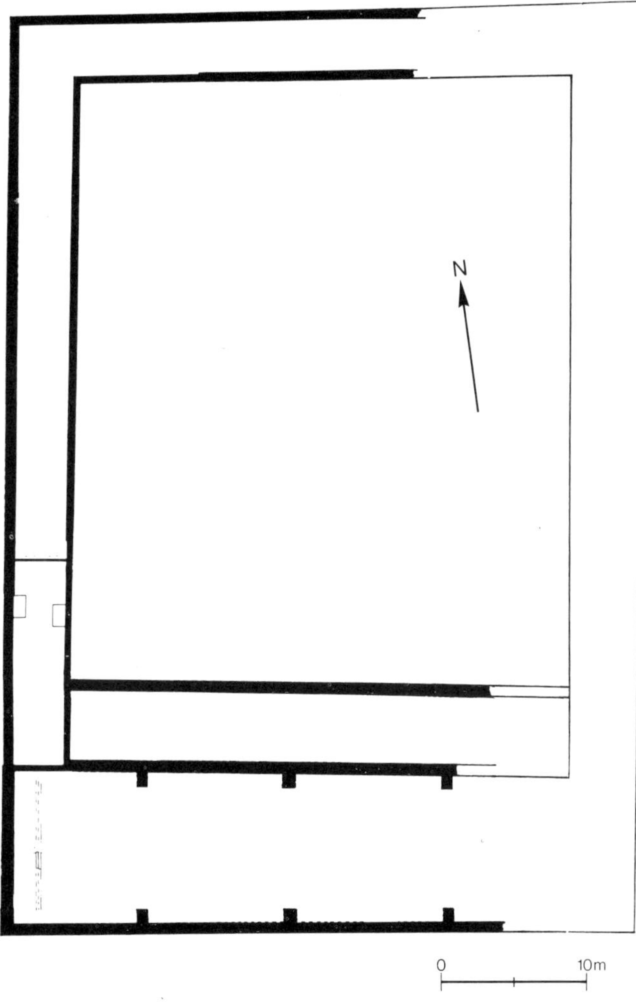

Fig. 13 Alet: the principia (after Langouët).

THE CASTELLUM OF SOLIDOR

The breaching of the coastline in the bay of Solidor in the middle of the 4th century was to cause topographical changes which enhanced the role played by a sugar-loaf shaped rock which lay outside the small gate serving the harbour (Fig. 14).

The *castellum* has a very narrow elongated shape. It is surrounded by a 180 m-long wall with brick-courses, which is sometimes concealed below medieval masonry. The wall, 1 m wide and bonded with crushed-tile mortar, was discovered in a series of *sondages*. The base of the medieval round tower, situated on the west point, is Roman.

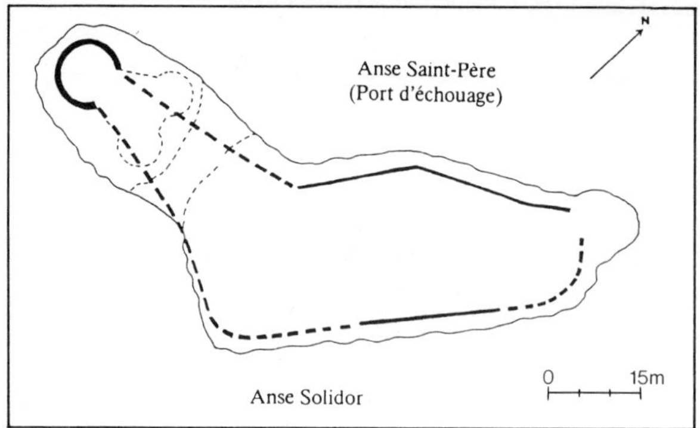

Fig. 14 Alet: the castellum of Solidor (after Langouët).

The recent excavations, apart from allowing us to locate the line of the walls, have also revealed the remains of a lean-to structure against the southern rampart. The archaeo-magnetic dating of tiles, fallen after a fire, lies between 375 and 405. Pieces of military equipment have come from this excavation: a bronze belt-buckle and a spear-butt.

The absence of Argonne ware is striking evidence of the late character of the occupation of this structure, as is the presence of a large percentage of imitation coinage.

In the rest of the *castellum* roller-stamped samian ware of groups III and VI has been recorded, and coins minted up to the end of the 4th century. The abandonment of the military installations must have taken place in the 5th century.

THE HARBOUR

The identification of the harbour of *Reginca* in the Peutinger Table with the harbour-site of Alet, at the mouth of the Rance, no longer presents any problems. The same name designates the river and the harbour on the right bank in the bay of Solidor.

In the early imperial period the coastal and river installations were grouped in the shelter of a bar of alluvial deposits which cut off from the sea a lagoon suitable for beaching ships. A fresh-water pumping station was discovered during the recent excavations. Two pools for storing fresh water, brought to the site from a nearby spring in an aqueduct open to the sky, and some very complex wooden machinery equipped with pumps, have been identified in the course of underwater excavation.

With the intensification of occupation at Alet at the end of the 3rd century, harbour activities continued to develop, until the middle of the 4th century when topographical changes occurred, no doubt naturally. The sea, having invaded the lagoon protected by the old offshore bar, wiped out the earlier installations. The harbour drew closer to the rock of Solidor.

Literature
Brenot 1974, 131-42; Langouët 1974, 3-5: 1976, 57-81: 1977, 38-45: 1983: 1987: 1988; Mitard 1974, 42-8.

AVRANCHES: *praefectus militum Dalmatarum, Abrincatis*
On the grounds of its being the main town of the *civitas Abrincatuorum*, the identification of *Abrincatis* with Avranches poses no problems, inasmuch as the city is also mentioned in the list of towns as well as by the Notitia Dignitatum.

The urban site occupies a dominant position 100 m above sea level. Recent discoveries allow us to regard the old town as still being occupied in the 4th century. From the end of the 3rd century the town of Avranches tended to withdraw to the high ground and surrounded itself with a rampart, the line of which can be partially reconstructed on the basis of the course of the medieval enclosure walls (Fig. 15).

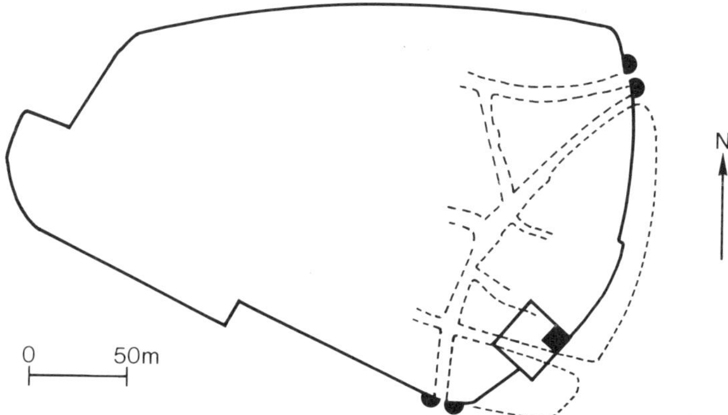

Fig. 15 Avranches: plan of the Gallo-Roman and medieval fortifications (after Levalet).

In the 19th century the driving of a road through the medieval castle led to the discovery of foundations made of re-used blocks, columns and capitals. In the castle keep a section of wall in small stonework can still be seen, and on an old drawing one can still make out the same small stonework and the brick courses that appear in the fragments of demolished walls.

We do not, however, have sufficient evidence to determine the whole area of the walled town. A small rectangular shape, as was recently suggested, would reduce the area enclosed by the walls to a bastion 26 m by 30 m, which is ridiculous and appears improbable.

Another location has been proposed as the base of the *milites Dalmatarum*, at the site of the Grand Dick de Vains, a defence-work strategically better sited, but without known Gallo-Roman occupation.

Literature
Levalet 1982, 361-75.

COUTANCES ?: *praefectus militum primae Flaviae, Constantia*
Coutances, the main town of a *civitas*, has not been proved archaeologically to have had an enclosure wall, even though its identification with *Constantia* is rarely called into question. The site of Coutance dominates its area from 90 m above sea level.

Given the lack of archaeological evidence, other sites have been sought to accommodate the soldiers of the *prima Flavia*, notably the Camp de César which, lying on the left bank of the Sienne at the widening of its estuary and close to the Roman road from Coutances to Granville, offers more strategic advantages. Unfortunately the defences known there are far removed from the *castella* of the *litus*, and the finds of Roman date are too few.

Literature
Langouët & Josseaume 1979, 3-9; Levalet 1982, 361-75.

CHERBOURG
Following the demolition of a residential quarter on the site of the medieval castle of Cherbourg, it was possible to sink some trial pits and then to undertake excavation there from 1976. This led to the observation that the medieval fortifications had been built on ancient ones.

From the end of the 17th century there have been reports of numerous discoveries of 4th-century coins in the rue Notre Dame, rue Maréchal Foch and impasse Laurent. Recent excavations have brought to light the relationship between these finds and a late medieval cemetery. In 1977 a section of wall in small stonework was discovered, related to 4th-century levels, which bear witness to the existence of an ancient *castrum*.

The occupation of the site does not appear to have been earlier than the last decade of the 4th century, dated by about 800 coins of Theodosius and Arcadius and by Argonne ware. The site was continuously occupied during the 5th and 6th centuries.

Literature
Gallia 37, 1978, 320-1; 38, 1980, 378; 40, 1982, 319-21.

Fig. 16 (opposite) Insignia of the dux Belgicae Secundae (Bodleian Ms. Canon Misc. 378 fol. 164 recto).

DVX BELGICAE SECVNDAE.

Sub dispositione viri spectabilis ducis belgice secunde.

Equites dalmate marcis in litore saxonico.

Prefectus class sambrice in loco quartensi siue hornens.

Tribunus militũ neruiorũ portuepatiaci.

Officium aũt habet idẽ
vir spectabilis hoc mõ.
Principẽ ex eodẽ corpe.
Numerarium.

Comentariensẽ.
Adiutorem.
Subadiuuam
Regerendarium.

Exceptores.
Singulares.
et reliquos
officiales.

THE AREA OF INFLUENCE OF THE DUX BELGICAE SECUNDAE

The problem of identification of the sites

The Dalmatian cavalry, a prefect of the fleet and a tribune of a contingent of Nervii were subject to the duke of Belgica Secunda, at least at the end of the late Empire (Fig. 16). The corresponding fortifications have not yet been identified with certainty (Fig. 17).

equites Dalmatae, Marcis in litore Saxonico
praefectus classis Sambricae, loco Quartensi sive Hornensi
tribunus militum Nerviorum, portu Aepatici

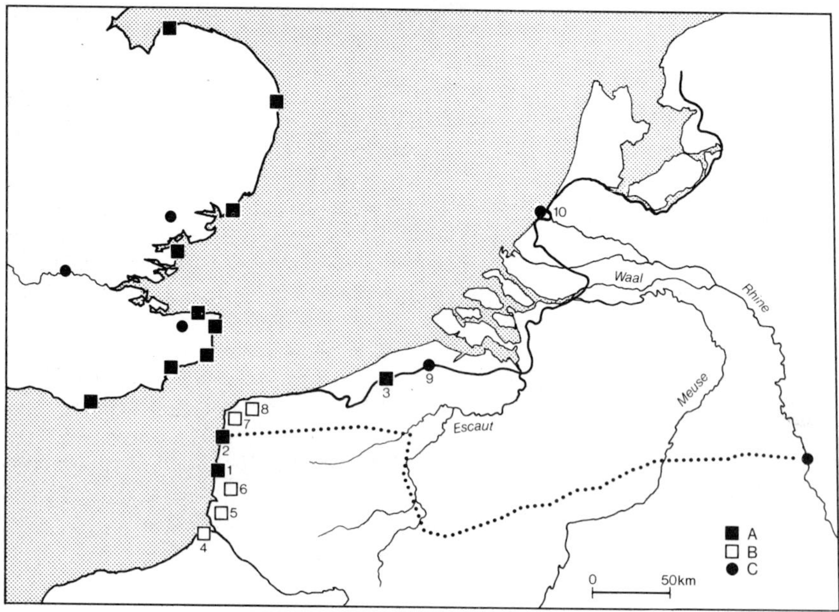

Fig. 17 Area of influence of the dux Belgicae Secundae at the end of the Late Empire. A. Late Roman coastal fortifications: 1-Etaples (Château), 2-Boulogne, 3-Oudenburg, B. Evidence for fortified sites at present based principally on place-name evidence: 4-Cap Hornu, 5-Le Crotoy, 6-Quentovic, 7-Marquise, 8-Marck, C. Coastal urban fortifications: 9-Aardenburg, 10-Brittenburg.

With regard to the site of Marcis, the names of Marck, Marquise and Mardyck have been considered on etymological grounds. Today, without its identity having been established, we can accept the proposals of Marck and Marquise in particular, since in the first case we now know of 4th-century Argonne ware from Marck, and in the second instance some 4th-century graves with cruciform brooches and bracelets have been found (Seillier

1987). Marquise, lying inland, nevertheless remains a site of strategic importance on the road-network.

Two sites are disputed for the location of the naval base of the *classis Sambrica*: the archaeological sites of Etaples or Quentovic at the mouth of the Canche, and the site of Cap-Hornu at Saint Valéry or Le Crotoy at the mouth of the Somme. The two banks of these waterways thus provide alternative hypotheses which cannot be rejected, given that the relevant passage in the Notitia Dignitatum lists two distinct sites placed under the command of the prefect of the fleet.

However most of these suggestions are still based on etymology without any new archaeological evidence. As regards the site of Visemaretz, on the left bank of the Canche, evidence of a 4th-century origin is still lacking, despite the Franco-British programme of investigations there, aimed at finding the late medieval harbour area of Quentovic (Leman 1981).

For the time being, only the site of the castle of Etaples seems to bring together the requirements for a late Roman military establishment. The proposal to identify *Portu Aepatici* with Oudenburg has not been confirmed.

Research during the last few years, especially in the Pas-de-Calais, has shown that the occupation of the coast very clearly extended into the 4th and 5th centuries, cemeteries of this period having been located (Seillier 1987). In Belgium new sites with late occupation have been located not far from the coast at Roksem and Zerkegem.

The notion of seeing a cordon of watch-towers set up along the Belgian and Dutch coastline has even been put forward, but without any firm evidence (Brulet 1989).

As for the settlements of Aardenburg and Oudenburg, the best interpretation recently put forward is to see these not as *castella* but as settlements of an urban nature, surrounded by walls towards the end of the second into the third centuries.

Known sites

ETAPLES

The proposal to identify Etaples as one of the home bases of the *classis Sambrica*, for which a prefect is listed in the Notitia Dignitatum, remains today the most sound of the various theories. It rests on the discovery at Etaples in 1890 of fragments of tiles bearing the stamp CLSAM.

On the right bank of the Canche, not far from its mouth, lies the site of the medieval castle which occupies a strategic position resembling that of other fortifications sheltering in an estuary. Furthermore the site has produced roller-stamped samian and, next to the castle, an important 4th-century cemetery, at least 30 of whose graves date to the middle and second half of the 4th century in particular.

Literature
Sennequier & Tufreau-Libre 1977, 933-41; Souquet 1865, 270-4; Piton 1985.

New Research

BOULOGNE-SUR-MER

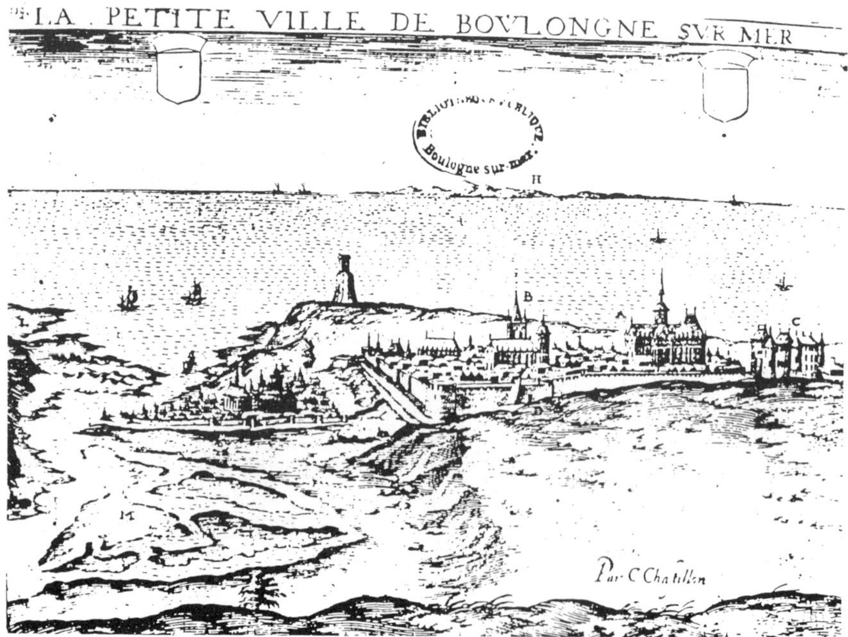

Fig. 18 Boulogne-sur-Mer: French topographical print by Chastillon (1648).

THE HISTORICAL PROBLEM OF BOULOGNE
The existence of the port of Boulogne is already attested from the beginning of the Roman period, prior to its use as a naval base by Claudius for the conquest of Britain. In Pliny and Pomponius Mela the name *Gesoriacum* is used, and it has long been suggested that the name *Bononia* was substituted for it at the end of the 3rd century. However, a letter sent by Tiberius Caesar between AD 4 and 14 in Phrygia proves that the name *Bononia* was already in use considerably earlier. It is therefore accepted today that the

two names, *Gesoriacum* and *Bononia* could have been in use at the same time, denoting two districts of the same town, the harbour area and the upper town.

The traditional explanation designates *Bononia* as the site of the upper town, essentially of a later period, the name of which alone survived into the Middle Ages. This idea assumes that the rise of *Bononia* was linked to the establishment of a fortified town, and that the harbour area was in decline in the 4th century, which was in fact far from being the case. It has recently been proposed that this traditional explanation be reversed, on the basis particularly of the interpretation of the place-name evidence for the two-sites, whereby *Gesoriacum* indicates the hill and *Bononia* the harbour area. So it would be the harbour area that finally imposed its name on the whole site formed by the two districts, for the harbour still remains the *raison d'être* of Boulogne.

TOPOGRAPHY

A bird's-eye view of Boulogne of 1648 gives a good impression of the urban topography (Fig. 18). The Liane estuary was much wider and deeper than it is today, with huge cliffs, providing a reception-point for an important fleet. The harbour installations could have extended into the small valley of the Tintelleries (which also sheltered the medieval harbour), and into the bay of Bréquerecque, sanded up after marine transgressions (Fig. 19). In the Roman period this bay could have stretched as far as the present-day rue Nationale.

The harbour of Boulogne is therefore divided between the small valley of the Tintelleries and the mouth of the stream of Val Saint-Martin in the bay of Bréquerecque. The location of the Roman naval base is generally placed in this bay, with logistic installations alongside it, given the numerous stamps of the *classis Britannica* which have been found there. Neither is the possibility excluded that the little valley near the Tintelleries had once been used in the same way, at least as a commercial harbour.

One particular characteristic of Boulogne is the duality of both its occupation areas and its names. There is indeed a very clear distinction between the lower town and the upper town, while texts show that the two names, *Gesoriacum* and *Bononia* coexisted in Antiquity.

The layout of the lower town is structured around a road running north-south which crosses the Bréquerecque quarter, and another running south-east/north-west, acknowledged to be the road running along the old shoreline, which forms the alignment to the lighthouse of the Tour d'Ordre. Recognised streets are adapted to the topography, and are not integrated into a regular plan. The town had an urban core measuring about 60 hectares in the early Empire, and its occupation was earlier than that of the upper town. The existence of a wall protecting the lower town in the late Empire remains very conjectural, and is, as yet, unproven. But the military policy of Carausius would suggest that it did exist.

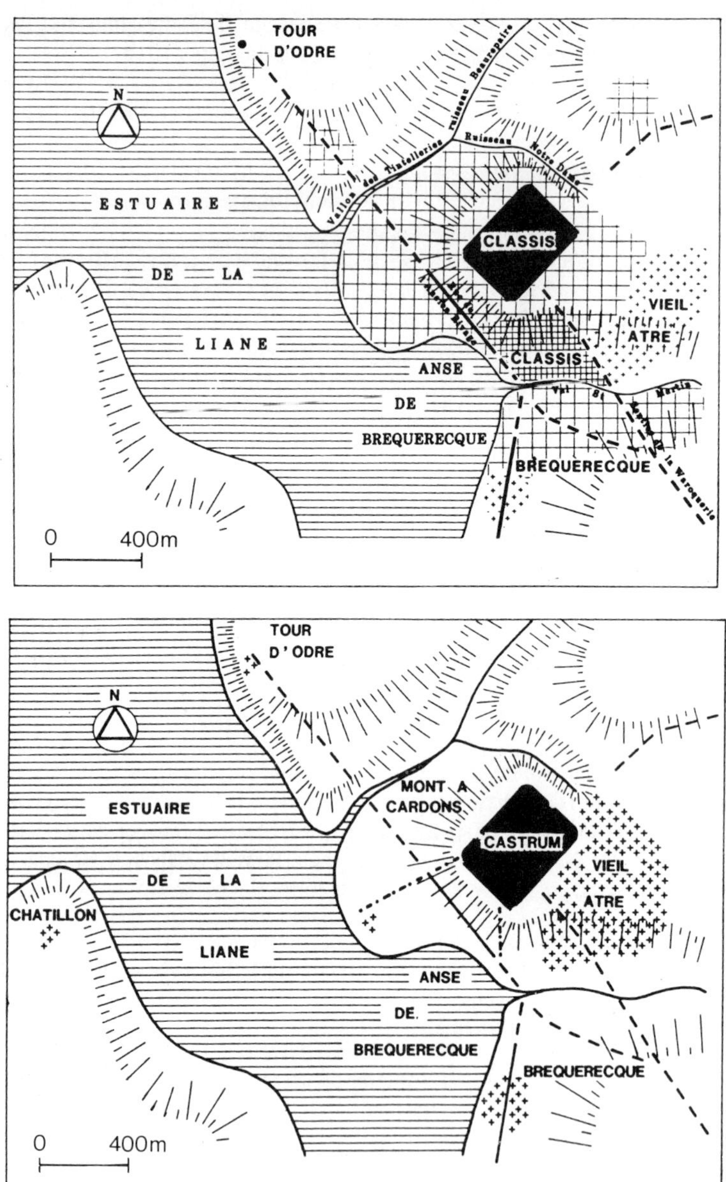

Fig. 19 Boulogne-sur-Mer: top - during the Principate; bottom - in the late 3rd to 4th centuries (after Gosselin and Seillier).

The arrangement of the upper town is structured around the plateau that dominates the harbour, and the ancient road of the Sentier de la Waroquerie which served as its *decumanus*. The upper town had a homogeneous rectangular enclosure which surrounded the area occupied by the camp of the *classis Britannica*. The presence of inhumation tombs around the ramparts proves that there was a contraction of the settlement, which was concentrated in a walled town 12 hectares in area.

Two early imperial cemeteries have been brought to light. They continued in use into the 4th century and indeed beyond. They are the cemeteries of Bréquerecque and of Vieil-Atre, situated respectively along the coast and at the foot of the upper town. The first marks the southern limit of the early imperial town. In the cemetery of Vieil-Atre there was one area for inhumation burial, another for cremation. The cemetery of Mont à Cardons, to the west, has produced some inhumations, some of which, of late Roman date, were in sarcophagi or lead coffins. Its limits have been poorly defined.

THE CLASSIS BRITANNICA

Research undertaken in 1967 and the years following, brought to light the camp of the *classis Britannica*, sited in the upper town of Boulogne. Numerous stamped tiles collected on the plateau already indicated the presence there of this unit, even though similar discoveries had been made in the past in the lower town in particular. Two barracks were excavated at the north corner of the site and then, in 1980, five others in the same area. From now on we can distinguish the camp of the unit, upper town, from the harbour and its installations, lower town.

The fleet

Epigraphic evidence has confirmed the importance of Boulogne as an operations base of the *classis Britannica*: witness the funerary stele of Graecia Tertia, daughter of a trierarch of the fleet, and the monument to the trierarch of the same fleet, Arrenius Verecundus, both discovered at Boulogne (CIL XIII 3546; 3540).

There are innumerable tile-stamps from Boulogne, bearing the monogram CLBR. For example, about 50 were found in the 19th century opposite the bay of Bréquerecque. From the 10 recorded findspots of *classis* stamps, two large groups emerge. The first lies between the road along the old shoreline, the stream of the Val Saint-Martin and the hill of the upper town where the warehouses of the fleet must have extended. The second group comes from the upper town.

The tile-stamps

The first finds date back to 1862, in the Bréquerecque area, and about fifty of them were known by 1967. Right at the start the new research resulted in the discovery of 40 stamps in the upper town. Since 1969 further stamps have been added, bringing the total of those known at present to about a hundred.

Fig. 20 Boulogne-sur-Mer: tile-stamps of the classis Britannica (after Seillier).

The abbreviations have very varied forms (Fig. 20). They can be impressed or in relief, in a rectangular or circular frame. The abbreviation can be CLBR, CL.BR or CLASBR.

Likewise, a classification can be considered on the basis of the appearance of the clay used. The least important group is of the same type as those from Beauport Park and attest a British origin, though the reverse may be true.

The fleet base in the upper town

The new excavations have not allowed us to establish whether the plateau which overlooks the Liane estuary harboured a temporary camp serving as a base for Claudius's conquest of Britain. The excavations have revealed the remains of a permanent fort dating to the beginning of the 2nd century and occupied by the *classis Britannica* (Fig. 21).

Its enclosure wall has been traced over a length of 62 m in the rue Saint-Jean (Fig. 22). It is built of a rubble core poured into a 2-metre wide trench, with a last layer of stones placed edgewise. The superstructure is only 1.8 m wide and is faced with small elongated cubic blocks which survive up to a height of 1.80 to 2.90 m. A rectangular tower has been located, against the inside of the curtain wall. It too is built of small stones, but after its abandonment it appears to have been restored with large blocks. Another tower, on the opposite side of the wall, is in the course of excavation in 1989. A ditch ran in front of the wall.

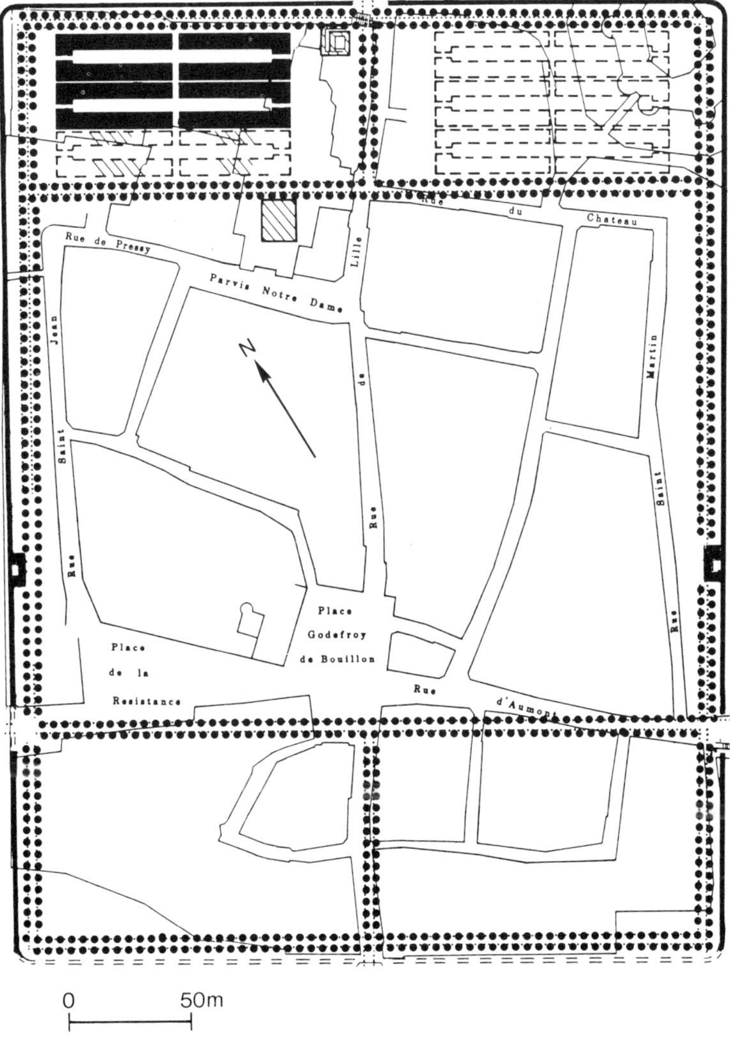

Fig. 21 Boulogne-sur-Mer: plan of the classis Britannica fort in the upper town (after Gosselin and Seillier).

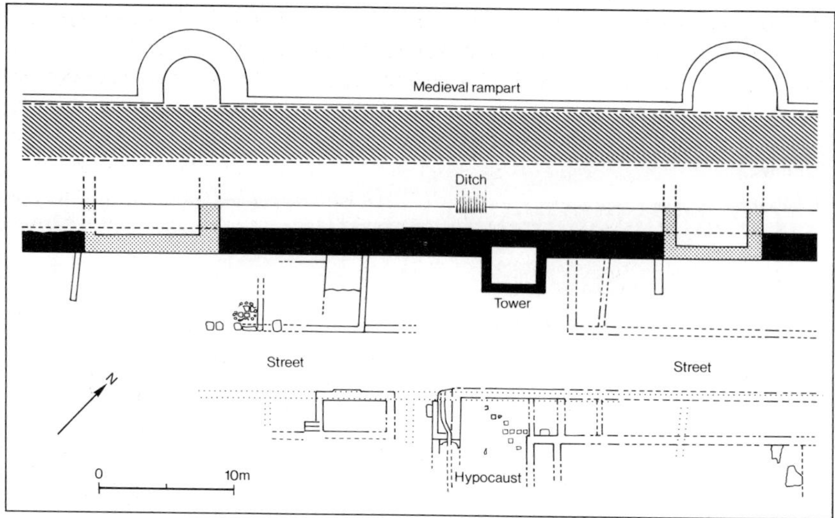

Fig. 22 Boulogne-sur-Mer: plan of the excavations in the rue Saint-Jean; via sagularis, curtain-wall and tower of the classis Britannica fort (in black); late Roman defences (cross-hatched); facing added and semi-circular towers (in white) and two rectangular towers of intermediate date (stippled) (after Gosselin and Seillier).

The stretch of fortification which has been brought to light forms part of the north-west flank of the fort defences which have been seen to lie about ten metres behind the outer face of the medieval rampart. The late Roman wall was built in the fort ditch.

In the same area, the excavators have located the *via sagularis* of the fort, as in the north-east, so it follows that the relationship of the fort defences to the medieval wall was identical on this side.

The space between wall and road is 5.50 m and the width of the *via sagularis* is 4 m with a main drain on its outer edge. Various structures survived on either side of the roadway: domestic ovens, hypocausts and a room with a mosaic floor.

The fort must have been 300 m wide, with its *porta decumana* on the site of the present Porte de Calais. Given the absence of discoveries in the south-western area, the exact length of the fort remains unknown, but it is at least 280 m and there is every reason to believe that the layout cannot have been dissimilar from that of the later period, which would bring the probable length to nearly 400 m, with the *porta praetoria* situated level with the medieval Porte des Degrés. The Porte des Dunes - Porte Gayole axis probably constitutes that of the *via principalis*.

In 1980 the demolition of the old bishop's palace allowed the undertaking of a large area excavation in the northern corner of the fort, permitting new and interesting discoveries in the fort interior, that is to say in its *retentura*.

Seven barrack-buildings were investigated (B to F, H and I), and there were probably originally ten. They were between 46.70 and 48.70 m in length (indeed, 51.20 m in the case of B), and 8.10 m wide (Fig. 23). The buildings date from the beginning of the second century, though the superior length of barrack B is the product of a later lengthening. They comprise ten pairs of rooms opening onto a verandah, with a larger room at the end. The painted wall- and ceiling-plaster from one of the rooms of barrack B has been collected. The motifs used are very restrained, notably two birds with foliage, and date from the late 2nd and third centuries. The plaster fell after materials had been retrieved from the building, but before it was burnt.

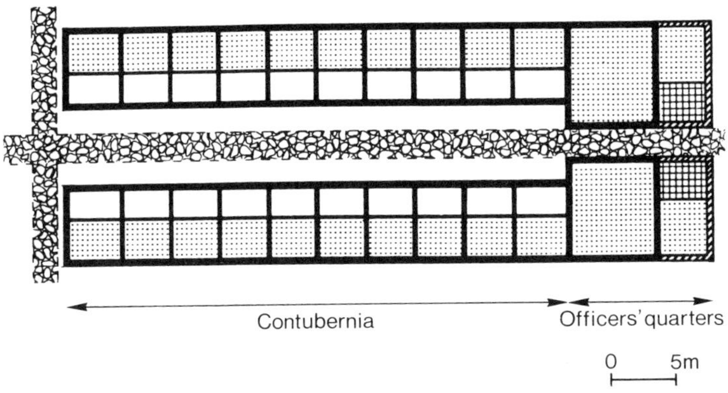

Fig. 23 Boulogne-sur-Mer: plan of the barracks of the classis Britannica (after Gosselin and Seillier).

The main drain has produced coins of Postumus and Tetricus which suggests that the fort was abandoned towards the end of the third century, before the construction of the urban enclosure. The site was filled in and was then reoccupied in the late Empire, as is attested by walls built at this time. Indeed, according to the latest coins found in the destruction level in the middle of the fort, it must have been abandoned after 269. However, some barracks could have been disused before this date, and left abandoned for some time, since the ceiling referred to had fallen prior to the fire. Finally, in the fort ditch coins of Tetricus I and Tetricus II and their imitations have been found.

Hence everything points to a partial closing down of the fort, too big for a reduced number of troops, in the course of the third century; and everything indicates that it nevertheless survived until about 270 at least. Moreover it is finally worth noting that the one tower recognized bore evidence of a restoration in large stones.

THE LATE IMPERIAL TOWN

The medieval walls of Boulogne, built towards 1230, surround the upper town and describe a rectangular circuit, 235 m by 410 m. At the end of the 19th century some

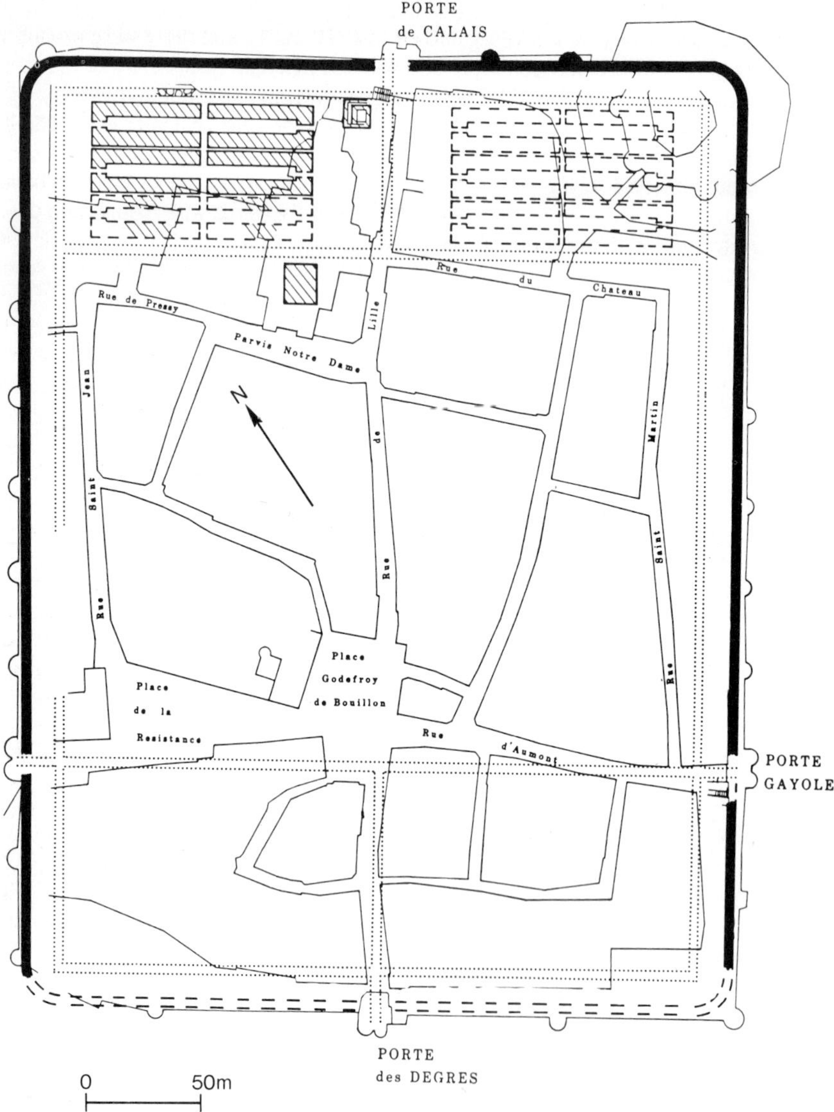

Fig. 24 Boulogne-sur-Mer: plan of the late Roman urban enclosure in the upper town (after Gosselin and Seillier).

stretches of Roman wall were observed within the thickness of the medieval enclosure walls. When work was carried out in 1895 opposite the Porte de Calais the existence of an ancient wall was recognized, as on the western side of the town. It is then readily apparent that the medieval wall was butted up to the late Roman town wall which is often correlated with the *Gesoriacensibus muris* of 293.

Since 1967 C. Seillier and J.Y. Gosselin have regularly directed excavations in the upper town. They have exposed new stretches of the late Roman wall as well as the earlier fort which can be identified as the place of garrison of the *classis Britannica*. It can at least be estimated that the walled town of the late Empire extended over 320 m by 400 m giving an area of between 12 and 13 ha (Fig. 24). As has twice been observed, the ditch of the fort of the early Empire served as a foundation trench for the late Roman town wall, and this was used as a support for the medieval enclosure wall, so accurately that the different alignments prove to be identical, give or take a few metres. The unity of construction of the late Roman circuit is obvious from its foundations of large reused blocks, the same vertical facing in small stonework but without tile-courses, at least in its lower part, and coarse rubble.

Several points of the enclosure have been recognized since 1975, in the eastern angle of the site. The Roman foundations are preserved there in the sub-foundations of the Château Comtal. Layers of moulded, sculpted or inscribed blocks make up the foundation of a wall with a facing of small stonework bonded with a lime and crushed brick mortar and without a tile bonding-course. Other *sondages* conducted in 1983 have allowed the recovery of the rounded shape of the corner of the urban fortification. The line of the eastern rampart can therefore be reconstructed, like the other three, behind the facing of the medieval enclosure. Only the south-west wall has not revealed the secret of its course.

In rue Saint-Jean the destruction level of the buildings of the early imperial fort contained coins from Gallienus to Claudius II. The deposits covering the foundations of the wall contained coins of Tetricus (and copies). The site of the fort was clearly levelled after materials had been recovered, then reoccupied at the time of the erection of the urban enclosure. This evidence, as well as the famous passage of the panegyric, seem to agree in attributing to Carausius the authorship of the new wall built in the ditch of the fort. Moreover, the late 3rd-century enclosure wall offers a considerable unity in its construction technique and its establishment.

Investigations undertaken during extension-work on the Palais de Justice exposed a stretch of the late Roman wall, knowledge of the construction technique and context of which could be retrieved. The wall is wedged between the medieval ring of walls and the rampart of the early Roman fort. It was built in the partially back-filled ditch of the fort on reused blocks which were piled up in tiers. The superstructure, built in rubble bonded with a grey-coloured lime mortar, does not have a tile bonding-course. The thickness of the wall can be estimated to be rather less than 4 m.

In 1988 the first towers of the enclosure were discovered on the north-east side. They are semi-circular, project from 2.65 to 2.70 m from the wall face and are 5.80 to 7.30 m in diameter.

If the construction of the enclosure to a single plan can probably be dated to the end of the third century, one problem remains. On the west as well as the east wall a distinct construction phase has been observed. On the west it takes the form of two rectangular features, similar to quadrangular towers, situated outside the wall of the fort and inside the late Roman circuit. The same phenomenon can be seen on the eastern side where excavations are in progress. These constructions are of late date since they rest on the walls of the fort; on the other hand their connection with the late Roman enclosure is not known. Are they evidence of a chronologically intermediate circuit, preceding the erection of the town wall set up only in the 4th century? Are they a later development than the town wall? The absence of strategraphic links between the foundations does not allow us to resolve the problem. The archaeological observations seem to lean in favour of the latter theory, but the positioning of towers inside the wall speak in favour of the former.

Literature
Belot 1981, 29-31; Delmaire 1978, 25-8; Gosselin, Seillier & Leclercq 1976, 5-15; Gosselin, Seillier & Florin 1978, 18-22; Gosselin & Seillier 1978, 50-7: 1981, 19-21; Heliot 1958, I, 158-82: II, 40-64; Heurgon 1948: 1949; Johnson 1976, 83-5; Johnson 1983a; Le Bourdelles 1988, 77-82; Seillier 1977, 35-8: 1984, 169-80: 1987, 25; Seillier & Gosselin 1969, 363-72: 1973, 55-6: 1975, 71; Seillier, Gosselin & Leclercq 1971, 669-79; Will 1960, 363-80.

OUDENBURG

TOPOGRAPHICAL SITUATION AND DISCOVERIES

The military site is located in the centre of the town of Oudenburg, between the Vulderstraat, Nordstraat, Weststraat and Cuperstraat. In the late Roman period it could have been sited on the coastline of the North Sea. Two cemeteries contemporary with the fortifications are known.

The existence of an old town (Aldenborg) is mentioned from 866, and the chronicle of the Abbey of St Peter at Oudenburg, dating from 1084-1087, notes the discovery of antiquities. In 1957-60, 1970 and in 1976-7 there has been archaeological investigation of the *castellum* and of one of the associated cemeteries. The north-west side has been the object of regular and recent research, as has the north-east quarter of the fort interior.

PLAN AND DEFENCES

Examination of the north-east sector of the fort has allowed the observation of a succession of three occupation phases of a military nature:

OUDENBURG I: the fort is demarcated by a ditch about 4.50 m wide and 1.40 m deep, and by a rampart of earth and sand. The ditch in question seems to have been situated

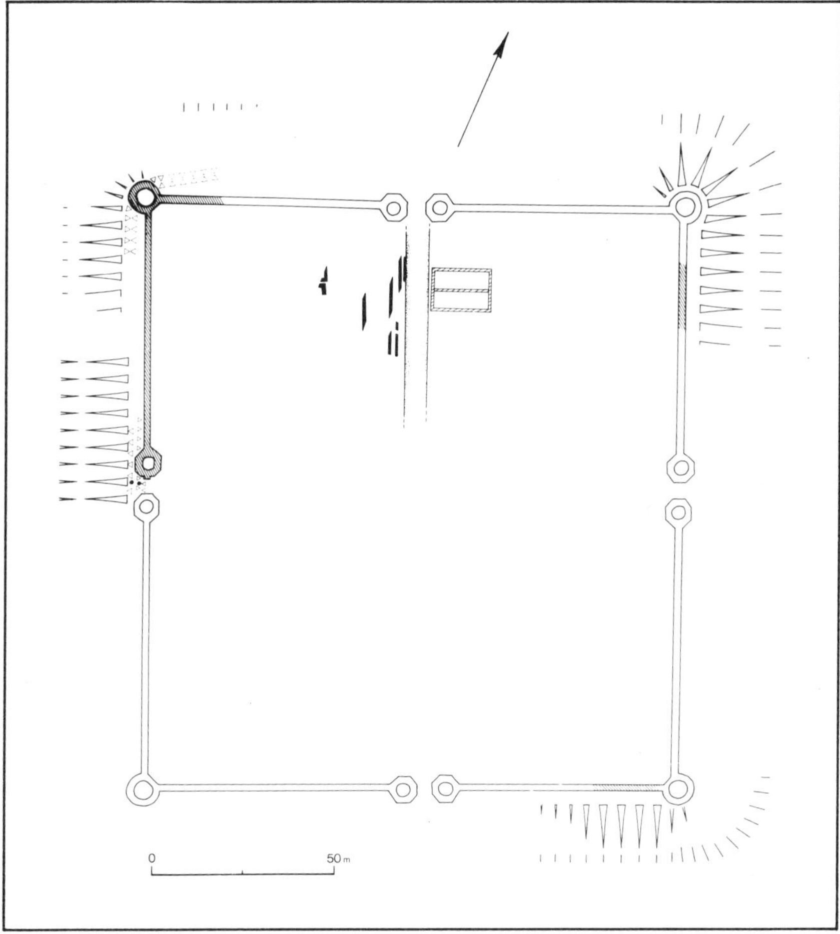

Fig. 25 The castellum of Oudenburg: plan of recent research (after Mertens).

towards the north, inside the later enclosure. The plan of Oudenburg I is not known. It must have been smaller than Oudenburg II and III and on a slightly different orientation.

Oudenburg II: the fort is demarcated by a ditch 3 m wide and by a rampart of earth and blocks of heather, reinforced with timber on the outer face.

Oudenburg III: the fort is demarcated by a ditch 20 m wide, and by a wall 1.30 m thick, sited only 2 m from the defensive ditch (Fig. 25). This wall, built from small ashlars of Tournai stone against which rested an internal earthen rampart, was strengthened by towers, circular at the corners and octagonal at the gates. The diameters of these towers attained 9 m and 7 m respectively, with walls 1.80 to 2 m and 1.55 m thick. The *castellum* is practically square in plan: 146 by 163 m (area: 2.4 ha).

FORT INTERIOR

In the north-west quarter of the fortification some hearths, a well and traces of buildings on a N-S alignment were brought to light. A N-S road metalling undoubtedly corresponds to the *cardo*. This was bordered by a two-phase stone structure 13.50 m by 18.50 m.

CHRONOLOGY

According to recent coin finds the construction of the fort dates to the end of the 2nd century or the beginning of the 3rd. Occupation continued until the beginning of the 5th century. Burials of the second half of the 4th century, in the cemetery, prove that the place was still occupied at this time.

Relative chronology:
Oudenburg I: late 2nd or mid-3rd century - 275; fortification of unknown plan; the ditch was filled in at the time of the construction of Oudenburg II.
Oudenburg II: 275 - beginning of 4th century; rampart of earth and heather blocks; wattle and daub buildings of elongated plan (III); destroyed by fire; ditch filled in at the time of the digging of the ditch of Oudenburg III.
Oudenburg III: after 275 and 4th century; the enclosure wall was built in the filled-in ditches of Oudenburg I and II; reconstruction of buildings to match the new alignment of the walls.

Literature

Mertens 1962, 51-62: 1978, 73-6: 1987; Mertens & van Impe 1971, 9-18; *Romeinen* 1978.

AARDENBURG

THE SITE

The site is located in the centre of the modern town. The first research dates from 1955 and after 1961. New excavations, conducted after 1975, revealed the presence of an important establishment surrounded by a ditch and an enclosure wall with circular towers.

The plan of the fortified site corresponds to a rectangle 3.8 ha in area, the wall of which, 1.20 m thick, is strengthened with towers 8 m in diameter (Fig. 26). The recessed rectangular gate structures are flanked by round towers. The ditch is at a distance of 7 m from the walls.

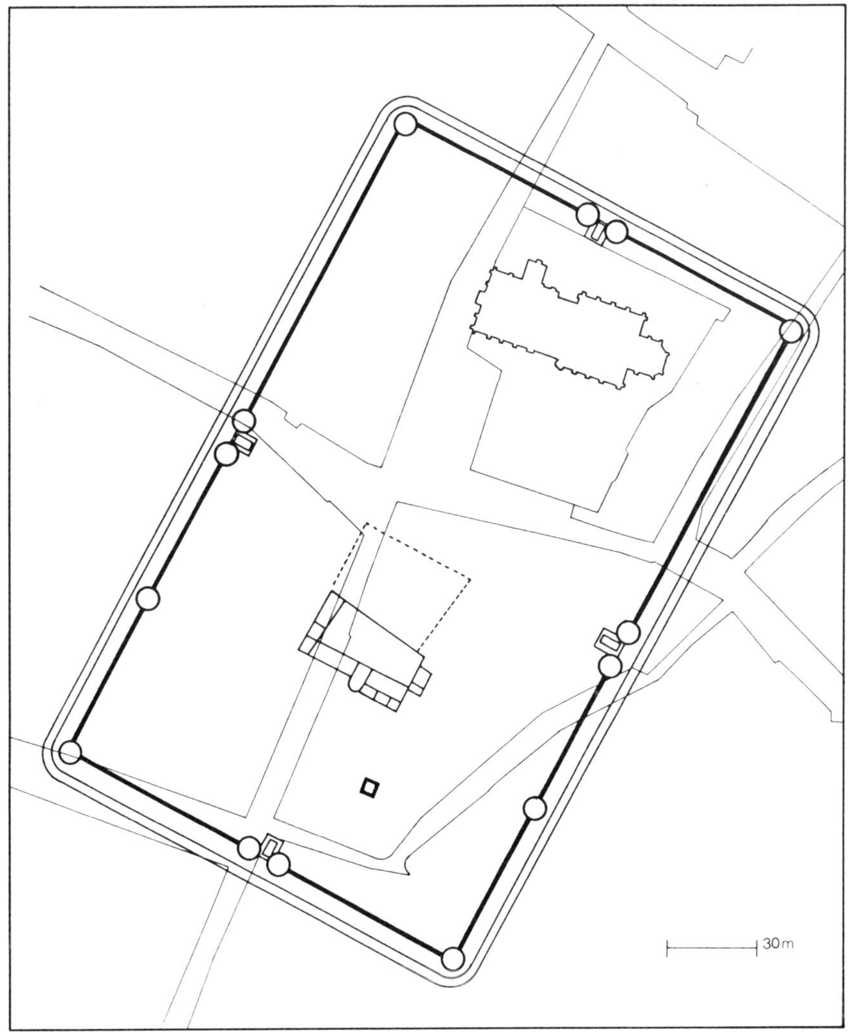

Fig. 26 Aardenburg (after Trimpe-Burger).

Inside the site there is a large building with an apse, undoubtedly the *principia*, insofar as it is a building of military character.

The construction of the enclosure wall can be dated to the end of the 2nd or the middle of the 3rd centuries. Two coin hoards buried after 271-273 confirm that the site was abandoned towards 275. In any case there is insignificant archaeological material of the 4th century and given the marine transgression of Dunkirk II the site no longer assumed any importance in the late Empire.

INTERPRETATION

Whether the nature of Aardenburg was essentially urban or military remains a matter of dispute. The abandonment of the site by the 4th century prevented it from playing its role as a military post of the *litus Saxonicum*. The very developed appearance of its defences in the 3rd century favours a civil interpretation of the site. It may be suggested, rather, that Aardenburg was regarded as an important urban establishment, but at high risk during the 3rd century, which led to the erection of an enclosure to protect the civil settlement. But Aardenburg could temporarily have assumed a mixed function a little before 275, the date of its abandonment. The monumental building considered to be a *principia* certainly bears witness to the use of the site as a military fortification at a some given time.

Literature

de Melker 1987; de Vries 1968; Johnson 1983a, 196-7; Trimpe-Burger 1985, 335-46.

THE BRITTENBURG

Since 1520 when the Brittenburg fortification became known, it has always been regarded as the northernmost base for military operations in the defence system protecting the Atlantic coast in the late Empire. New research undertaken at Katwijk and Valkenburg as well as new interpretations clearly undermine this view.

Generally speaking, the sector at the mouth of the Rhine has produced tile-stamps of various military units which, at least in the early Empire, were linked more with the defence of the Rhine frontier: *exercitus Germaniae Inferioris, legio XXX, I Minervia p.f.* and *classis Germanica p.f.*

A *horreum* in use in the 4th century in the fort at Valkenburg no longer entails the necessity of interpreting the Brittenburg as a late Roman military granary. At Katwijk, believed to be the *vicus* of Brittenburg, recent excavations have shown that there was no archaeological material of 4th century date, any more than at the Brittenburg, indicating that these two sites were not occupied later than the 3rd century.

The proposed interpretation suggests that the Brittenburg be regarded as a civil establishment of an urban nature which, just like Aardenburg, acquired an enclosure wall towards the end of the second or in the third century, for reasons of security or linked to the rising water level. It has even been suggested that the civilian urban settlement of *Lugdunum* be sited at the Brittenburg.

Literature
Bloemers & de Weerd 1983, 245-51: 1984, 41-51; de Weerd 1986, 284-90; Groenman 1986, 159-68.

RAYMOND BRULET

THE SOUTH-EAST AFTER THE ROMANS: THE SAXON SETTLEMENT

That great pioneer Alfred Plettke, when he was laying the foundations of Migration Period chronology in North Germany, used the historical evidence for the so-called *Adventus Saxonum* - the migration of Continental Saxons, Angles, Jutes and Frisians into Britain - as his yardstick for establishing a formula for the fifth century (Plettke 1921). With reference to the archaeological objects, principally the pottery and metalwork which are our prime sources of evidence for these folk movements, he wrote 'Types found both in Britain and Germany are in principle fifth century; those found in Germany alone are fourth-century or earlier, and those found in Britain alone are sixth century or later'. That the passage of time has left this simple definition substantially correct still is due to the fact that the historical information he used, though slight, was reasonably authoritative because independent and nearly contemporary. He used just the snippets of information about Britain recorded by the late fifth-century Byzantine historian Zosimus, two passages from *The Gallic Chronicle of 452* and extracts from the 'History of Britain' which prefaces *The Ruin of Britain* by the British cleric Gildas. Plettke was not seduced by the mid-fifth century dates for the first coming of the ancestral English computed by the Venerable Bede of Jarrow, in his *Chronica Majora* of 725 and his *Historia Ecclesiastica Gentis Anglorum* of 731, nor those given in the partially Bede-dependent *Anglo-Saxon Chronicle*, compiled in the ninth century. So he, and following him, most North German chronologists, escaped the error of nearly half a century which, until all too lately, bedeviled English writings, archaeological and historical alike, about the date of the first Anglo-Saxon settlements.

Turning first to the historical evidence, it must be said that though our sources are slight indeed they have generated an enormous critical literature in recent years. Obviously it would be impossible to do justice to all of it in a short synthetic survey such as this. In any modern study of the chronology of the Anglo-Saxon settlements it is necessary at once to dismiss the testimony of the Venerable Bede. He was by no means a primary source for the *Adventus Saxonum*: indeed for events in the fourth and fifth centuries he had very little factual evidence at all. From external sources, notably Constantius's *Vita Germani* he could cull only incidental references; from the English side there were only undated oral traditions, mainly Kentish, and probably a collection of Anglo-Saxon royal genealogies. Therefore, his only major source for historical narrative was that in the *De Excidio et Conquestu Britanniae* which the British cleric Gildas had 'published' between 545 and 549 (Miller 1975a). Modern historical criticism has done much to validate the coherence and intelligibility of the Gildasian narrative (Stevens 1941b; Miller 1975b; Dumville 1984), but enormous problems remain and for Bede the unfamiliar Latin style (Kerlouégen 1968; Winterbottom 1974-5) and general lack of absolute dates presented problems which led to misunderstandings, reinterpretation and wrong chronological computations (Miller 1975b).

We must look at Gildas again independently of Bede. He lived and wrote somewhere in western Britain, either in the north or south-east Wales, and clearly had no close knowledge at all of events and personalities in eastern Britain. By his own account he had little documentary evidence to draw on and relied heavily on tradition, which sometimes, as when he misplaced the building of Hadrian's and the Antonine Wall in his historical narrative, led him astray. He told a horrific disaster-story about Britain in the fifth century, which some have dismissed as borrowed from foreign literary models, but which increasingly we find illustrated and vindicated by archaeological findings. Gildas based the history of Britain after the death of Maximus in 388 on a triad of appeals from the Britons to Rome for help against their northern enemies the Picts: the first two were answered by Roman military expeditions, the third to *Agitius ter consul*, was ignored. Despite a famine and a civil war, the British succeeded in driving off the northern barbarians, who thereafter raided only sporadically. A time of unexampled prosperity then ensued, marred however by the rise and fall of kings (*tyranni*), and vice and corruption amongst laity and clergy alike. Meanwhile another attack threatened from the north, and this, combined with the debilitating actuality of a serious plague, led one *superbus tyrannus*, who was probably called *Vertigernus*, sixth-century form *Vortigerno* (Miller 1975b, 252-3; Dumville 1977, 183-5), to commit what Gildas, with benefit of hindsight, castigates as the ultimate folly of inviting in Saxons as mercenaries. The first three ship-loads were established with the status of *foederati* somewhere in the east of England, and seem to have done their job effectively, for Picts are not mentioned again. They were followed by a larger contingent of reinforcements who were also accepted as *foederati*, all of whom as a matter of course expected their hosts to provide them with food supplies, the technical military terms for which Gildas mentions, *i.e. epimenia*, monthly rations, *annona*, supply of corn. After some time, *multos annos*, they complained of insufficient rations and making good their threat to break their treaty obligations, they overran and pillaged the British territory to the west of them, besieging and sacking towns, and carrying the fire of destruction to the western ocean. Many Britons were killed, including magnates and priests, others were driven overseas, others were driven to take refuge in the high hills, 'menacing and fortified'.

In time the British rallied under a noble leader, Ambrosius Aurelianus, and from that time first one side then the other was victorious down to the siege of *Mons Badonicus*, when the Britons won a notable victory which bought them a long interval of peace. This still endured at the time Gildas was writing. In a complicated passage Gildas tells us that the battle of Badon was fought in the year he was born, which was the forty-fourth before his 'publication' of the *De Excidio*. This backward computation apparently baffled Bede, who interpreted the text from the Anglo-Saxon viewpoint as meaning forty-four years after the *Adventus Saxonum*, but this we may dismiss (Miller 1975a, 171-3). The two versions have given rise to lengthy and conflicting debates about the date of *Mons Badonicus*, but it is generally agreed nowadays that it cannot be placed more precisely than around AD 500.

If the early sixth century saw the end of the first phase of Anglo-Saxon aggression, when did it begin? For Bede, having no other source of information, it began after the letter to *Agitius ter consul*, whom he identified, rightly in the opinion of most modern scholars, with Aetius, whose third consulship lasted from 446-454. But as a *terminus post quem* for the whole sequence of events leading to the beginning of the Anglo-Saxon settlements it hopelessly constricted the timetable, as Bede himself was unhappily aware. So he silently emended Gildas's text to reduce to a minimum the interval between letter and the invitation to the Saxons. His consequent dates for the coming of the English, variously about 445, 446/7, 449, 450-55, all seem computed and are now generally discredited.

The problem posed by the letter to Aetius has been much debated. Miller argued that it belongs in a section of Gildas's narrative dealing exclusively with the Pictish wars, and removed it altogether from the prologue to the five chapters dealing with the Saxon mutiny (Miller 1975b). Thompson (1979) suggested that the whole narrative of events refers to the north of Britain and has no relevance to anything recorded in southern tradition about the coming of the Saxons, so the dating of the letter becomes immaterial in any but the very localized context of a few federates in Northumbria. Dumville goes much further in warning us off reliance on Gildas: 'the problems involved in viewing his account as a straightforward history of sub-Roman Britain as a whole are so appalling as to imperil any credence which we might give to Gildas as a source for any period before his own adult lifetime. What this means, in turn, is that ideas of the place of Vortigern, Hencgest and Horsa, Ambrosius Aurelianus, the Battle of Mount Badon....in the development of southern English history must be abandoned, completely and at once.' (Dumville 1984, 79). This bitter pill may take some time in the swallowing and there may yet be rebels who prefer to agree with earlier writers that Gildas's letter to Aetius is indeed relevant to affairs in the south but was confused by him with the last of his dimly remembered triad of appeals for military assistance, which were actually sent in the last days of Roman Britain; namely the so-called 'rescript' of Honorius in 410, telling the *civitates* of Britain that they must defend themselves (Myres 1946, 1951, 1986; Hawkes 1956). The argument is that Gildas had no means of dating the third consulship of Aetius. This remains a very tempting option, and one I shall adopt for present purposes, for if Gildas's third appeal is removed back to just before 410, the succeeding events he describes fall beautifully into place, and though we must exchange Picts for Saxons his story bears a close resemblance to the early fifth-century history of events we can piece together from other sources.

In 407, the newly elected British Emperor, the usurper or, as we may now begin to call such men, the tyrant Constantine III, removed what must have been the last of the Roman army from Britain to prevent the Vandals, Alans and Suevi, who had invaded Gaul, from seizing the port of Boulogne and thus cutting off Britain from the Continent. He never came back. In 408 he took the army to Spain, leaving Britain undefended, and in 410 (Jones & Casey 1988), as the *Gallic Chronicler of 452* tells us, 'The British provinces were devastated by an incursion of Saxons.' We learn from Zosimus (vi.3.3) that the British rebelled against Rome and Roman laws, and 'taking up arms and fighting on their own behalf, freed the cities from the barbarians who were pressing upon them.' They also expelled the Roman officials and established a sovereign constitution on their own authority, so that when Honorius wrote in 410 (Zosimus vi.10.2), presumably refusing an appeal for military assistance, he had to address himself to the *civitates*, who were now governing themselves. In 411, Procopius (Vandal War iii.2.38) tells us that 'The Romans were no longer able to recover Britain, but it remained from that time under tyrants.' One of those tyrants was Vortigern, perhaps another usurping Emperor, who was not only mentioned in Gildas and Bede but also in the semi-legendary material, some of it clearly ancient, incorporated in the ninth-century *Historia Britonnum*, where he figures as the chief opponent of St Germanus who, in 429, visited Britain to combat the spread of the Pelagian heresy. Vortigern was presumably a Pelagian, while his enemy Ambrosius belonged to the Catholic party (Myres 1960).

And the quarrelling which was to be the downfall of the magnates of Britain extended also to the question of military defence. According to the Kentish traditions narrated in the *Historia*, Vortigern's policy of employing Germanic federates against the Picts divided him from his colleagues, whose decision not to go on feeding and clothing them after they had done their job, but to send them home, led directly to the federate revolt. Vortigern, who is said to have feared Ambrosius on the one hand and Roman intervention on the other, took the advice of Hengest and sent for yet more of his people, ceding them land for their maintenance in East Kent and, displacing its British ruler Guoirancgon, the city of Canterbury itself. Afterwards Vortigern's son Vortemir attempted to drive them out, fighting three battles, apparently identical with those mentioned in the *Anglo-Saxon Chronicle*, but Hengest survived to betray Vortigern and to force him to cede more territory, namely Essex, Middlesex and Sussex. The *Anglo-Saxon Chronicle* makes no mention of the two former, but reports the Anglo-Saxon landtakings in the order Kent, Sussex, southern Wessex and the Isle of Wight.

Though Bede was led by his Kentish informants to believe that Hengest was the leader of Gildas's federates, there can be no proof of this. It has been suggested that Hengest was remembered when other early leaders were forgotten because he was a "Woden-born royal" (Miller 1975b, 254). He may have been, but a more likely explanation for the survival of heroic stories about him is that Kent acquired a stable royal dynasty early enough to preserve oral traditions of original founder figures and events. Further, Kent became dominant from an early date and Kentish `dynastic propaganda' probably disseminated the Hengest stories more widely than those of other kingdoms. Hence Hengest's appearance in heroic literature and the strong Kentish emphasis in Bede and the *Historia*. The latter gives us two computed dates for the arrival of Hengest and his federates, 428 (Dumville 1974) and *c.* 430 (Ward 1972). If neither is exactly correct they cannot be far wrong (Morris 1965) if we accept that Vortigern may have recruited Hengest to help counter possible interference from Aetius, who was active in Gaul at this date (Wood 1987, 252), and that the federate revolt took place in 441/2, when, as the *Gallic Chronicler* tells us, `The provinces of Britain, which up to this time had been harassed by various disasters and accidents, are brought under the control of the Saxons.' It seems that something decisive happened which, ten years later across the Channel, appeared to mark the end of a process of Saxon conquest (Myres 1946, 1951; Morris 1965; Jones & Casey 1988), not of all the British provinces, of course, but of those closest and best known to Gaul. If we allow it in this context, `The Groans of the Britons', the appeal to Aetius in 446 or later, with its lament `The barbarians drive us to the sea: the sea drives us back on the barbarians: between them two kinds of death await us, we are either slaughtered or drowned' - will have been occasioned by the federate revolt. For subsequent events on the English front we have to return to the early traditions preserved in annalistic form in the *Anglo-Saxon Chronicle*, whose chronological framework, based on Easter Tables, is probably artificial and liable to nineteen-year dislocations through scribal error in copying from lunar calendars (Harrison 1976, 127 f.). The events were tabulated in relative order beginning with an *Adventus* in Kent in 449, and if we accept that this derives from Bede and is probably too late by about twenty years, `it follows that, to recover the form and intent of the compilers, all fifth-century entries must be set back about twenty years' (Morris 1965, 157). Such a calibration of the Chronicle would place the fighting in Kent before and after 441/2, the colonization of Sussex in the third quarter of the fifth century and of Hampshire before its end.

With this revised history of events, archaeology is now marvellously in accord. The earliest Germanic settlers do seem to have come to eastern England. They were the founders of the great cremation cemeteries (Fig. 27), in East Anglia, Lincolnshire, the Midlands and East Yorkshire (e.g. Caistor-by-Norwich, Spong Hill, Loveden Hill and Sancton). Amongst their earliest urns we find vessels comparable not only with those from Anglian areas of north Germany, but also with those from Saxon lands between the Elbe and Weser. 'In the earliest days it would seem that folk of Angle and Saxon, and indeed other, antecedents were establishing themselves indiscriminately over the regions that were later dominated by Anglian regimes' (Myres 1970). The Saxon component is reflected also in the less numerous finds of metalwork from these cemeteries, and is exceptionally useful for dating purposes. Alone amongst the peoples of north Germany, the Saxons were in close enough contact with the Late Roman Empire in the West, with Gaul and with the Rhineland, in the late fourth and fifth centuries, for their material culture, their pots and brooches *etc.*, to be closely dateable, directly or indirectly, by association with Roman finds (Böhme 1974 and 1986; Schmid 1977). Further north, in Schleswig, Fünen and Jutland, the chronological framework is much more problematic (Morris 1974; Kidd 1976).

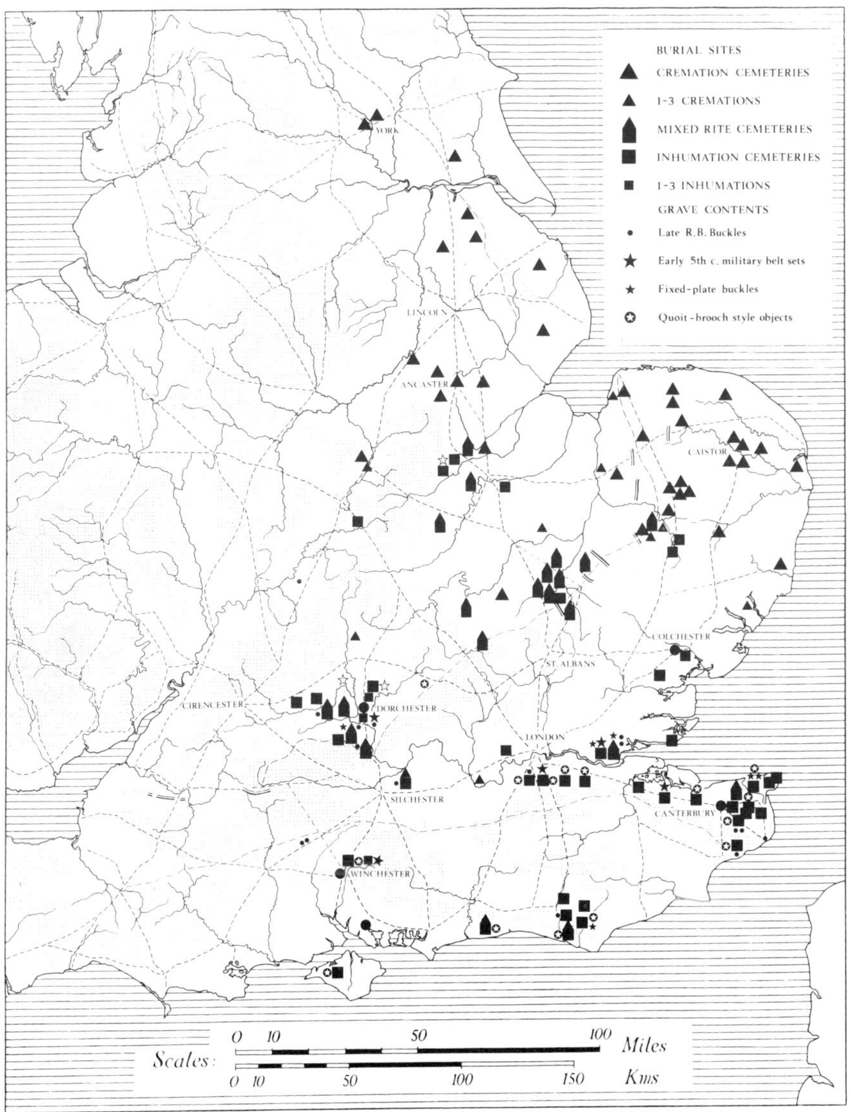

Fig. 27 Distribution of Anglo-Saxon cemeteries, to show the distinction between cremating and inhumating peoples, and the occurrence of Late Roman and Quoit Brooch Style metalwork.

In his various works on Anglo-Saxon pottery particularly and the Anglo-Saxon settlements in general, Myres has clung tenaciously to a theory of north German settlement in eastern England during the fourth century (Myres 1969, 62 ff., 1986, 98 ff.; Myres & Southern 1973, 14 ff.; Myres & Green 1973, 13, 43 ff.). He has come under heavy and justified attack for his mishandling of north German ceramic 'parallels', for his uncritical use of Albrectsen's too early chronology for Fünen and, in the Saxon area, his bias towards the earliest date possible for ceramic types which, in fact, enjoyed considerable longevity (Morris 1974; Hawkes 1974; Kidd 1976; Schmid 1976). Since north German chronological systems are normally constructed in broad overlapping phases to allow for such longevity of artifact manufacture and use, and Schmid (1976) has suggested that Caistor and the other eastern cremation cemeteries came into use in Böhme's critical but for Britain all-too-broad Phase II (380-420), it is no wonder that Kidd doubted whether 'archaeological material from Germania can be directly used to elucidate calendrically based, historical problems where the span of a generation is critical' (Kidd 1976). For the period 380-420, we need even greater precision: as the historical discussion has shown, these forty years saw the beginning of the end of Roman Britain, and critical events were taking place every few years. The challenge, then, is to see how far our hard-won history can refine on north German archaeological chronology.

Myres's dating of the first coming of the English to 'at least one generation before the complete collapse of Roman rule in Britain' (1969, 72), *i.e. c.* 380, stems directly from his observation that many of our early cremation cemeteries are situated very close to Roman towns, and his assumption that these early north Germans were being employed by the British as mercenaries to defend the towns. In human terms the scenario was never convincing. These were out-and-out barbarians, many from regions beyond the zone of previous direct contact with the Roman Empire, who, even after they arrived in Britain, remained totally unromanized both in their burial customs and their material culture. Germans employed in a military capacity in fourth-century Gaul (Böhme 1974), whether garrisons of the forts or units of the field army billeted on towns or country estates, inhumed their dead after Roman fashion and created a whole proud new fashion of burying their weapons and officially produced belt-fittings (the insignia of status for men) and brooches (the distinctive clues to the ethnic dress of their women), along with an often large assemblage of Roman vessels, according to rank. If we had excavated more Late Roman cemeteries in Britain we might see something comparable here, but there are positive indications from the headquarters fort of the Saxon Shore at Richborough (Hawkes & Dunning 1962-3, *passim*) that the garrison included such Germanic troops. Böhme (1986), reappraising all the finds of official Late Roman belt-fittings and weapons from other forts, towns and rural sites, has expressed himself more positively than I felt able to, in a pioneering work nearly thirty years ago, that these may represent the dispositions of at least some of the various units of the army in Late Roman Britain. There is a particularly important group of such 'military' finds from within the walls of Roman Caistor-by-Norwich, but significantly not a scrap of such equipment from the Anglo-Saxon cremation cemetery outside the walls. In fact there is not a scrap of official Late Roman military gear, whether fourth or fifth-century in date, from any one of the great cremation cemeteries north of the Thames. Their total independence from Roman influence makes these people very unlikely recruits indeed, either as *laeti* in the fourth century or, as Morris (1974) would have them, *foederati* deliberately introduced by *c.* 420. Indeed, it is difficult to imagine how the authorities of Late-Roman or Sub-Roman Britain could have contacted such peoples to recruit them by deliberate policy.

So let us consider a third hypothesis, that these were the Anglo-Saxon invaders who devastated Britain in 410. The evidence fits this hypothesis quite neatly. Böhme (1974, 1986), in his study of Germanic finds in Britain, has shown that except for the occasional broken and outworn heirloom, there is no fourth-century Germanic metalwork in any of our Anglo-Saxon cemeteries. In his more recent paper he rightly stresses the difference between fourth- and fifth-century metalwork types in England. Except for a few probably heirloom pots, there is nothing buried with these cremating peoples that need imply a date of arrival before the early fifth century. Historically, of course, the invaders of 410 are said to have been defeated, but, faced with what seems to have been a folk migration of whole families, how were the British authorities to get rid of them? Where, after all, with their homelands rendered uninhabitable by severe flooding, had the Saxon and Frisian immigrants to go? The participation of the Angles, and in Kent the Jutes, suggests that there must have been good reasons at this time for people to abandon homes in the Jutland peninsula too. These may have been both ecological and political. In sum then, Britain may have been faced with a major refugee problem. There are no weapon burials in the Anglo-Saxon cremation cemeteries in Britain, so it is very difficult to judge how warlike these people may have been. Presumably there were some trained warriors, perhaps erstwhile pirates who knew eastern Britain well, amongst their leaders to help organize the crossing from north Germany and the taking up of land on arrival, and, particularly as we are dealing with mixed ethnic groups, to keep order amongst the firstcomers.

Elsewhere at this time, Germanic refugees were often settled with some kind of federate status, and this may well have happened in eastern England, which, after long years of piratical raids during the fourth century, may have been a severely depopulated zone. From the fate of the towns (Wacher 1975), it seems clear that, in most parts of eastern England, control by the British *civitates* must have lapsed early in the fifth century. Positive archaeological evidence for the survival of the British in areas occupied by the Anglo-Saxons is virtually non-existent at present, but can sometimes be inferred from gaps in the pattern of Germanic settlement, notably around towns such as Verulamium and Lincoln, for example. British presence in the countryside is harder to detect but, in East Anglia certainly, the first Anglo-Saxon settlers seem to have respected and indeed avoided what had been major Roman villa estates, the implication surely being that these were still under the control of powerful British magnates capable of defending them (C. Scull, pers. comment). So the first Anglo-Saxon settlers in this region may well have been encouraged to take up some of the less attractive land, the sort of sandy land which they were in fact well used to farming in the north German homelands. The Anglo-Saxon settlement at West Stow, for example, on a sandy island in a marsh, was formed on the nearest thing to a north German *terp* or *wurt* that could be imagined in the English landscape. To what extent the British could have controlled these people once settled is debatable, but one suspects that our cremating Anglo-Saxons may have been to all intents and purposes free settlers from the outset. Except in a few cases where urban settlement and burial in Roman extra-mural cemeteries has been attested by excavation, *e.g.* Ancaster, Godmanchester (Rodwell & Rowley 1975), York, and as we shall see at Colchester and Canterbury, the first Anglo-Saxon settlers may have attached themselves to towns, not for military reasons, but for the sake of the townlands, the cleared and readily cultivable fields in their immediate vicinity. This seems certainly to have been the case at Caistor-by-Norwich.

By 420, or thereabouts, ten years after the Britons had apparently appealed unsuccessfully to Rome for military assistance, large tracts of country north of the Thames had perhaps already passed to the English. If so, we have a partial explanation for another phenomenon of the earlier fifth century. On both sides of the river Thames, which is both the principal route of entry into central England and a major frontier between north and south, we find the burials of other Germanic peoples. But these are very different. They consist of small numbers of people who had adopted the Roman funeral rite of inhumation; the men buried with their weapons and wearing fifth-century versions of the late Roman military belt; the women a mixture of Romano-British ornaments and their own north German brooches. Remains of such people have been found in two places very close to the Roman town of Dorchester, at a major crossing and customs's post on the Upper Thames; at Croydon south of London; at Mucking in Essex, on a hill overlooking the Thames estuary; and at Milton Regis in Kent, beside a creek on the south bank of the river (Hawkes & Dunning 1962-3; Evison 1968, 1981; Hawkes 1986; Böhme 1986). They were mainly Saxons, perhaps admixed with Franks, and are very reminiscent of, perhaps recruited from, Germanic troops who served as *comitatenses* and *foederati* in northern Gaul and the Rhineland during the later fourth and fifth centuries (Böhme 1974). Certainly their burial customs and equipment speak for an established relationship with the late Roman Empire. They are just the sort of people, familiar and available across the Channel, whom the magnates of Britain would have sought to recruit to their own defence, against potentially hostile north Germans as well as Picts, after 410 (Hawkes 1986). From their distribution, they will have been protecting southern and south-western Britain, against the Midlands, the North and ingress from whatever quarter up the Thames. They will have been hired to protect London and its communications upriver to Cirencester, whence came necessary supplies of grain and wool. Their small numbers suggest that their employers were the local *civitates*, rather than that they were units of any continuing official army of Britain after 407 (*pace* Böhme 1986). However, the simple fact that anyone bothered to hire such small numbers of militarily trained German soldiers in this period suggests that a few armed men at strategic places would have been effective.

At Dorchester-on-Thames and Milton Regis, their equipment comprises the broadest form of the military belt, with narrow end-plates, plain lanceolate strap-ends, rosette attachments with suspension loops and, in the case of Dorchester, a buckle with repaired hinge-plate (Hawkes & Dunning 1962-3, Abb. 1 and 3). They are of a type (Ypey 1969) which began its development during the last decade of the fourth century, but which, in the forms in which we have them in Anglo-Saxon contexts, outlasted the circulation of the last western coinage, of Constantine III (407-11) and Jovinus (411-13), and so occur in largely undated contexts. Yet the contemporary womens' brooches at Dorchester, the famous early cruciform brooch and trio of applied brooches (Kirk and Leeds 1954), indicate a relatively early date in the overlap between Böhme's phases II and III, *c.* 420. The earliest graves in the more recently excavated cemeteries at Mucking, Essex, contain a British made version, in early Quoit Brooch Style, of an elaborate five-piece military belt-set in flat chip-carving style, modelled on Ypey's Form A (I, grave 117); an unusual version of Form B, with fixed-plate buckle cast-in-one piece with one of the end-plates (II, grave 989); and a hybrid form of Stützarmfibel similar to Böhme's Type Mahndorf (II, gr. 987; Evison 1977, 128 f., fig. 1.i), found in association with a worn late fourth-century Romano-British buckle with horse-heads on the dolphin-head loop (Hawkes Type IB; Hawkes & Dunning 1962-3; Hawkes 1973 and 1974a; Böhme 1986). These founder burials in Cemetery II at Mucking appear to be perhaps a little later than that in Cemetery I and the graves at Dorchester and Milton Regis, and may be dateable nearer the middle of the fifth century (Hawkes 1986, 71).

These groups along the Thames are likely to represent some of the first real federates, whose terms of employment were correctly transmitted to and by Gildas. It has been suggested by Stevens (1941, 368 f.) that, in using the terms *annona*, *epimenia* and *hospites*, 'Gildas gives what seems to be a correct description of *foederatio* in its early stages of allowance of victuals (and billeting arrangements) which preceded the grants of portions of landed estates.' (See also Jones 1964, 199 ff.). Since the first recorded occasion when Late Roman authorities were forced by financial stringency to cede land in lieu of victuals occurred in 418, when the Visigoths were settled in southern Gaul, we may have here a precious historical indicator of the latest date by which federate settlement, under the old terms, may have taken place in Britain. As always the attention focuses on the Dorchester Saxons, who seem to have been billeted in the Late Roman town, perhaps still in receipt of Late Roman pay (Frere 1966), but who seem not to have been the founders of Anglo-Saxon dynasties like the people at Mucking. At this early date these may not have been Vortigern's federates but part of the defensive measures taken by the *civitates* of Britain in general after AD 410. The military men at Mucking and Croydon, who became founders of cemeteries, may have been recruited slightly later. There may have been several separate phases of federate employment.

Vortigern's federates in Kent seem certainly to have been different. In the first place, Kentish tradition remembered that from the outset they were granted the island of Thanet; a land grant, therefore, in keeping with their later date of recruitment. In the second place they were a different kind of people. Tradition recorded by Bede, the *Historia Britonnum* and the poems *Beowulf* and the *Finnsburg Fragment*, makes Hengest and his following a band of exiles from Jutland via Frisia; unemployed warriors with no previous Roman service and hence no distinguishing military equipment, seeking service with a new lord in Britain. Most of the earliest Germanic settlers in Kent were indeed Jutes or other South Scandinavians, as their pottery (Myres 1970, 28 ff.), their cruciform brooches (Reichstein 1975, 90 ff.; Hawkes & Pollard 1981, 322 ff.), their relief and square-headed brooches, and their gold bracteates, all combine to show (Bakka 1958, 1973 and 1981; Chadwick 1958, Hawkes 1969, Hawkes and Pollard 1981; Haseloff 1974 and 1981; Leeds 1946). Moreover, the Jutish connexion seems to have begun and continued at a high aristocratic level, despite a Frankish connexion, beginning around the middle of the fifth century, which strengthened during the first half of the sixth. So archaeology supports historical traditions of a Nordic ancestry for the Kentish royal house. The real problem in Kent is the apparent lack of fifth-century graves: most of the fifth-century metalwork that survives was buried later, in rich inhumation graves of the sixth century. The distorting factor seems to be that the first Jutes may have practised cremation and that a high percentage of their burial urns can have been destroyed by intensive ploughing of Kent's chalk downland since the last century. However, where early ceramic material survives, as at Sarre, Westbere and Patrixbourne (Bifrons) near Canterbury, and in and around Canterbury itself, Myres seems confident that some at least dates from the 'Hengest period', before the middle of the fifth century (1969, 77; 1970, 29). One of the more remarkable features of Jutish archaeology in Kent is the way it has confirmed the tradition of the takeover of Canterbury. Fifth-century Jutish burials have been found in the Roman cemeteries outside the walls and, in the town itself there is evidence of quite extensive early settlement in Germanic dug-out huts (Frere 1966, 91 ff., figs. 18-20). Canterbury was the first town to yield up evidence of early Germanic intramural settlement, but recent finds in Dorchester-on-Thames and Colchester, where the situation closely resembles that in Canterbury (Crummy 1974, 22 ff.), shows that the phenomenon was not so uncommon after all. However, in Canterbury, apparently Jutish occupation was short-lived: the town was abandoned during the sixth century and only reoccupied after the establishment of the Archbishop within the walls in the seventh (Tatton-Brown 1984, 5).

The rapid growth of Kent to prosperous kingdom status owed much to its surviving Roman sub-structure of towns, villa estates, and above all the roads and ports which served its continuing overseas connexions and soon-to-be-resumed cross-Channel trade. Other regions developed, too, though less dynamically. The evidence of pottery and brooches shows how, from the time of the first settlements, eastern and midland England continued to fill up with more and more peoples from north Germany and south Scandinavia throughout the fifth century. Myres's demonstration of the 'complete and unbroken range of ceramic fashions' represented (Myres 1969), speaks for a free and continuous process of settlement, uncontrolled by the political events of the period. His published maps of pottery types were never adequate to illustrate this process. However, as an indispensible supplement to my own overall map (Fig. 27) of the early cemeteries

Fig. 28 (opposite) Distribution of North German women's brooches in the first half of the fifth century (after Böhme 1986, Abb. 57).

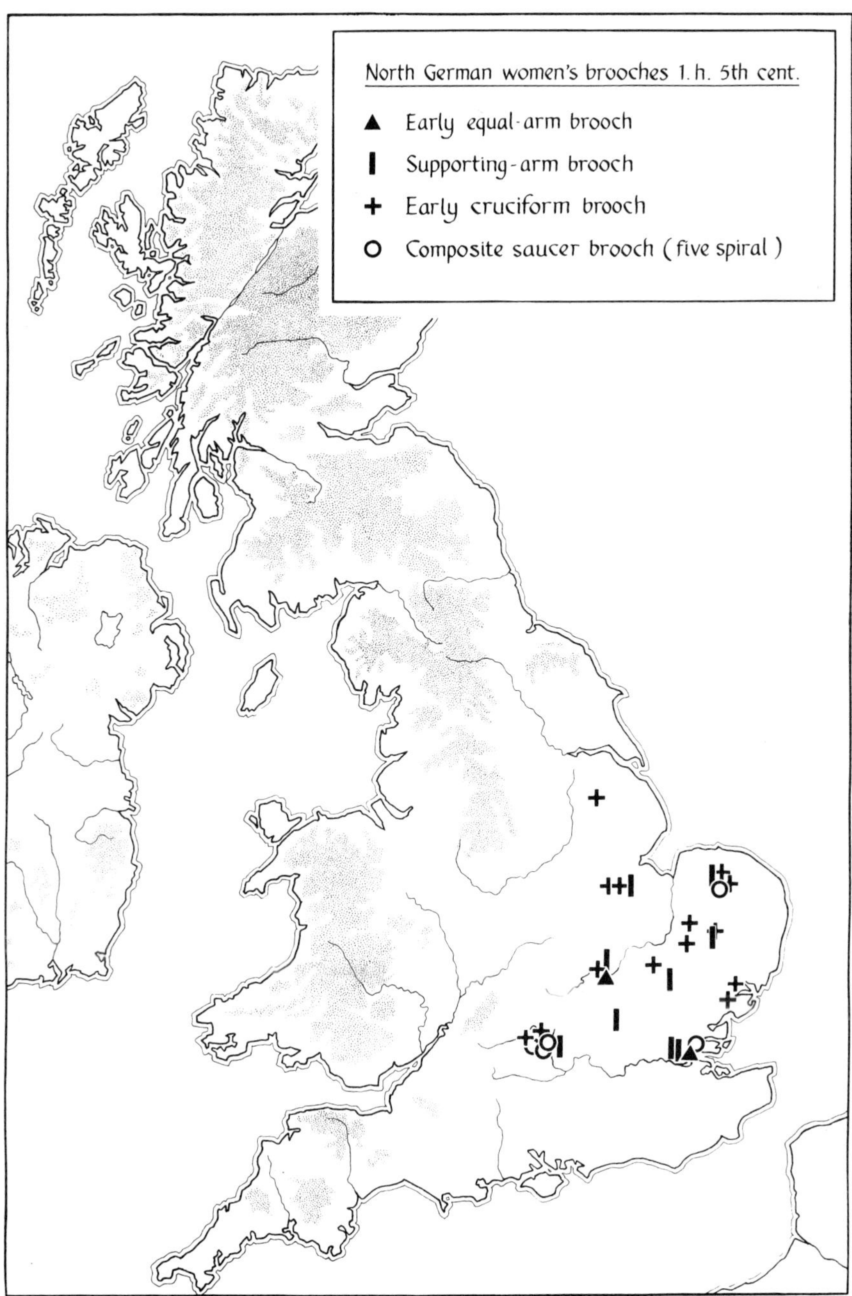
North German women's brooches 1. h. 5th cent.
Early equal-arm brooch
Supporting-arm brooch
Early cruciform brooch
Composite saucer brooch (five spiral)

(Hawkes 1986, fig. 5), Böhme (1986) has produced a series of well-documented distribution maps of mainly Saxon women's brooch-types in Britain during the fifth-century, which greatly increase our understanding of the progress of the Germanic settlements. The first of these (Fig. 28) shows that during the early fifth century Germanic settlement was mainly confined to East Anglia, Essex, the East Midlands and the Thames valley. The second (Fig.29) shows how, during the second half of the century, Saxon settlement spread much more widely in the Upper Thames and into the West Midlands, Surrey, Sussex and Hampshire. But of course Böhme's distributions mostly ignore the Jutish and Anglian component in the settlement, so I have added yet another map (Fig. 30), which fills in some of their early types, cruciform and small-long brooches, down to *c.* 500. These nicely populate Kent, of course, but also indicate further landtakings by people of Anglian and south Scandinavian origin in West Norfolk and the east Midlands, all around the fen country of the Wash, to the north of the majority of Saxons. The sixth century was to sce this Scandinavian element much strengthened in all regions which Bede called Anglian (Hines 1984). All that is beyond the scope of this paper, however. It is time to look in more detail at Saxon doings in the south.

In the Upper Thames valley, the Dorchester Saxons were quickly reinforced by more of their kindred, and other early Saxon communities were established not far away, notably at Abingdon, Berinsfield and Frilford. These early fifth-century groups may still have been controlled by *foedus*, but by the middle of the fifth century further colonization was under way, upstream from the Oxford area towards Cirencester. This movement coincided with the takeover of erstwhile Roman villa estates in the Darenth and Cray valleys off the Lower Thames in West Kent, and the contemporary appearance in Saxon cemeteries in both regions of burials with aristocratic weapons and other equipment from the Lower Rhine and Meuse valleys, perhaps indicating the arrival of Frankish warleaders. However we interpret the situation, the river Thames had now become a highway for the Saxons and their Frankish allies, who seem to have been able to pass freely up river direct from the Continent, reinforcing earlier comers. Later, the increasing power of Jutish Kent, with its apparent maritime monopoly assisted by an archaeologically as well as historically attested Jutish colony placed strategically on the Isle of Wight, appears have to cut off these Thames valley settlers, as also the colonists of Sussex and southern Wessex, from direct contacts overseas. But that was not until the sixth century.

One very clear result of the federate revolt as described in the *Historia Britonnum* was the foundation of the kingdom of Sussex, by an alliance of Saxons and Franks. Thanks to the close dating now possible for such things as the applied and cast saucer brooches of the former and the inlaid iron metalwork of the latter (Böhme 1974, 1986; Evison 1965; Welch 1975, 1976, 1983), we can safely place this event in the middle years of the fifth century. The early cemeteries are restricted in their distribution to the country between

Fig. 29 (opposite) Distribution of Saxon women's brooches in the second half of the fifth century (after Böhme 1986, Abb. 70 with additions).

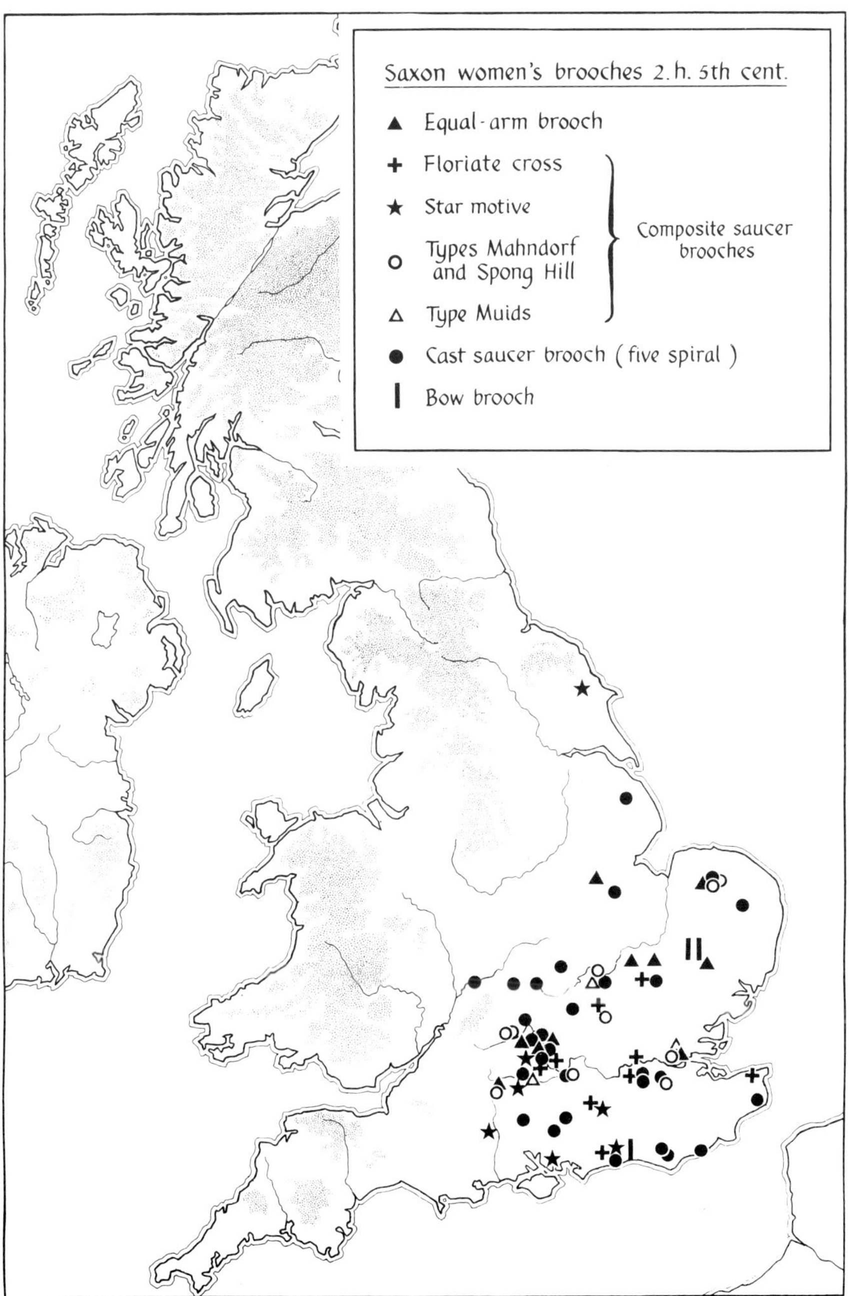
Saxon women's brooches 2. h. 5th cent.
Equal-arm brooch
Floriate cross
Star motive
Types Mahndorf and Spong Hill
Type Muids
Composite saucer brooches
Cast saucer brooch (five spiral)
Bow brooch

the rivers Ouse and Cuckmere, in east Sussex, where we find such sites as Alfriston and Bishopstone, and to the old hillfort of Highdown, near Worthing (Welch 1976, 1983), a site which, like Mucking, clearly had a strategic importance. It has been suggested, most plausibly, that these firstcomers were settled on ceded lands, by foedus with the surviving British magnates of the Roman cantonal capital, *Noviomagus*, now Chichester, in west Sussex (Morris 1965, 167 f.; Welch 1971, 1983). If so, the entries in the *Anglo-Saxon Chronicle*, dated approximately twenty years too late, would suggest a rapid outbreak, culminating in a successful attack on a British force in the Saxon Shore fort of *Anderida* (Pevensey). In English tradition Sussex was one of the earliest founded independent kingdoms, its first king Aelle a warlord of importance beyond the confines of his own small territory. Possibly his was the mastermind behind the next Germanic push along the coast into southern Wessex.

Thus far in the story of the Anglo-Saxon settlements, the invaders have been coming direct from the Continent, from north Germany, south Scandinavia and northern Gaul and the Rhineland. The exodus from the Saxon homelands can be shown to have started in the west, in the country between the rivers Weser and Oste, where most cemeteries and settlements were abandoned by *c.* 450 and where pollen analysis has shown that the arable land, on marsh and Geest alike, was not cultivated again for several centuries (Schmid 1977). West again, in Frisia and Drenthe, the situation seems to have been quite similar: Frisia's prosperity as a trading power did not begin before the early seventh century (Mazo-Karras 1985). After the federate revolt in the 440s, not only the Jutes but more Saxons, this time from the east side of Niedersachsen, between the rivers Oste and Elbe (Böhme 1976), joined the exodus. These, with their Buckelurnen, their composite and cast saucer brooches and their elaborate equal-arm brooches, went partly to the Cambridge region and partly to the Upper Thames, as we have seen, presumably to join their pioneering kindred. It was the final wave of these Saxons, now somehow allied and admixed with Franks of equal status, who colonised Sussex.

During the fifth century Britain had born the brunt of migrations from many different quarters of north Germany, and eastern, midland and southern England had absorbed them, in different ways and to different degrees. By the last third of the century, it seems, the flood of immigrants had been reduced to a trickle, for the next recorded advance of the Saxons, along the south coast into southern Wessex, seems to have been carried out by second-generation colonists. These apparently came from Sussex, Kent and perhaps other parts of southern England, with newcomers in the minority and those mainly Franks.

On present evidence, one of the first place to be settled in Hampshire may have been the Saxon Shore fort of Portchester in Portsmouth Harbour. Here, recent excavation of the interior has disclosed evidence of Saxon occupation from the second half of the fifth

Fig. 30 (opposite) Distribution of Anglian and Jutish women's brooches in the second half of the fifth century.

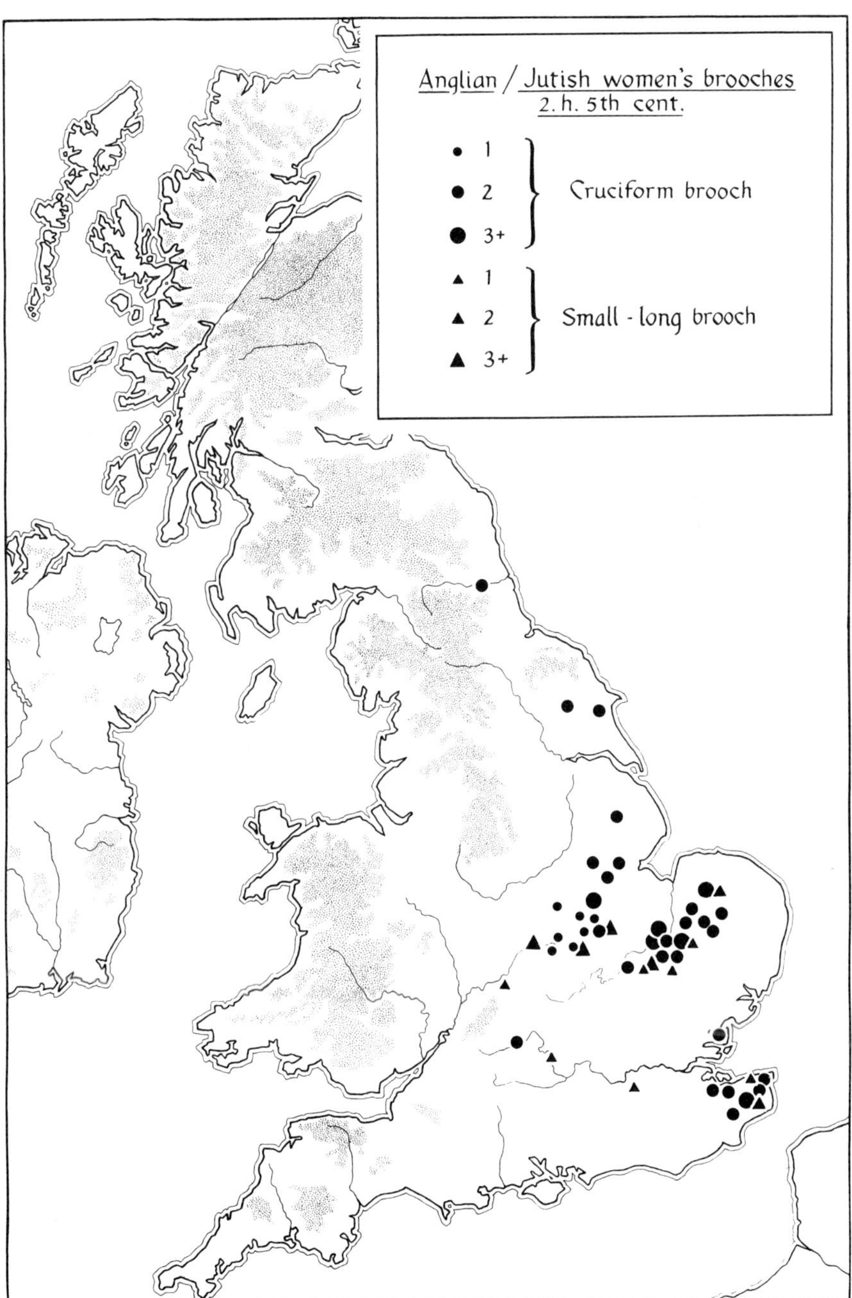

Anglian / Jutish women's brooches
2. h. 5th cent.
1
2
3+
Cruciform brooch
1
2
3+
Small - long brooch

century (Cunliffe 1976). Fifth-century pottery was also found in Winchester, though the context is uncertain (Biddle 1972, 233). But Hampshire is producing a few surprises from recently excavated cemeteries. A grave in what may have been a Roman cemetery at Itchen Abbas has yielded an early spear of Swanton (1974) type K1 and fittings of a fifth-century military belt (Youngs, 1985, 180-1) and there is a Dorchester-type lanceolate strap-tag from Cremation 2 at Alton (Evison 1988, 23, fig. 39). At Alton, at Andover (Cook & Dacre 1985) and my own unpublished cemetery at Worthy Park, Kingsworthy, downstream of Itchen Abbas on the river Itchen, the Anglo-Saxon graves contain quite a number of late fourth and early fifth-century Roman belt-fittings, some of which had been kept in use for generations (Fig. 27). It is conceivable that the officials of Roman *Venta Belgarum* (Winchester) had recruited officially equipped federates similar to those at Dorchester-on-Thames, and that some of these, or their families, later dispersed to found independent settlements in the countryside. Alternatively, men of families owning such equipment may have joined in the confederacy, notionally under the leadership of Aelle, which sought to bring southern Wessex under Germanic control in the second half of the fifth century. They seem to have succeeded in Hampshire, because at Alton, Andover, Kingsworthy and Droxford (Aldsworth 1978) there are graves at least as early as the late fifth century. Considering the sparsity of excavated sites even today, these argue for a high success-rate in the initial takeover of Hampshire. Progress into southern Wiltshire, however, seems not to have been effected until early in the sixth century.

Despite the dislocation of dates in the *Anglo-Saxon Chronicle*, it is remarkable how well archaeology is now bearing out the main lines of the story it told about the conquest of southern Wessex. It is tempting to equate the Portchester settlement with the aftermath of the victory scored by Baeda and Maegla over a young British nobleman (whom Morris 1965 identified as Geraint of Dumnonia) at *Portesmutha*, and to associate the settlement of the Salisbury region, via the river Avon up from Christchurch Harbour, with the deeds of Cerdic, the eponymous ancestor of the royal dynasty of the West Saxons. Had the coastwise advance continued, the next landfall should have been at Poole Harbour in east Dorset, but the Chronicler makes no claim of further westward expansion, and archaeology can show only one tiny Anglo-Saxon community of sixth-century date, with a precarious foothold on the coast of west Dorset. Evidently the southern adventure had run out of steam, and the British kingdom of Dumnonia, whose embattled state at this time is so dramatically illustrated by the total refortification of the huge Iron Age hillfort at South Cadbury in Somerset (Alcock 1972), proved too powerful to overcome. Not until the seventh century did the Saxons finally annex Dorset. This is the only part of England where we can actually see the Anglo-Saxon advance being stopped in its tracks in the early sixth century.

Probably there will never be agreement about the site of *Mons Badonicus*, especially if it has now to be thought of in the north. But, for those who still cling to the hope that the Gildasian story illuminates events in the south, there are good grounds, philological (Jackson 1958) as well as archaeological and historical, for considering Mount Badon to have been Badbury Rings in east Dorset. This is another Iron Age hillfort, unfortunately unexcavated, but so strategically significant that one would expect it to have been refortified at the same time as South Cadbury, for it commands the approaches by Roman roads to Poole Harbour. It stood at the very portals of Dumnonia. A major British victory here would explain why, while the Anglo-Saxon peoples in the Upper Thames and the Midlands were busily expanding their territories in the sixth century, the southerners were held in check, perhaps by one last *foedus*, for at least two generations. It would fit Gildas's timetable and, if he were writing in the British south-west, also his very limited viewpoint. He was interested in Dumnonia (Miller 1975); and this might support the case for our seeing the siege of *Mons Badonicus* as a localized Dumnonian victory.

The 'peace of Badon' came to an end about a decade after Gildas 'published' the *De Excidio*, when hostilities broke out afresh on the accession of Ceawlin of the West Saxons. By this time most of the regions settled by the Anglo-Saxons had time to stabilise and develop economically, sufficiently to support a political and social superstructure. Except for the precocious kingdom of Kent, which was already well developed, most other regions of Anglo-Saxon England began to acquire royal dynasties and the beginnings of a kingdom structure in the middle years of the sixth century. A new story is about to start, and it is time to bring this account of the Saxon settlement to an end.

SONIA CHADWICK HAWKES

DEFENCE OF THE REALM: MEDIEVAL AND LATER DEFENCES

The factors influencing the defence of the south-east of England have remained constant: proximity to the continent of Europe, a coast-line open to landings, short and good land access to London, and a direct water-borne route up the Thames Estuary. Although the coasts of Sussex and Kent provide convenient beaches for an invader, access immediately northwards is hampered by poor communications through the heavily wooded, undulating, wet claylands of the Weald. A way has to be found round it, and Canterbury acts as the hub of a road system which provides the most direct route to London following the line of Roman Watling Street from Dover through Canterbury, skirting the edge of the North Downs and at Rochester crossing the river Medway, which is the only major natural obstacle on the way. The defences of the south-east therefore pivot on Dover on the one hand and Rochester and Chatham on the other. Apart from the Roman and medieval city wall, London has never had a system of permanent defences in comparatively modern times, and only on rare occasions has it even had temporary defence works. Despite London's increasing importance as the centre of government and the commercial capital of the country, its topographical position has at

Fig. 31 (opposite) Defences of South-East England: 1-North Weald, 2-Tilbury Fort, 3-Coalhouse Fort, 4-Gravesend, New Tavern Fort, 5-Shornemead Fort, 6-Cliffe Fort, 7-Slough Fort, 8-Grain Fort and Battery, 9-Garrison Point Fort and Sheerness Lines, 10-Queenborough Lines, 11-Fort Darnet, 12-Hoo Fort, 13-Twydall Redoubts, 14-Fort Darland, 15-Fort Luton, 16-Fort Horstead, 17-Fort Bridgewoods, 18-Fort Borstal, 19-Chatham Lines and Fort Pitt, 20-Farningham, 21-Fort Halsted, 22-Westerham, 23-Woldingham, 24-Fosterdown, 25-Mersham, 26-Reigate, 27-Betchworth, 28-Box Hill and Denbies, 29-Pewley Hill, 30-Henley Grove, 31-Newhaven Fort, 32-Seaford, 33-Eastbourne Redoubt, 34-Pevensey Castle, 35-Camber Castle, 36-Dungeness Batteries, 37-Dymchurch Redoubt, 38-Sandgate Castle, 39-Western Heights, 40-Dover Castle, 41-Walmer Castle, 42-Deal Castle, 43-Sandown Castle.

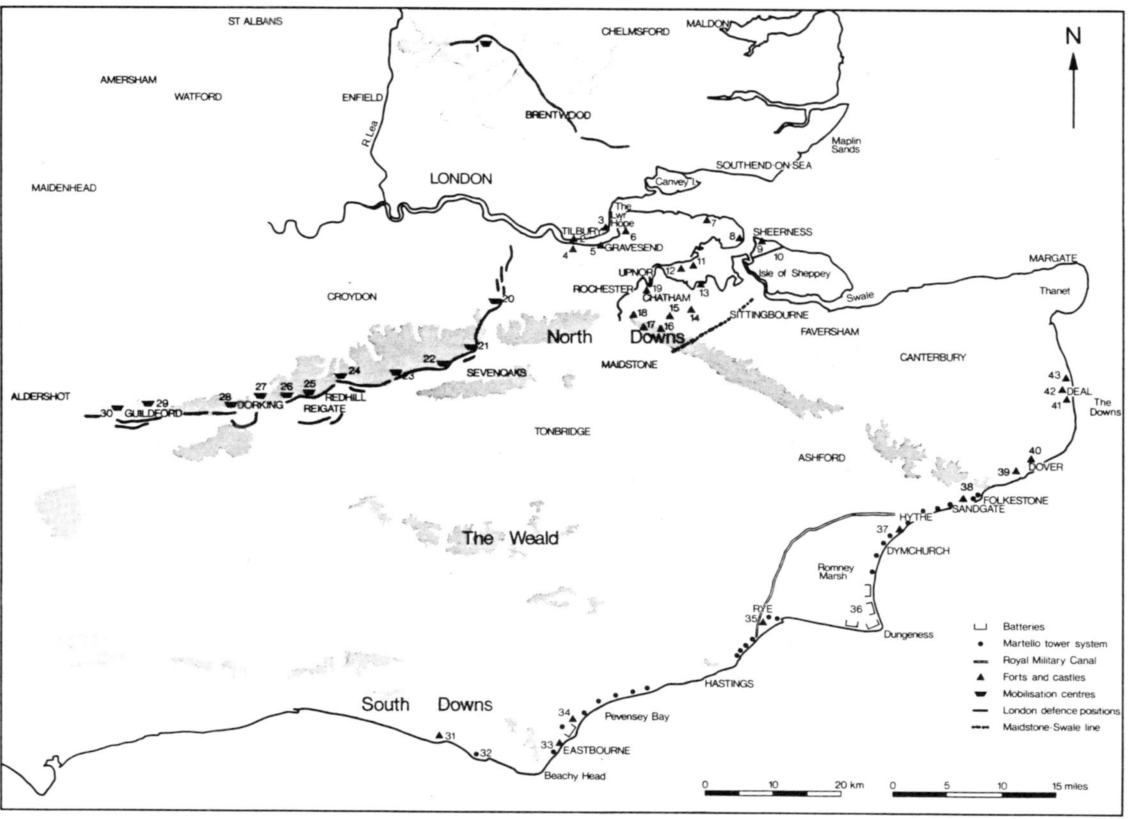
N
ST ALBANS
AMERSHAM
WATFORD
ENFIELD
R Lea
MAIDENHEAD
LONDON
CHELMSFORD
MALDON
BRENTWOOD
Maplin Sands
SOUTHEND-ON-SEA
Canvey I.
The Lwr Hope
TILBURY
GRAVESEND
SHEERNESS
Isle of Sheppey
Swale
MARGATE
Thanet
UPNOR
ROCHESTER
CHATHAM
SITTINGBOURNE
FAVERSHAM
CANTERBURY
CROYDON
North Downs
MAIDSTONE
SEVENOAKS
ALDERSHOT
GUILDFORD
DORKING
REDHILL
REIGATE
TONBRIDGE
ASHFORD
DEAL
The Downs
DOVER
FOLKESTONE
SANDGATE
HYTHE
DYMCHURCH
Romney Marsh
RYE
Dungeness
The Weald
HASTINGS
South Downs
Pevensey Bay
EASTBOURNE
Beachy Head
Batteries
Martello tower system
Royal Military Canal
Forts and castles
Mobilisation centres
London defence positions
Maidstone-Swale line
0 10 20 km
0 5 10 15 miles

times been said to be indefensible. It has looked for its defence primarily to the navy at sea or to the spasmodically constructed and maintained defences of the south-east coast (Fig. 31).

Medieval Castles

The locations of the royal castles constructed in the years immediately following the Norman Conquest reflect this strategic pattern. Dover Castle was set within a prehistoric hillfort on the Eastern Heights above the harbour, and included within its enclosure one of the two Roman lighthouses. Canterbury Castle lay within the south-western part of the city, and Rochester Castle commanded the bridge-crossing of the Medway. Each in their final form had as their core a massive tower keep. The significance and strength of these castles was brought out during the period of civil war in the closing years of the reign of King John early in the 13th century. At Rochester, the king carried out a successful siege and mining of the keep in order to regain this castle. Later, John's adherents held Dover, 'the key of England', in another well documented siege against the forces of the Dauphin of France, who had exploited the rebellion of the English baronage in an attempt to seize the throne.

Along the coast of Sussex were military commands or *castellariae* based upon the ancient administrative districts called rapes which run northwards from the coast in parallel strips. From east to west the castles were placed at Hastings, Pevensey, Lewes, Bramber, Arundel and Chichester. While these castles were built by the leading companions of William the Conqueror and were not directly royal, they were part of William's policy for maintaining Norman rule. Subsequent kings ensured that these castles did not fall into hostile hands and as a result they were frequently in royal possession. There were numerous castles elsewhere in the south-east which were associated with particular honours and land-holdings and had no substantial strategic function. In the later Middle Ages, however, there was to be royal encouragement of castle construction with coast defence in mind.

By the feudal system of sea-service the Norman and later kings inherited a sea-borne organisation which could provide for the defence of the coast and the cross-Channel passage, based upon the ancient organisation of the Cinque Ports. The original five ports were Hastings, Romney, Hythe, Dover and Sandwich. In return for the supply of a specific number of ships and seamen the kings granted legal and economic privileges to these towns, but by the end of the Middle Ages the naval value of the Cinque Ports had greatly declined. This was largely due to the ruin of their harbours by silting and erosion.

Dover Castle is the most significant monument. No trace remains of William the Conqueror's castle, and what we see today owes its origin to Henry II, who in his later years undertook the entire rebuilding of the castle between 1168 and 1174. This included the great tower keep, the finest in England, the curtain of the inner bailey with two gates and two barbicans to north and south, and a stretch of outer curtain to the north-east.

The late Allen Brown considered that the technical interest of Henry II's works at Dover is considerable. For example, the curtain walls incorporate what is the earliest surviving extensive system of interdependent flanking towers in English medieval architecture, and Brown believed that Dover represents the first known instance of concentric fortification in Western Europe. King John completed the outer curtain, and major repairs and re-adjustments of the gatehouses took place after the siege of 1216, to bring the castle to its maximum development by the mid-13th century (Fig. 32).

Fig. 32 Aerial view of Dover Castle.

Introduction of gunpowder artillery

The Hundred Years' War between England and France saw the development of an increasingly 'national' emphasis to a conflict which was primarily feudal in origin. It was also the time, in the late 14th century, when gunpowder artillery was being introduced into warfare and subsequently affecting the character and design of defensive structures. Destructive cross-Channel raiding and more serious threats led the English royal government to react, both on its own account by building new castles, such as Queenborough Castle in the Isle of Sheppey, constructed in the 1360s and 70s at the junction of the Swale with the mouth of the Medway, and by encouraging prominent landowners to fortify their coastal houses and estates. Townspeople were also expected to look to their town walls, and their improvements could be subsidized by the Crown. In 1381, Sir John de Cobeham received licence to fortify Cooling Castle, 5 miles (8 km) north of Rochester, overlooking the Thames Estuary. In 1385, Sir Edward Dalyggrigge was empowered at Bodiam, Sussex, 'to make a castle ... in defence of the adjacent country against the King's enemies'. In 1380, the West Gate of Canterbury was under construction, followed by the refortification of the city walls. Sandwich and Rye were coastal towns which were often attacked and also kept up their defences.

These new castles and town walls in the south-east are significant in being among the first defences in England to show evidence for the use of guns. At first this appears archaeologically as specialised gunports for handguns, such as the three levels of inverted keyhole-shape loops in the external faces of the Canterbury West Gate. The evidence for the use of the heavier guns of the period is more difficult to find since these were frequently mounted in earthwork positions at ground level, or sometimes on top of towers whose parapets have now vanished or have been substantially altered. The evidence for the use of a wide range of guns is more often documentary than archaeological. The defensive improvements were, however, innovatory in a technical sense, a piecemeal response to a threat which was itself transitory if highly destructive. The whole concept of defence in terms of a coherent national policy did not emerge until the 16th century, and with it a form of warfare wholly dominated by gunpowder artillery.

The castles of Henry VIII

The 'castles' built by Henry VIII in 1539-40 and throughout the rest of his reign marked the emergence of fortifications designed, from the outset, for and against artillery. Revolutionary as they were in England, they marked in fact only a transition from the medieval castle to the employment of the Italian-derived angle-bastioned earthwork fortifications which were to become the basis for military engineering throughout Europe, and wherever European influence spread, from about 1550-1850.

The greatest concentration of defences during the 1540s was in the south-east of England in response to an expected invasion by the combined forces of Francis I of France and Charles V of Spain, the two Catholic monarchs drawn into a brief alliance as a result of Henry's assumption of authority over the Church in England, his divorce from Catherine of Aragon and the dissolution of the monasteries and dispersal of their wealth;

Fig. 33 (opposite) Deal Castle.

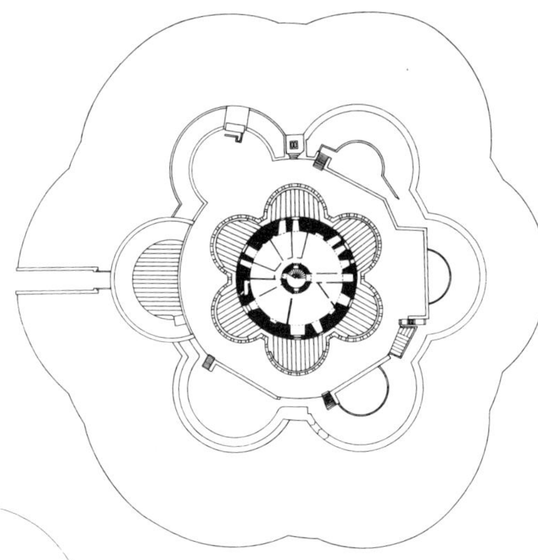

First-floor plan

Ground-floor plan

Basement plan

N

0 50 100 200 Feet

0 5 10 20 30 40 50 60 Metres

in effect the establishment of Protestantism in England. Henry did not attempt the protection of the whole coastline. Instead, defences were directed to the main anchorages and harbours. The chief castles in the south-east were Deal (Fig. 33), Walmer and Sandown, set close in line guarding the much-used anchorage of the Downs (a stretch of sheltered water between the Kent coast and the Goodwin Sands). Others were Sandgate Castle, near Folkestone (Fig. 34), guarding the western flank and approaches to Dover, and further west, Camber Castle, beside the now silted-up harbour near Rye. At Dover, a number of blockhouses protected the new harbour works. There was a short-lived blockhouse at Sheerness, at the mouth of the Medway, and five blockhouses were placed on either side of the Thames at the point where the river narrows considerably and also to protect the crossing-point between Tilbury and Gravesend.

The major castles were begun in 1539-40 and share the same basic elements. They were centrally planned and were given rounded forms both in terms of the plans of their structural elements and in the profiles of their parapets. The principal element was always a central round tower or keep rising above three, four or six substantial rounded bastions projecting from an enclosing curtain. The armament was arranged in tiers, with usually three levels of offensive fire-power, and one or two tiers of gunports for self-defence, usually for handguns, controlling the moat or an internal courtyard. The smaller blockhouses were much simpler but they too had D-shaped fronts, and the earthwork bulwarks between the Downs castles were circular.

The inspiration for the design of Henry's castles comes from northern Europe, and it may owe something to a theoretical treatise on fortification written by Albrecht Dürer and published in Nuremburg in 1527. Within five years of the start of Henry's defence programme, however, the angle bastion forms, derived from Italy, were rapidly being applied to English fortification, and by the 1550s they had become the established norm for fortress construction. Because the new defences in the south-east were among the first to be built, the distinctive changes in defensive fashions took place elsewhere along the coast.

The angle-bastion system of fortification

The Henrician castles in the south-east, though out-of-date, were still sufficiently substantial to be garrisoned and armed to combat the next major invasion crisis, which arose fifty years or so on, from the forces of Philip II of Spain. This was to materialise into the threat stemming from a conjunction of the Great Armada sailing up-Channel from Spain, with the army under the Duke of Parma from the Spanish Netherlands. There was a greater desire among the military in 1588 than there had been in Henry VIII's time to meet the invaders on the beaches, so the existing fortifications were amplified by numerous trenches and fieldworks of a temporary nature manned by the militia. The field army was encamped at Tilbury in order to meet the invaders should they land to the north in Essex, or to cross by ferry to Gravesend and into Kent if the landing took place

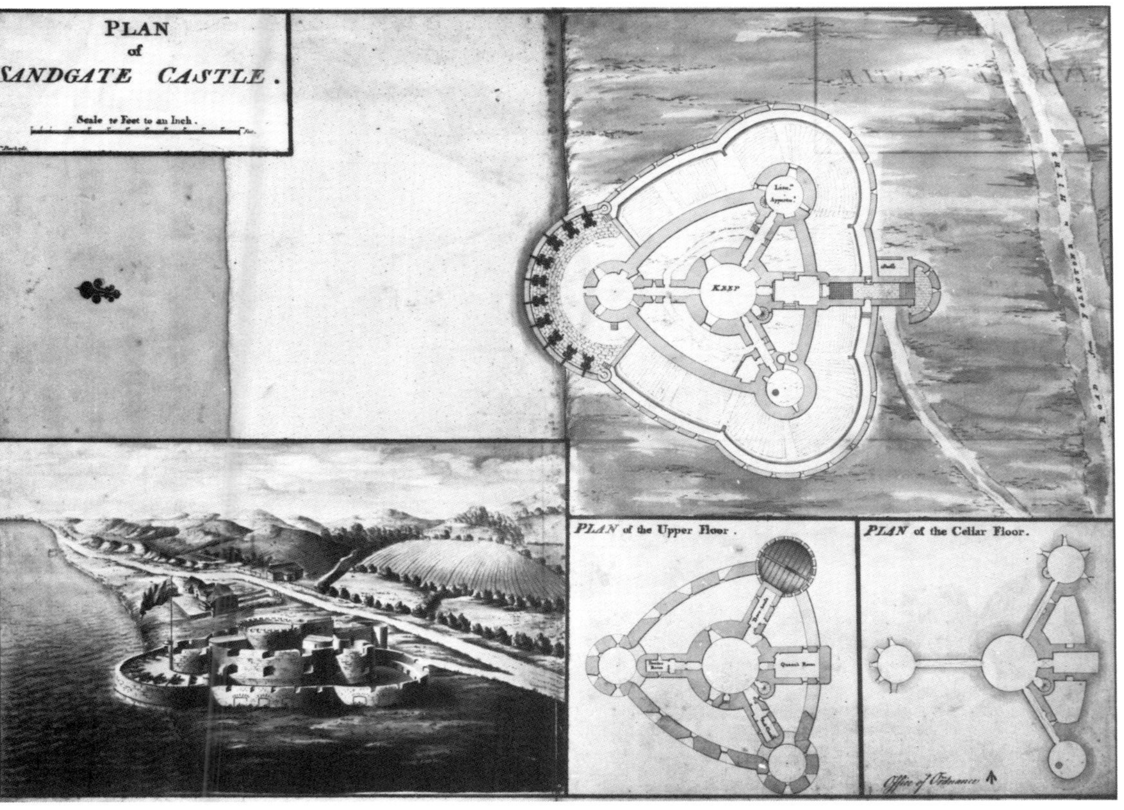

Fig. 34 Sandgate Castle.

there. The blockhouse at West Tilbury was subsequently given up-to-date outer defences to match the emergency.

No new permanent fortifications were built in this area in Queen Elizabeth's reign, except for a small idiosyncratically designed fort at Upnor opposite the later Chatham Dockyard. This was a significant development for it marked a shift in naval policy by using the upper reaches of the river Medway below Rochester Bridge as a place for laying up the Queen's ships when out of commission and making use of the developing dockyard at Chatham. Upnor Castle was built in 1559-67 to protect this new naval base. The growing value of the Medway soon spread to the mouth of the estuary with the development of dockyard facilities at Sheerness as well, and together this changed the strategic balance of the south-east.

This factor was borne out a century later during the Anglo-Dutch Wars. The wars were mainly commercial and naval conflicts but the Dutch raid on the Thames and the Medway in 1667 was a destructive and psychologically damaging blow. It involved the capture and burning of warships at anchor in the Medway and the destruction of a newly built fort at Sheerness. In the fifteen years which followed, two new powerful batteries were built on either side of the river below Upnor Castle, which was now relegated to be a magazine, and a new fort was built at Sheerness enclosing the new dockyard. These works were all designed by Charles II's chief engineer, Sir Bernard de Gomme. They were built at the high tide of the bastion system, at the time when the most famous military engineers of all, Vauban and Coehoorn, were fortifying France and the Low Countries.

Eighteenth century: wars with France

The 18th century was a period of intermittent war between Britain and France, and there were the occasional invasion alarms. By now the strategic pattern represented by the Rochester/Chatham and Dover axis which was to influence the south-east during the ensuing three centuries was beginning to emerge. In the middle of the century Chatham Dockyard, the associated barracks and the town of Brompton were enclosed by a continuous, bastioned line, stretching across the high ground east of Chatham, from cliff to cliff (Fig. 35). At the same time, Dover Castle, which was then in a forlorn state of medieval decay, was revived as a barracks with new ranges constructed inside the inner bailey, and new gun batteries were built to provide landward defence.

In 1779, Britain was at war not only with her American colonies but also with France and Spain. As the two latter powers possessed a combined fleet numerically superior to the British, which was already engaged in the Atlantic and elsewhere, there was a rare opportunity for an invasion. A combined French and Spanish force was prepared, 'the other Armada'. There was public alarm at the prospect of attack all along the south coast and hasty defences were thrown up. Both ends of the Chatham Lines were retrenched,

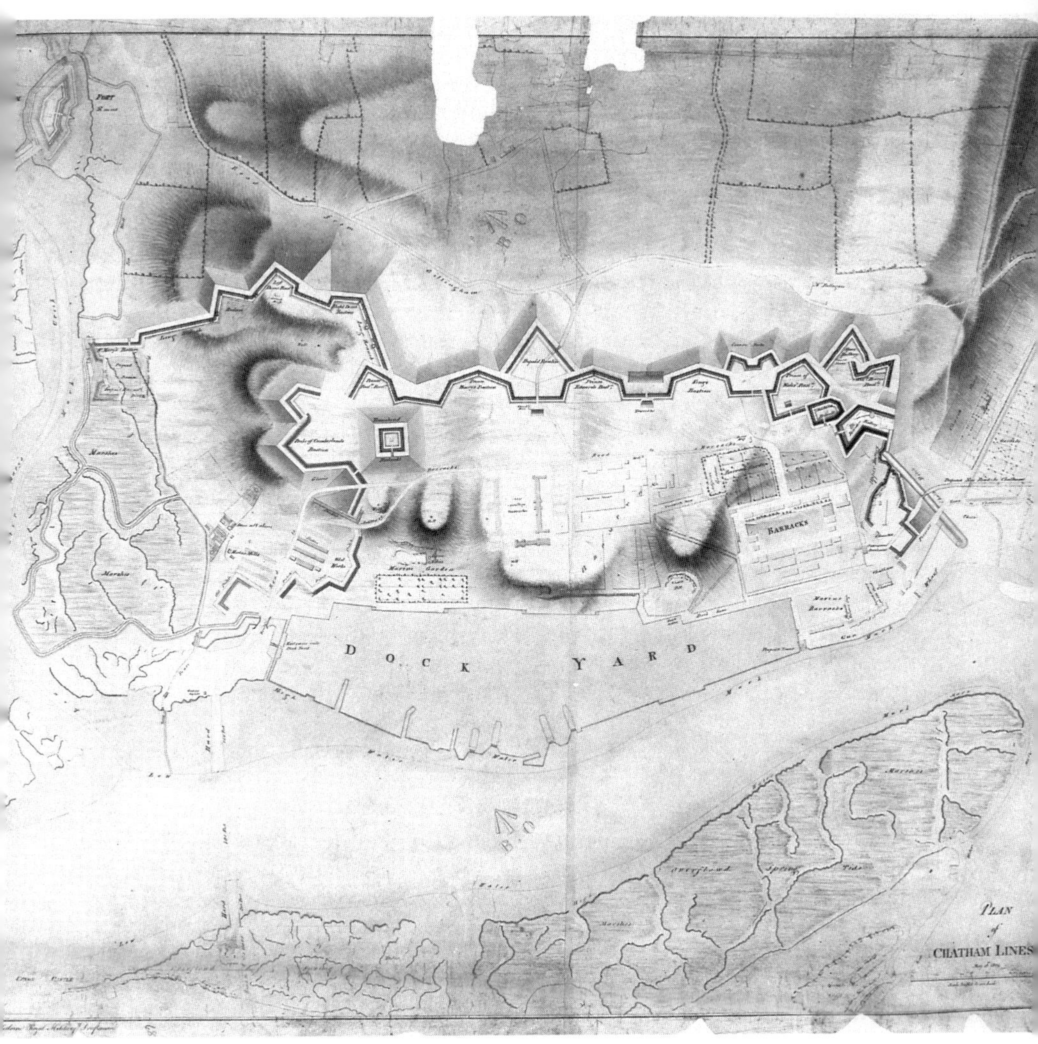

Fig. 35 Chatham Lines.

the existing Thames defences were enhanced and new batteries built downstream. The town which had grown up outside the dockyard at Sheerness was enclosed by a new bastioned trace. But the most conspicuous work was done at Dover. As well as earthen batteries to protect the harbour and seafront, there was a drastic remodelling of the Castle, which continued into the early 19th century. The Spur to the north, the gate-houses and the whole of its eastern length were refortified by the construction of detached works, bastions, caponiers and galleries cut into the chalk. The medieval mural towers were cut down in height to allow the mounting of guns, and the armanent of the castle was fixed at over 200 guns. In 1798, the then Secretary of State for War summed up the importance placed on Dover; 'Without Dover Castle the enemy can have no certain communication .... The conquest of this alone would be to him a sufficient object could he arrive with the means of immediately attacking it. Its preservation to us is most important ....'

The 1779 crisis was just the start of a far more intensive period of warfare between Britain and France which was to develop, under Napoleon Bonaparte, on a European scale. The fear of invasion was never far away but reached its climax during the period 1803-5 when Napoleon's invasion forces were assembled in readiness along the western coastline of the Continent. In 1801, Hythe Bay, south-east of Dover, was considered to be one of the most likely objectives. Four new batteries were constructed here, and Henry VIII's Sandgate Castle was remodelled for the emergency. There were, besides, four batteries at Dungeness, roughly formed works at Ramsgate, Broadstairs and Margate, and about twenty batteries of various sizes along the Sussex coast from Rye to Selsey.

At the height of the emergency in 1803-5, quite fundamental measures were devised in the south-east. These involved, for the first time, permanent beach defences to inhibit actual landings, and, simultaneously, defence in depth should those landings succeed. Seventy-four gun-towers, later called Martello Towers (after a gun-tower in the Bay of Mortella, Corsica, which successfully held off two British warships in 1794), were arranged in two divisions along the shore from Folkestone to Romney Marsh and from Bexhill to Seaford in the west. Each had at least one 24-pounder gun on its platform, capable of 360-degree traverse, and was intended, with the support of its neighbours, little more than 500 metres apart, to bring a hot and concentrated artillery fire upon the flat-bottomed barges, the horse-boats and the covering men-of-war of the invading force. Martello towers have remained the most visible reminder of the Napoleonic Wars. Associated with them were other forts and batteries which either had been in existence prior to 1803 or were built to defend certain places beyond the scope of the towers. Among these new works were the circular eleven-gun redoubts at Eastbourne and Dymchurch.

Behind the towers, Romney Marsh was isolated by the digging of the Royal Military Canal under the direction of the engineer, Rennie. Closer to London, a defence line of earthworks was planned ringing the capital, and a military road, known as the 'Chalk Ridge Communication' ran along the North Downs from Guildford to Rochester. In Essex, there were entrenched camps for a field army to move against any landings north of the Thames. On the Western Heights, on the opposite side of the valley from Dover Castle, a more substantial entrenched camp was created capable of housing 5-6000 men 'in readiness to move against an enemy wherever required' (Fig. 36). On the expected line of advance of the invaders, the defences of Rochester and Chatham took on the mantle of a barrier fortress. The Chatham Lines had already been substantially im-

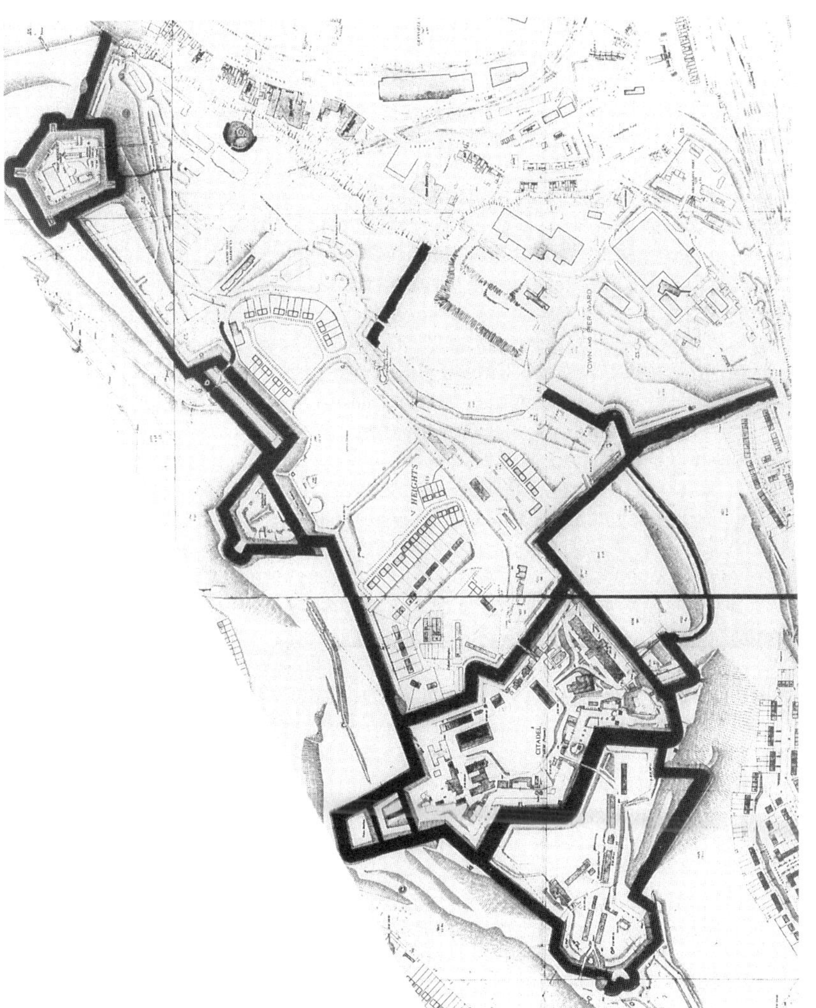

Fig 36 *Dover: Western Heights.*

proved, now an outer line of defence on the fringes of Rochester was created with Fort Pitt as its core, and with towers and a defended ditch system controlling the approaches from the south and west. All this represented a novel and flexible response to an invasion threat which was not to be paralleled until 1940.

Polygonal fortification

The character of military engineering began to undergo a gradual yet major change at about this time, and is reflected in some of the measures adopted by the British engineers during the Napoleonic Wars. There was widespread dissatisfaction with the conventions and restrictions of the bastion system, with its continuous lines and with its costly requirement for vast numbers of men and weapons to operate it. Concentrations of earthwork redoubts and trenches were now shown to be effective obstacles. Permanent fortification moved in the direction of rings of individual, self-defensible forts which could also support others of their kind. This form of defence, known as the 'Prussian' and later as the 'Polygonal' system of fortification, developed in Germany and the Low Countries after the defeat of France in 1815. Replacing the system of enfilade fire from one bastion to another, 'polygonal' fortification placed greater emphasis on the offensive fire-power mounted on the ramparts, and defensive control was effected by guns in caponiers covering the bottoms of deep wide ditches. Greater use was made of casemated guns in massive masonry works particularly for coast defences. Examples of these changes can be found in the British Isles during the first half of the nineteenth century and particularly in the Thames Estuary at Shornemead Fort.

There had been occasional invasion scares during the 1840s and 50s, but in 1859 there was much popular alarm over the ambitions of Napoleon III of France and the recent fortification of Cherbourg, combined with a widely appreciated technological revolution in armaments and warships in which it was felt Britain lagged behind. The introduction of the rifled gun and development of the explosive shell advanced enormously the range, accuracy and destructiveness of artillery. The use of steam power and armour plate in warships was an area where France had taken a temporary lead, and mistakenly these factors were thought to place an undue advantage in the hands of the would-be invader. Such was the level of public concern at British vulnerability that a Royal Commission was set up in 1859 to report on the state of the Defences of the United Kingdom. Its report was published the next year, and was to result in the most extensive programme of fortress construction that the country had, and was ever to see. Recommendations for defences concentrated on the naval bases and dockyards and the Thames. They included Dover which was said to be 'the only place in England which partakes of the nature of a strategical fortress or entrenched camp in its primary object'. With modifications, the main force of the 1860 Report was adopted and construction got under way which was to continue for most of the 1860s.

The early forts of Tilbury and Gravesend in the Thames Estuary were relegated to the second line, with three new casemated forts, Coalhouse at East Tilbury on the Essex bank and Cliffe and Shornemead on the Kent side, built further downstream. At the mouth of the Medway a powerful two-tiered casemated fort was built at Garrison Point, Sheerness, on the site of the Henrician blockhouse. It was matched by extensive batteries on the Isle of Grain opposite. Further upstream were two circular, casemated forts on islands either side of the main channel leading to Chatham dockyard. The whole of the Sheerness dockyard complex was now enclosed by yet a third line of defence consisting of a continuous wet moat and defended rampart two miles (over three kilometres) long. In the case of Dover, so much had already been done that it was a matter of improvements rather than drastic innovation. The Western Heights defences were largely in existence and required only completion and bringing up-to-date by adding caponiers to improve the ditch defences. The main new work at Dover was a large 'polygonal' land-fort on the higher ground immediately north of the castle and remedying this traditional area of weakness. It was named after Field Marshal Sir John Burgoyne, who had begun his career as a military engineer in 1798 at Dover Castle and completed it as Inspector General of Fortifications, and responsible for putting into practice the recommendations of the 1860 Royal Commission.

Improved artillery technology

The ring of detached forts to the south and west of Chatham which were in the Royal Commission plan were omitted on grounds of economy.. However the ground had been bought, and by dint of convict labour the forts were built during the 1870s and 80s. They reflect the accelerating technical improvements that had taken place since 1860. Breech-loading guns were now accepted, and quick-firing and even machine-guns were coming into increasing use; ranges were longer and high explosive more powerful. Exposed masonry fronts could be quickly shattered, even caponiers in ditches were vulnerable to high angle fire. There was a move towards greater concealment and use of earthwork and concrete. While the Chatham forts were being built, the lessons of the siege of Plevna in Bulgaria were noted by British engineers. There, simple earthworks combined with the use of the new magazine rifle produced sufficient protected firepower to resist numerically superior attackers. While on the continent of Europe greater weight was placed on ever more powerful fortresses and the use of armour plate and guns mounted in steel cupolas, the shift in Britain was towards mobile artillery and simple earthwork infantry positions. The latest of the Chatham forts demonstrate this development while the only armoured turret to be constructed in Britain was that for two 16-inch (400 mm) guns in 1882 on the Admiralty Pier at Dover Harbour.

Defence of London

The cheapness and simple construction of the Chatham infantry redoubts led to a change in political attitudes to the defence of London itself and its feasibility in military engineering terms. A defence line of thirteen positions known as Mobilisation Centres was constructed in the early 1890s with associated trench systems and ran for 70 miles (112 km) along the escarpment of the North Downs, from Guildford in the west to the Darenth valley, concentrating on the strategic gaps in the Downs through which the road and rail communications passed to London (Fig. 31). Then the line ran to the Thames at Dartford, resumed at Vange on the north bank of the Thames, and continued along the low hills to North Weald near Epping. The 'forts' had a dual purpose. They were to be mobilisation storehouses for the Volunteers, and they were also useable as redoubts in an emergency. Even so, they were short-lived since by the turn of the century invasion was then considered impossible by the Imperial Defence Committee.

Defence concerns for the south-east changed amid the realities of the First World War. For the past decade or more, the north-east coast harbours and naval ports had received most attention as the threat was seen to come from growing German naval power. After the battle of Jutland in 1916, home defence became more urgent. The line of the London Defence Positions was brought back into use, equipped with some 6-inch (152 mm) guns and 9.2-inch (233 mm) howitzers. The Chatham line also returned to favour. Further out still, there was a line of entrenchments and pill-boxes constructed between Maidstone and the Swale. There were also three trench systems north of the Thames.

The defensive strategy after the war differed little from that adopted at the beginning of the century. Britain was not tempted to adopt a Maginot Line approach. Before 1939 there had been a more radical decision to invest in fighter planes and radar early warning systems. After the fall of France in 1940 the defensive strategy had three main elements: an 'extended crust' along the probable invasion beaches and a ring of gun batteries around the coast. The second defence line was a series of road blocks with some local 'stop lines' of pillboxes. The third element was the main 'GHQ' stop line of pill-boxes which followed the course of rivers and canals and was intended to cover London and the industrial Midlands, leaving the mobile reserve to the rear. These tactics were changed after a few months to bring the field forces much closer to the possible invasion points and allow them greater mobility. For the Dover Straits, long range guns were needed to combat the German batteries between Cape Gris Nez and Calais. At first the only answer lay with two 14-inch (356 mm) railway guns at Dover. These were later augmented by three new batteries in the Dover area for the harassment of shipping and for counter-battery fire. Some of the old land forts now mounted anti-aircraft guns. An innovation resulting from the changing nature of warfare were the 'flak-towers' far out into the Thames Estuary. There were two types. The Navy forts consisted of cylindrical concrete towers which were towed out and sunk into position. The Army towers, more suitable for a shifting seabed and closer in shore, consisted of seven tubular steel towers connected above water by lattice steel bridges. The objectives of these sea-forts were to break up enemy aircraft formations approaching London, to prevent the laying of mines in the estuaries and to prevent enemy E-boats carrying out raids on shipping and coastal targets.

After the Second World War a few batteries in the south-east remained in commission but nuclear weapons had changed the character of warfare fundamentally. In 1956, coastal defence was abolished and the forts and batteries finally were redundant, some to become historical monuments as are their Roman counterparts, the Saxon Shore Forts.

ANDREW SAUNDERS

GAZETTEER

LONDON

The origins of London and its Roman history have been the object of archaeological curiosity since the early sixteenth-century. Successive, and often destructive, events have provided major opportunities for archaeological investigations from the Great Fire of 1666, the metropolitan improvements of the nineteenth-century, the bomb damage of World War II and more recently two phases of commercial office development in the late 1960s and the 1980s. Increasing archaeological resources have been employed over the last twenty years in an attempt to keep pace with this urban regeneration and as a result a basic framework for the development of the Roman city has been established. However, a great many gaps in this picture remain, not least the paucity of information surrounding the origin of the Roman settlement, and, at the end of the Roman period, the survival of the city in the fifth-century AD. In addition much work has been done to establish the date and character of the important settlement of Southwark on the opposite south bank of the River Thames. By contrast, the study of the nature of the surrounding countryside (now the built-over area of Greater London), the density and pattern of its Roman settlement and the nature of its relationship to *Londinium* itself, is in its infancy.

The Roman city of *Londinium* lies underneath the area of modern London colloquially known as 'The City', and now the area that serves as the financial centre of the modern metropolis. This area on the north bank of the River Thames, delineated in the Roman period by a stone defensive wall in the early third-century AD enclosing an area of *c.* 130 ha, formed the shape of London until its rapid expansion in the early seventeenth-century (Fig. 37).

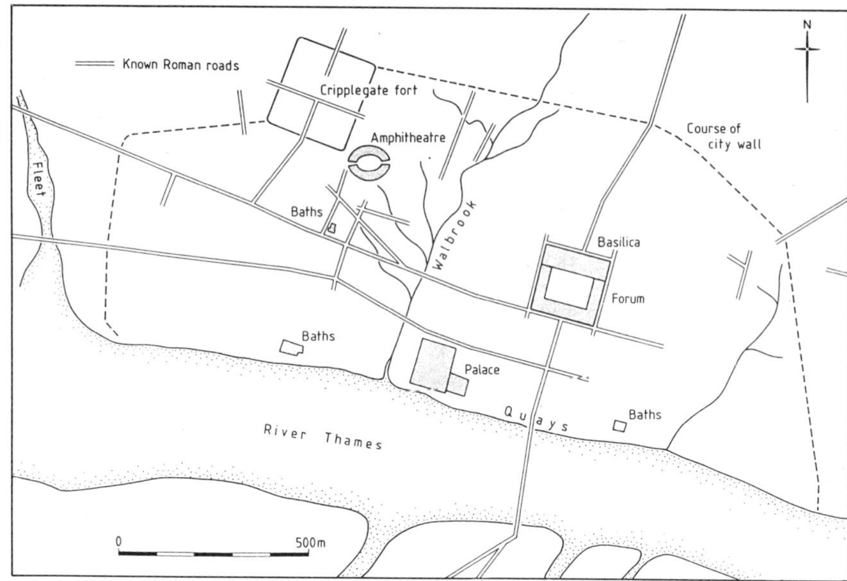

Fig. 37 Roman London.

Though the Latin name *Londinium* is attested epigraphically and in literature (*e.g.* Tacitus *Annals* 14.33) its full meaning is unexplained, though it embodies non-Roman Celtic elements. Despite the considerable evidence for trade between south-east England, Gaul and the Mediterranean basin at the end of the first-century BC and the first half of the first-century AD, the River Thames appears to have been primarily a frontier between rival Celtic kingdoms rather than a main trade route. There is no evidence of a major Celtic oppidum as a precursor on or near the subsequent site of *Londinium*.

The Roman town owes its origin to a decision to bridge the River Thames during, or soon after, the Claudian invasion campaign of AD 43. The choice provided a regular crossing point that became the focal point for the developing road system in southern Britain. The River Thames, wider than today and with a limited tidal aptitude of *c.* 1.5 m in the mid-first century AD in the area of the city, provided a primary route connecting the lowland of Britain with the North Sea and the River Rhine, and a way into the provinces of Gaul and Germany and the heartland of the Roman empire. The River Thames and its water-borne trade served as the catalyst that fired the growth of the Roman settlement on both banks of the river from 50 AD to the later second-century.

The full character of the first phase of building is uncertain. Timber buildings laid out parallel to two roads in the Lombard Street - Fenchurch Street area on the east of the two low (11-12 m above OD) hills of brickearth and gravel on which the city developed, indicate a regular plan, but whether they are part of a military installation, or of 'civil' character is not clear. Large scale comprehensive excavation of the earliest Roman levels in London is much needed. By AD 60 Tacitus says that London was full of merchants and a famous centre for commerce (*copia negotiatorum et commeatuum maxime celebre*) though the settlement apparently had no defined status, either as a *colonia* or *municipium*. Evidence of the destruction of the settlement in AD 60 in the nearly successful rebellion of Boudica indicates how rapidly the settlement had spread in seventeen years east-west either side of the centre on Cornhill and across the River Walbrook. The hapless procurator Decianus Catus was also apparently based in London, suggesting that London had already begun to exercise some central administrative functions. His successor, Julius Alpinus Classicianus, who died in office, was buried in one of the cemetery areas in the eastern edge of the city limit (RIB 12).

AD 70-125 marks a period of change and development of the Roman city on a scale and at an intensity unmatched by any other Roman urban development in Britain. After an initial hesitation caused by the destruction wrought by the Boudican rebellion, and overcome by the pre-eminent geographical advantages of the site, an extensive programme of civic or official building resulted in a succession of fora in the central Cornhill area (the second some 170 m square including the basilica), a major terraced complex (the *praetorium* of the *legatus*?) on the river edge, an extensive public bath building again near the river in the south-west area of the city, and most remarkably a fort (of *c.* 4 ha) with stone wall on the north-west edge of the urban settlement. The recently (1988) discovered amphitheatre in close proximity to the south-east corner of the fort suggests a close relationship between the two. This energetic public and military building programme was matched by a similar vitality in the building, initially with timber frame and wattle and daub infill, and in places mud brick, of planned strip buildings, fronting on to the street grid, and providing domestic and workshop accommodation.

The most remarkable evidence of this extraordinary economic vitality of London in the second half of the first century has been the discovery of successive waterfronts along the river bank stretching ultimately for a distance of at least 550 m, and extending upstream of the bridging position. Constructed of massive oak timbers (up to 0.6 x 0.4 m in section) in interlocking boxed compartments, successive replacement waterfronts were built in front of each other in a reclamation process extending the waterfront southwards, and provided the port facilities through which came a great flood of imports from the provinces of Gaul, Germany and from the Mediterranean.

Although not directly attested epigraphically, at least until the mid-third century, it can be argued from the existence of the fort (to house *equites et pedites singulares* (?), though little of its internal arrangement is known), the palatial terraced complex at Cannon Street Station, and hints (RIB 5, 21) that the imperial cult had moved here, that London had become the administrative and religious capital of the province, certainly by AD 100 and perhaps more likely directly after AD 61. It remained as capital of Britannia Superior after the Severan division of the province, and an altar found in 1975 built into the riverside defences near Blackfriars records Marcus Martiannus Pulcher, described as *propraetor*, commemorating the rebuilding of a Temple of Isis between AD 251-259. A mint founded by Carausius in AD 283, continued under his vanquisher, Allectus, was again revived by Constantius Chlorus, and minted coins under Constantine I until 325. It was briefly restarted by the usurper Magnus Maximus in 383.

If the history of Roman London in the first and second centuries AD can be described with some degree of confidence, from the late second-century the picture becomes more problematical. Excavation has shown a number of sites where the intensive occupation that characterised the earlier period, ended during the later half of the second century. Subsequent activity on many sites is marked by a layer of ubiquitous dark earth, the content of which has proved difficult to interpret with confidence. The causes of this decline, seen both in London and elsewhere in south-east Britain, remain debated, but there can be no doubt that the city's character and economic life had reached a major point of change. In contrast to this picture of stagnation in economic prosperity, signalled by a great reduction in the amount of material that can be dated with confidence to the third and fourth centuries, are two major construction programmes. The first of these was the building of the city wall protecting the east, north and west sides of the settlement and incorporating within its circuit the earlier fort. Numismatic evidence indicates that it was constructed after AD 190 and before AD 217. Built with remarkable regularity throughout its 3.2 km length, it used Kentish ragstone, carried up the Thames by boat, for both its core and for the squared coursed blocks on both faces. 2.7 m thick at ground level, where it had along the outer face a chamfered sandstone plinth, levelling and bonding courses of flat bricks (three deep for the first, and with two above) ran through the width of the wall. Four brick courses have been recorded, the highest at *c.* 4.4 m above the plinth. The total height of the wall including parapet walk and crenellated breastwork was perhaps *c.* 6.4 m. Coping stones from the crenellations have been found re-used as fill in the mid-fourth century towers. The wall was accompanied by a V-shaped ditch, *c.* 3 - 5 m wide, 1.35 - 2 m deep, and lying between 2.7 - 4.4 m in front. A bank about 2 m high, with a base of 4 m, strengthened the back of the wall. The wall was later reinforced in the mid-fourth century by semi-circular projecting towers on at least the eastern side, at intervals of *c.* 60 m. One of the most important discoveries of the last fifteen years has been the confirmation that the defended circuit was completed by the construction, along the waterfront, of a wall built in the late third-century, running from Blackfriars in the west to the south-eastern extent of the landward wall within the confines of the later Tower of London. The discovery in 1974 at Shadwell, *c.* 1.2 km eastwards downstream of the city, of the foundations of an 8-metre-square tower of masonry build of late third-century date, perhaps hints at the existence of a series of signal towers providing early warning of Saxon raiders in the Thames estuary.

The second major and previously unsuspected development was revealed by the discovery and subsequent interpretation of fifty-two re-used architectural blocks in what is probably a later rebuild of the riverside wall near its eastern end. Analysis of this material by Blagg indicated that a major building complex embellished the city's south-western corner, reflecting an official function and administrative character of the city in the third-century and later. The individual elements of this great building scheme so far identified are a monumental arch (8 m + high) and a curious double sided 'screen' wall, both decorated with figures of deities, a temple dedicated to Isis, the rebuilding of which was commemorated by M. Martiannus Pulcher as *propraetor* between 251-9, and a second temple perhaps to Jupiter. In addition, a remarkable sculptured relief panel of *four* mother goddesses suggests the presence of yet another religious dedication. The inferred scale and obvious quality of the building and the direct involvement of an acting governor indicate public building. The exact position of these buildings and their relationship to one another is unknown, though a massive foundation of masonry blocks at Peter's Hill, Upper Thames Street, may be connected.

London was renamed *Augusta* probably after AD 368. It is listed in the Notitia Dignitatum as the place where the treasury was and the *praepositus Thesaurorum Augustensium* stationed (perhaps as late as *c.* AD 395), which may explain why the south-east corner of the city (the site of the late eleventh-century Norman keep and fortress of the Tower of London) received special strengthening in the late 390s AD. If the fortified nature of London in the second half of the fourth century and the early years of the fifth century is clear, the degree to which civic life continued within the walls, or within a sub-enclave, remains uncertain, although a reduction in the population and deterioration in civic and communal life appears to characterise the change, rather than any wholesale destruction. During the fifth-century the focus of occupation appears to have moved away from the walled city of *Londinium*, and Saxon *Lundenwic* grew up to the west of the city in the area of the Strand.

Visible Remains

Little remains to be seen today of the largest Roman city of Britain. Most of what is visible are sections of the early third-century landward defensive circuit, which have survived encapsulated as property boundaries between post-medieval properties, and revealed now these properties have been demolished. The best sections are at Tower Hill and nearby Cooper's Row on the east side, and on the north-west in the Cripplegate area, where the bottom levels of the earlier fort can also be distinguished. A notable survivor is the remains of the north tower of the west gate in the Cripplegate area, where the bottom levels of the earlier fort can also be distinguished. A notable survivor is the remains of the north tower of the west gate of the fort, entombed under modern London Wall. No other Roman gate survives. A welcome recent addition has been the foundation base of a mid-fourth century projecting tower at Vine Street, incorporated into a modern office building, but viewable from street level. The towers surviving along the west side of the fort are of thirteenth-century date. The only surviving part of the riverside wall is the late fourth-century rebuild at its eastern end which can be seen within the Tower of London. An exception to the surviving parts of the defensive system is the foundation and lower courses of the early third-century Temple of Mithras, excavated on the eastern bank of the River Walbrook by Grimes in 1954, and subsequently reconstructed on a site along Queen Victoria Street some 60 m to the west and aligned on an incorrect north-south axis. It is to be hoped that a more enterprising approach to the Roman past will see the public display of the Roman house and bath at Lower Thames street discovered in 1848 and excavated in 1968, but not available to the public. Consideration is also being given to the public display of the east entrance to the amphitheatre located to the east side of Guildhall Yard and a massive public (?) building and baths currently being excavated on the north side of Upper Thames Street.

Literature
Merrifield 1965; 1983; Marsden 1980; Grimes 1968; Hill, Millett & Blagg 1980; Ordnance Survey 1983; Hall & Merrifield 1986; annual summaries of work in progress, in *Britannia*; the *Transactions* and Special Paper Series of the London and Middlesex Archaeological Society.

HUGH CHAPMAN

CANTERBURY

The first serious archaeological investigations began with the formation of the Canterbury Excavations Committee in 1944, when trenching under the direction of Audrey Williams took place within bomb-damaged street-frontage properties and in a number of back gardens and yards. From 1945 until the late 1950s, excavations directed by Professor S.S. Frere laid down the basic foundation on which an assessment of the Roman city can be made. (An account of the genesis and character of the excavations carried out in the period 1946-60 by the Canterbury Excavation Committee appears in Frere & Stow 1983, 7-9: Frere 1984, 29-46.) Two decades of intermittent seasonal excavation followed, mainly in the bomb-damaged city centre area. In 1975 the Canterbury Archaeological Trust was established, and has since undertaken numerous large and small scale excavations and observations in advance of redevelopment. These hectic years of almost continuous fieldwork have produced a corpus of new information which collectively allows the following brief assessment of the Roman city. Despite all of this, one is immediately struck by the gaps in our knowledge of Roman Canterbury (*Durovernum Cantiacorum*).

Pre-Roman occupation

Apart from tentative evidence for lower palaeolithic implements within the higher gravel terraces west and east of the city (Roe 1981, 204; Bennett 1978, 158-64), late Neolithic occupation at Whitehall Gardens (Frere *et al.* 1987, 45), a late Bronze Age site at Christ Church College (Bennett forthcoming a), and an early Iron Age settlement at Castle

Street (Jenkins & Boyle 1951, 145-7; 1952, 157-9; Blockley 1987a, 293-5), continuous occupation did not begin until a late 'Belgic' settlement grew up on either side of the Stour at this convenient crossing point in the closing decades of the first century BC. Evidence for 'Belgic' levels and structures contained by ditches, which may have formed part of a defensive screen (Blockley & Day 1978, 273; Blockley *et al.* forthcoming), have been found on various sites in the city. The extent of occupation can only be guessed at, but foci in the Whitehall Road area, west of the Stour and the St Margaret's Street area to the east, appear likely.

There can be no doubt that Canterbury was *Durovernum Cantiacorum*, the *civitas* of the *Cantiaci* and a city of considerable importance in the Roman period. The *Geography* of Claudius Ptolemaeus mentions *Darouernon* as a city of the *Cantii*. The Antonine Itinerary, in describing the roads of East Kent, places *Durovernum* at the correct distance from Richborough, Dover and Lympne. The Peutinger Table marks *Duroavernus* and the Ravenna Cosmography calls the place *Duroaverno Cantiacorum*, literally, 'the walled city of the *Cantii*, by an alder marsh'. The modern name is derived from Old English *Cantwara-byrig* - the *burgh* of the *Cantwara*, or Men of Kent.

The Early Roman Levels

Although there is clear evidence in the pre-conquest 'Belgic' levels for Roman imports of the early first century AD, the earliest phase of Roman occupation may have been military. Excavations in the south-west quarter of the city (Bennett, Frere & Stow 1982, 25-30) revealed long lengths of inter-cutting V-shaped ditches for what appears to have been the eastern side of a two-phase fort, established before *c.* AD 65. This base, protecting the eastern side of the important Stour crossing, was probably constructed shortly after the invasion of AD 43, evacuated *c.* AD 60 and then almost immediately re-occupied during the Boudican revolt. Final evacuation may have taken place in *c.* AD 69-70 in connection with troop movements for the Civil War or in *c.* AD 71 when troops were moved to the north. An alternative interpretation of the evidence is that the fort may have been established as a direct result of the Boudican revolt, abandoned during the revolt, reoccupied and then finally abandoned in *c.* AD 69-70 or in AD 71.

These early phases of military activity appear to have had little effect on the 'Belgic' settlement. Although some evidence exists for Flavian occupation in the area later contained by the city walls, including the construction of a few of the principal streets, a growing body of evidence now supports the theory that it was not until the early second century that the Roman city was really established. Recent excavations have provided evidence to suggest that 'Belgic' occupation continued relatively uninterrupted into the late first century when a period of re-organisation was instituted, which may have caused interruption and dislocation of occupation on selected sites for several decades. These sparse occupation levels, indicating continuity of 'Belgic' occupation, were sealed by dump deposits and levels associated with both major building activity and the formation of the street grid in the opening decade or so of the second century.

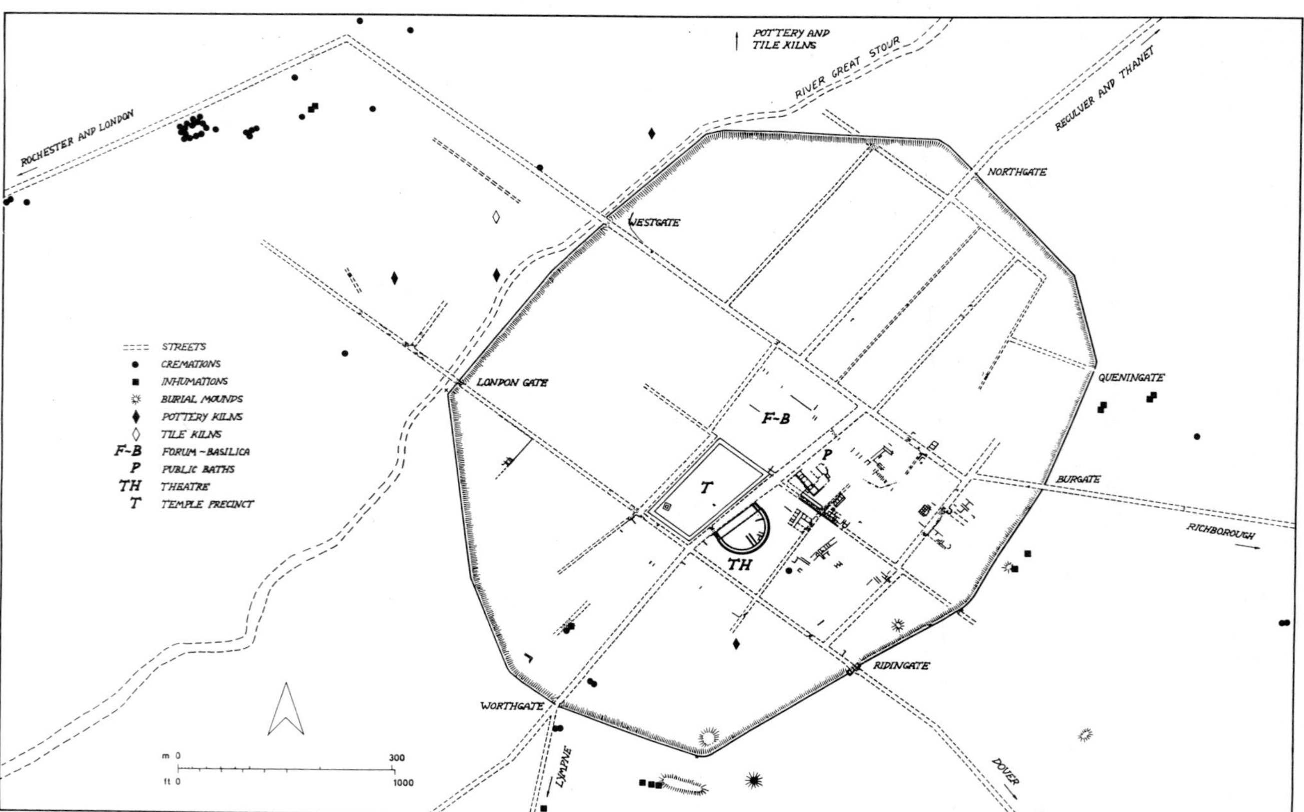

Fig. 38 Roman Canterbury (c. 70/80 - c. 450).

The Street Grid

Current knowledge from excavations and observation has radically modified the regular chequer-board street grid originally postulated by Professor Frere. (For Frere's current views on the street grid see Frere & Stowe 1983, 334-5 and fig. 144.) The network of streets shown on Fig. 38, though regular in many respects, suggests that the development of the street pattern was piecemeal, with modifications occurring through time, and with fundamental changes taking place in the late third century when the city wall was built. All the streets now located had been made of rammed gravel with the metalling often attaining a considerable thickness as a result of repeated repair. Masonry- or timber-lined side drains accompany most streets, many of them graded or aligned to discharge in the river or in centrally located soakaways.

The line of the late third-century city wall and external streets leading to the Saxon shore forts and to London, established by Professor Frere and confirmed by the Trust are the most dominant features of the Roman city plan so far located. Only three intra-mural streets aligned north-west to south-east (the Riding Gate - London Gate street, the West Gate - Burgate Street and a street located equidistant between them) and two others roughly at right-angles to them (south-east of the theatre and a second south-east of the St George's Street bath-house), indicate any regularity in plan. Elsewhere, known streets seem to follow differing and seemingly random alignments. Two streets aligned north-east to south-west, may have been first laid out in Flavian times (a small section of street located in the south-west quarter of the city and one separating the temple precinct from the theatre). These may hark back to the brief phases of military activity mentioned above. Their lines, together with a similarly aligned minor street, later covered by metallings of the temple courtyard, the line of Watling Street, and an early street which ran from Burgate to West Gate, may therefore have been established before formal and large-scale planning took place in the early second century. The line of the modern London Road, north-west of the city, may also have been of early Roman origin. The latter changes direction at the point of intersection, near St Dunstan's church, with the other leading from the West Gate, perhaps indicating that the London road originally extended further eastward to a pre Roman and early Roman settlement or fort on the north-west side of the Stour and in the area of Canterbury West railway station; but this has yet to be proved.

The Civic Centre

At the centre of this new street pattern were the civic buildings, the Theatre, the Temple Precinct, a Public Baths and the Forum-Basilica. The public building of which we know most was the Theatre which lay where present day Castle Street and St Margaret's Street meet Watling Street at a crossroads (Frere 1970, 83-112; Bennett 1984, 52-3). Excavations in the 1950s by Professor Frere revealed traces of a timbered structure utilizing a bank of earth and gravel to carry wooden seating, the bank being revetted by substantial masonry curving walls to the front and rear. This structure, dated by Professor Frere to the closing decade of the first century, was superceded just over a century later by a monumental building partly carried on massive vaulted masonry, the foundations of which still survive to varying degrees under existing roads and pavements and within cellars of houses, shops and gardens in the area. The only visible section of this once imposing edifice can be seen in the basement of Slatter's Hotel (Nos 7 and 8 St Margaret's Street). Recent excavations by the Trust have considerably added to our knowledge of this great theatre and an up-to-date postulated plan is included here (Fig. 39).

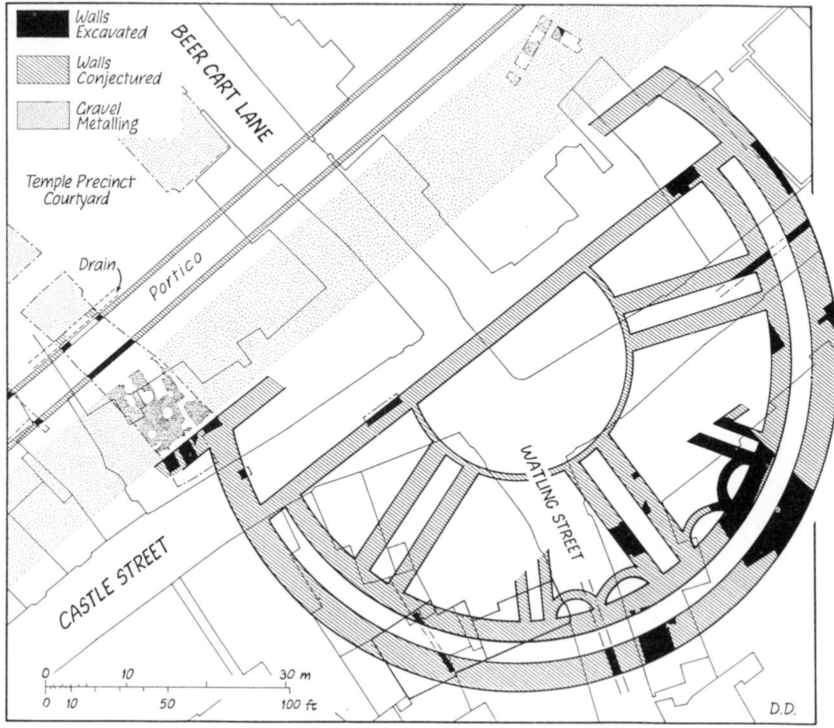

Fig. 39 Canterbury: plan of theatre.

Substantial parts of the temple precinct and a public baths have also been excavated in recent years and our cumulative knowledge of the plans of these structures is shown on Fig. 40, and in the artist's hypothetical reconstruction of the Roman city centre, Fig. 41.

The gravel-metalled temple precinct, constructed in the early second century, was surrounded on all four sides by a masonry wall, within which was a stylobate wall and drain of a colonnade. A small shrine has been located in the north-west corner of the

Fig. 40 (opposite) Canterbury: excavated structures.

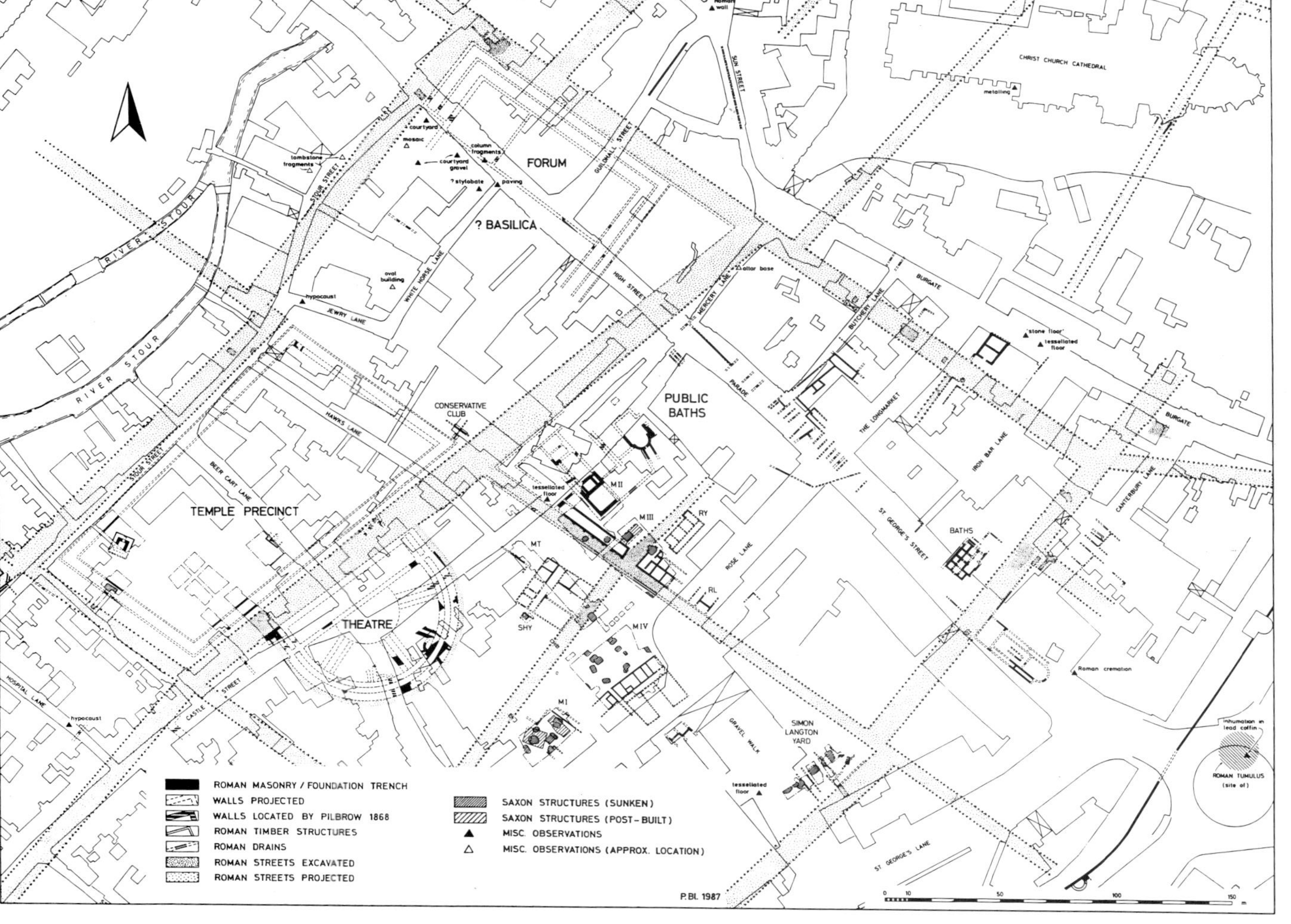

CHRIST CHURCH CATHEDRAL
metalling
Roman wall
SUN STREET
FORUM
? BASILICA
GUILDHALL STREET
courtyard
mosaic
column fragments
courtyard gravel
? stylobate
paving
tombstone fragments
STOUR STREET
RIVER STOUR
oval building
hypocaust
WHITE HORSE LANE
JEWRY LANE
HIGH STREET
MERCERY LANE
altar base
BURGATE
BUTCHERY LANE
'stone floor'
tessellated floor
PARADE
PUBLIC BATHS
THE LONGMARKET
IRON BAR LANE
CANTERBURY LANE
CONSERVATIVE CLUB
HAWKS LANE
BEER CART LANE
MII
MIII
RY
tessellated floor
ST GEORGE'S STREET
BATHS
TEMPLE PRECINCT
MT
ROSE LANE
RL
THEATRE
SHY
MIV
MI
Roman cremation
HOSPITAL LANE
hypocaust
CASTLE STREET
GRAVEL WALK
SIMON LANGTON YARD
tessellated floor
inhumation in lead coffin
ROMAN TUMULUS (site of)
ST GEORGE'S LANE
ROMAN MASONRY / FOUNDATION TRENCH
WALLS PROJECTED
WALLS LOCATED BY PILBROW 1868
ROMAN TIMBER STRUCTURES
ROMAN DRAINS
ROMAN STREETS EXCAVATED
ROMAN STREETS PROJECTED
SAXON STRUCTURES (SUNKEN)
SAXON STRUCTURES (POST-BUILT)
MISC. OBSERVATIONS
MISC. OBSERVATIONS (APPROX. LOCATION)
P.Bl. 1987
0 10 50 100 150 m

Fig 41 Canterbury: hypothetical reconstruction of the Roman city.

enclosure and the remnants of a fountain basin placed in line with the central axis of the theatre. Although a principal temple has not been found, architectural debris (marble mouldings and veneers and stone fragments of Corinthian column capitals, and a fluted column shaft) are assumed to have come from a large building within the precinct; this perhaps located north-west of the fountain opposite the central axis of the theatre.

Parts of the south-western range of a public baths constructed in the early second century have been excavated, together with the foundations of an associated *caldarium* with *praefurnium* to the south of it. The baths appear to have been flanked on the north-west and south-west sides by a wide colonnade; a gravel-metalled *palaestra* lay to the south-east. The *apodyterium* may have been situated mid-way along the south-west range. The baths were extensively refurbished in the mid-third century and appear to have been in disuse by the mid- to late fourth century.

Little has been discovered of the forum, or the basilica, the other great public building in Canterbury. A number of substantial masonry walls, a great expanse of courtyard metalling and a stone-paved portico and courtyard have been seen in recent observations under the High Street (Frere *et al.* 1987, 98-104). These finds add further weight to Professor Frere's assumption that the Roman forum was located in this area, in the *insula* north of the Temple Precinct and west of the Public Baths. Although insufficient evidence exists for a detailed assessment of the size and disposition of this building complex, a plan showing all the known excavated and observed remains is presented here (Fig. 40), together with a tentative reconstruction based on some of the surviving elements.

Private Town-houses, Shrines and Workshops

The period of expansion commencing in the early second century also saw the construction of many private town-houses, the two most completely known being of winged-corridor type; other more incomplete examples suggest similar plans. Many of these early structures continued in use with later alterations and additions for several centuries. New streets and lanes were also gradually added to the grid as the building density in *insulae* increased. The earliest of these buildings were of timber; later phases were of masonry or of timber on masonry foundations, while some were masonry from the beginning. It should perhaps be said that so far the evidence for houses has essentially been restricted to the area immediately to the east of the civic centre, and even here, no complete structure has yet been revealed.

Throughout the second and early third centuries new buildings were added while others received modifications which indicated an increasing degree of sophistication and pretension such as tessellated and mosaic floors, hypocausts, painted plaster and marble wall veneer. Part of one prestigious town-house with mosaic floors can be seen in a small museum under Butchery Lane (Williams & Frere 1948, 1-45; Frere & Stow 1983, 320-22 and fig. 138).

Besides the small shrine located in the north-west corner of the temple enclosure (Bennett 1981, 279-80; Bennett forthcoming b), parts of three other possible temples are known, these being constructed from the late second century onwards (Gas Lane: Bennett, Frere & Stow 1982, 43-4; St Gabriel's Chapel: Rady forthcoming; Burgate Street: Frere & Stow 1983, 41-9). The almost complete plan of a bath-house has been recovered from under St George's Street and adjacent buildings to the north-east. This structure, perhaps that of a city guild, was built in *c.* AD 220-30 and extensively altered, perhaps after a fire in *c.* AD 360 (Frere & Stow 1983, 27-40, 324-34). Part of a possible *mansio* or large town-house has very recently been uncovered just inside the London Gate, built beside Roman Watling Street in the early second century (Blockley 1987b, 300-3).

Some evidence for trade and industries exists. Bakers' shops (Rady 1987, 300-3) and a possible enameller's workshop (Day 1979, 275-6; Blockley *et al.* forthcoming) are known from the city centre; an extensive industrial suburb for metalworking and pottery and tile manufacture (Jenkins 1960, 151-61; 1958, 126-7; Bennett forthcoming c), with its own network of small streets is known to the west of the city outside and between the London and West Gates. This trans-Stour area, originally part of the expanding city only became extra-mural (and abandoned) in the third century. The present intra-mural stream probably did not exist in Roman times. The western branch of the present Stour almost certainly existed from earliest times and may have formed part of the outer western defences of the city from the late third century onwards. Chalk and gravel quarries in the eastern and south-eastern suburbs are also known.

Cemeteries

Cremation and inhumation cemeteries flanked most, if not all streets leading out of the Roman city. Most of them can only be deduced from chance finds and observations. Numerous burials have been reported from the suburbs, but few can be provenanced. Again, the sum of our knowledge appears in Fig. 38. The greatest number of burials yet found in a single place were produced in salvage work by the Trust south of the London road, where most of the burials dated from the early second century onwards (Frere *et al.* 1987, 56-73). Little can be said of the Romano-British burial mounds flanking the south-east side of the city, which probably date from the late first or early second century; none have been excavated. Two existed inside the walled area and they, together with a number of other scattered cremations, pre-date the construction of the defences. The south-east quarter of the city in which the internal mounds were situated, also provided a unique double inhumation burial containing military equipment dating to the mid second to mid third centuries, which may testify to a Roman murder (Bennett, Frere & Stow 1972, 44-46).

The City Walls

Excavations at a number of points on the city walls indicate that Canterbury was unusual in Roman Britain, apparently not being provided with a defensive circuit until the last quarter of the third century, *c.* AD 270-29 (Frere *et al.* 1982, 18-20).

The wall, of coursed locally available flints faced with a mixture of rough lower greensand 'doggers', water rolled flints and occasional fragments of re-used building material (mainly 'lumps' of Roman concrete and tiles) was backed by a contemporary earthen rampart. A cobbled berm separated the front of the wall from a wide and deep defensive ditch; bridges perhaps spanned the ditch at the main gates. Unlike Richborough no tile bonding courses have been seen in the wall fabric and there is little evidence to suggest that the defences were originally or later furnished with projecting external towers, although one certain internal tower is known from the present site of Canterbury Bus Station (Frere *et al.* 1982, 61-2. See also observations by Frank Jenkins in Frere *et al.* 1982, 61, 67).

The walled area, enclosing some 130 acres (52.6 ha) has exercised a controlling influence on the size of the city to the present day and is the most enduring reminder of Canterbury's Roman origins. Of particular importance and rarity is the survival of a section of Roman city wall still to be seen in the north wall of the Church of St Mary, Northgate (Frere *et al.* 1982, 82-5 and fig. 45). Here intact, the superstructure rises from its foundations to a height of 5 m and is capped by a continuous row of intact crenellations. Although these 'fossil' battlements, preserved when the wall was heightened (probably in the twelfth century), may be Roman work, the presence of occasional Caen stone blocks edging the merlons, may equally suggest Norman build, or repair of Roman merlons.

The Gates

Four of the six principal gates interrupting the defensive circuit, have been partially excavated ('London' Gate, Burgate, Riding Gate and Worthgate). Eighteenth-century prints of Worthgate and Riding Gate exist, these show, with varying degrees of accuracy, that Roman fabric survived until demolition took place (Frere *et al.* 1982, 33 (London Gate); 43 (Riding Gate); 56 (Worthgate). At Riding Gate recent comprehensive excavation and survey work (Blockley 1986, 205-9) has revealed a gate with a double-carriageway and flanking guard chambers. Its plan has now been marked out in brick on the street surface. London Gate, at the opposite end of Roman Watling Street, was less substantial, with only a single portal and apparently no guard chamber. Only a fragment of Roman Burgate (Bennett & Houliston forthcoming) survived later medieval reconstruction, but there is reason to suppose that a double-carriageway existed here. In addition to these, a gate survives at Quenin Gate, embedded in the existing city wall, and may still be seen at the back of the car park in Broad Street (Frere *et al.* 1982, 74 and fig. 31). It consists of some large weathered ashlars of lower greensand, forming parts of the two jambs and a few turns of the brick arch, spanning an opening 2.64 m wide. The street leading out of it probably gave a short-cut from the north-eastern part of the city to the Richborough road.

That Canterbury held a strategic position in Kent is indicated by the roads which radiate from its gates to the coastal forts at Reculver, Richborough, Lympne and Dover and to Rochester and London. Indeed, this key position, 'at the hub of the wheel', may indicate that the city was a seat of military command throughout the late Roman period. The increasing quantities of what may be military metalwork from Canterbury's latest Roman levels could reinforce this supposition (Ager 1987, 25-31).

The Latest Roman Levels

Great changes undoubtedly took place in the late Roman period. Although new buildings were being constructed and others refurbished during the early to mid- third centuries, others were significantly in decay. The portico of the temple was demolished at this time and far more finds from the latest courtyard surfaces strongly suggests a change in use, perhaps to that of a market (Bennett forthcoming b). By the mid-fourth century many buildings constructed during the second century including the public baths and the possible *mansio*, had fallen into decay or had been demolished. In some cases timber buildings were constructed over or within ruined houses (Blockley *et al.* forthcoming); other structures were re-used for industrial purposes. The southern carriageway at Riding Gate for example was stopped up at this time and the space contained therein used as a metalworker's workshop (Blockley 1986, 206-7). Occupation of this nature and some new building-works continued into the fifth century although their siting over Roman roads indicates a decline in urban standards or a possible change in needs and attitudes. Not only does the discovery of a silver hoard outside the London Gate, dated to *c.* AD 410 (Painter 1965, 1-14; Johns & Potter 1985, 312-52) suggest the continued presence of wealthy inhabitants at this time, but the decoration of some pieces with *chi-rho* monograms further indicates the presence of a Christian community.

Rapid decline in the early fifth century is attested by 'dark-earth' deposits which appear to indicate neglect and decay across the city. Only two sites have produced definite evidence for later fifth-century occupation. In the north-west corner of the temple precinct, a remarkable multiple burial, perhaps that of an entire family, including a 'pet dog', of mid to late fifth-century date was discovered (Bennett 1980, 406-10). In the Marlowe area part of a late fifth-century goldsmith's hoard, including a south Gaulish Visigothic gold *tremissis* of *c.* 480, was found in stratified soils over a late Roman courtyard (Kent *et al.* 1983, 371-2). Although these discoveries are hardly evidence for urban continuity, they do, together with other evidence for Jutish occupation in the middle or second half of the fifth century, suggest that the ruinous city was used for settlement of a sporadic or transient nature well into the fifth century (Brooks 1988, 99-114).

This brief survey and the accompanying figures underline the relative paucity of our knowledge of the Roman city, which within the walls is largely restricted to the south-east quadrant. Canterbury is presently undergoing a development boom which, with careful planning for excavation in advance of construction, may provide much more material evidence to support its status as one of the principal Roman cities of South-East Britain.

Acknowledgements:
The author would like to thank Professor S.S. Frere, Professor J. Wacher, Dr T. Blagg and Mr T. Tatton-Brown for reading earlier drafts of this text and for their helpful comments and suggestions.

Literature
Publication of the recent and ongoing excavation programme is in *The Archaeology of Canterbury*, a series of monographs, produced for the Canterbury Archaeological Trust by the Kent Archaeological Society: for detailed references see above.

PAUL BENNETT

BRANCASTER

The site of Brancaster fort and its surrounding settlement, detected through aerial photography and explored through partial excavation, lies on a slight elevation above salt marshes to its north. There is considerable evidence of silting of this part of the coast since the medieval period, and it is not unreasonable to suppose that in the Roman period the fort lay close to a navigable inlet.

The fort itself, whose walls were recorded as standing 12 feet (3.6 m) high in the seventeenth century, is now a low plateau, one of the least impressive of the Saxon Shore series, with none of its elements standing above ground. Limited excavation, confined in the main to the examination of the defences, has been supplemented by evidence from aerial photography (Fig. 42). The fort is almost square, with rounded corners, and measures 175 by 178 m, its longer dimension north-south, enclosing an area of 2.56 ha. There are indications of rectangular internal towers placed in at least one of the rounded angles, and there may have been similar towers flanking the east and west gateways, their fronts projecting slightly in advance of the fort's curtain wall. Where they have so far been examined, the walls, built of sandstone round a flint, ironstone and chalk rubble core, were 2.70 m thick, and backed by a rampart 6 m wide. At about 12 m from the west fort wall lay a ditch 13.5 m wide, and 2.40 m deep. A further shallow 'ditch' further out, apparently at least 25 m wide, may have been an additional defence on this side.

Results from aerial photography have been able to identify more features belonging to the fort's internal structures. From the air, the immediately discernible feature is the fort ramparts, but cropmarks have indicated the site of the *principia* facing the north gate at

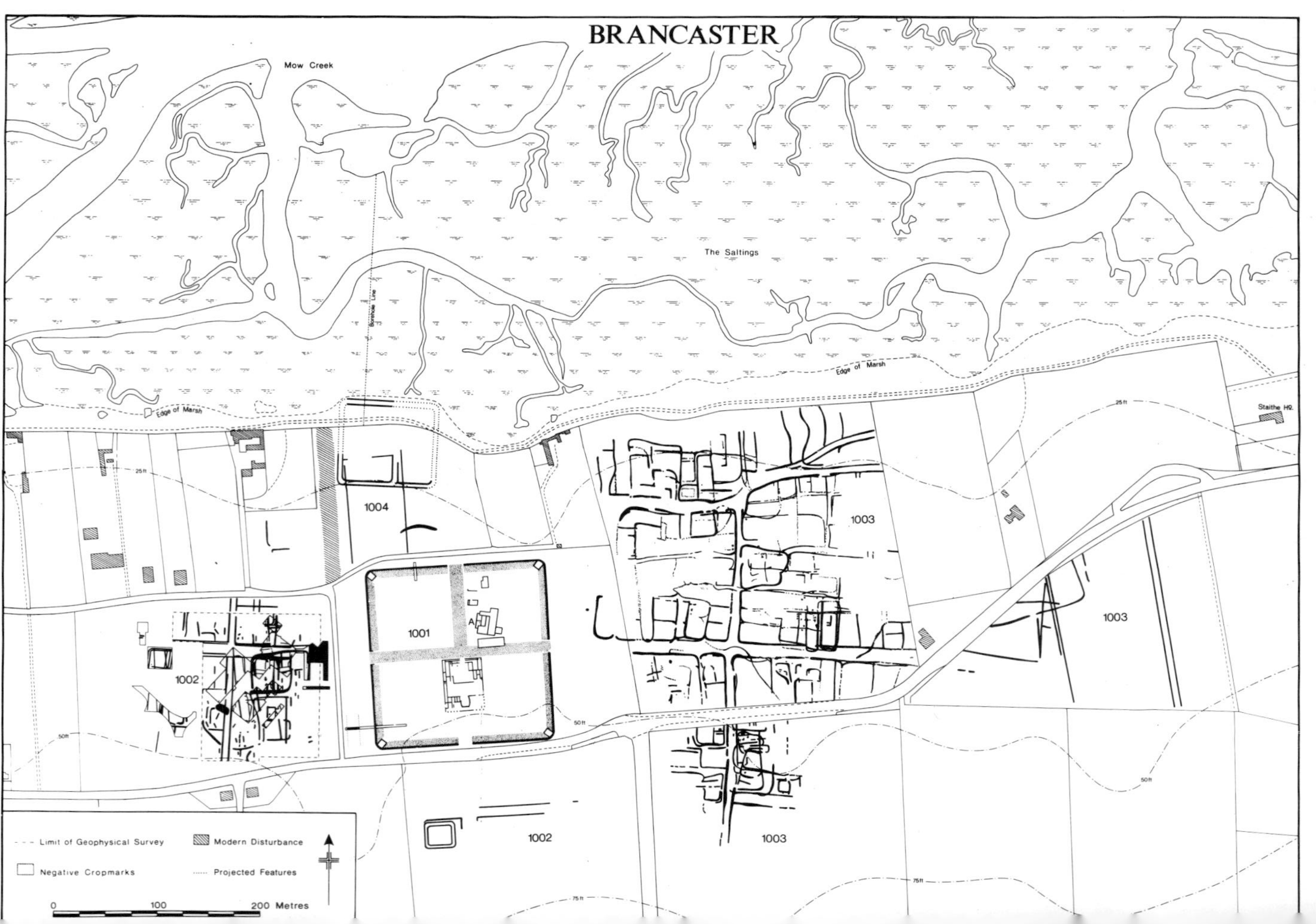

BRANCASTER
Mow Creek
The Saltings
Borehole Line
Edge of Marsh
Edge of Marsh
Staithe Hd.
25 ft
25 ft
50 ft
50 ft
50 ft
75 ft
75 ft
1004
1001
A
1002
1002
1003
1003
1003
Limit of Geophysical Survey
Modern Disturbance
Negative Cropmarks
Projected Features
0
100
200 Metres

the centre of the fort just south of its east-west road: it appears to measure 46 x 36 m overall, and follows an outline which is typical of such buildings: to the north a courtyard surrounded by rooms, and to the south a range of offices off the basilical hall, including a large central room, possibly the *aedes*. Two further buildings can be identified within the fort: north-east of the *principia* a building 26 x 9 m lies just north of the *via principalis*, while immediately to its north, on a slightly different alignment, is another building with a considerable number of separate rooms.

A combination of excavation and aerial survey has shown that the fort is placed within an area of regular ditched enclosures and trackways of Roman date. Most of the cropmarks so far recorded lie east of the fort, but a limited area west of the fort was excavated in 1974 and 1977. This work confirmed that the rectangular plots were probably linked to a planned settlement of mid- to late second century date, but few structures were found within the ditched plots, and only the presence of substantial amounts of pottery and domestic refuse buried in rubbish pits and in the ditches gives any clue as to the use of the enclosures, which were probably house-plots. These enclosures seem to be aligned on a small double-ditched fort measuring 80 by 90 m, which has not been examined.

Independent dating for the fort rests only on the limited excavations which have been carried out within it. The list of coin-finds from the fort suggests that it may have been in occupation as early as the late second century, a date confirmed by the pottery, and there is evidence that occupation continued up to the end of the fourth century. The fort's misalignment with the traces of the settlement suggests that it may have been planted over either part of it, or an earlier installation at its hub, some years after the settlement and its enclosures came into existence. It is not possible, however, to assign the fort's construction a precise date.

From the packing of a post-hole of a poorly-constructed timber building and from the fill of one of the enclosure ditches within the settlement came fragments of tiles stamped by the *cohors I Aquitanorum*, otherwise only attested in Britain in late second century inscriptions from Carrawburgh on Hadrian's Wall (RIB 1550) and Brough-on-Noe, Derbyshire (RIB 283). In the Notitia Dignitatum, *Branodunum* has a garrison of *equites Dalmatae*.

Literature

St Joseph 1936; Edwards & Green 1977; Hinchliffe & Green 1985.

STEPHEN JOHNSON

Fig. 42 (opposite) Brancaster: the Saxon Shore fort and settlement areas - the evidence of aerial photography and excavation.

BURGH CASTLE

The fort stands on high ground some 30 m above fenland and the river Yare, formerly the site of a large estuary fed by three rivers which afforded access deeper into parts of East Anglia. Burgh Castle stands thus at some distance from the present coastline but in the Roman period commanded a safe anchorage on a substantial stretch of inland estuary, whose outflow to the sea lay through the area now occupied by Great Yarmouth.

Originally a trapezoidal quadrilateral of maximum dimensions 90 by 135 m, the fort enclosed an area of 1.2 ha (Fig. 43). Its west wall, assumed to run parallel to the standing eastern wall, has fallen, and traces of fallen masonry have been located in the marshlands below. Much of the north, east and south walls stand to a relatively uniform height of around 4.6 m above original ground level. The walls are built of a rubble core faced with split flints and regularly spaced triple tile courses. About 3.2 m in width at their bases, the walls presently taper to about 1.5 m in width at their top: this is so uniform that it seems unlikely to have been merely the effects of erosion, and is probably the result of a number of stepped offsets on the interior.

Externally, the walls are protected by solid projecting towers of horseshoe shape in plan, exactly parallel in build and facing to the wall: for the bottom 2.2 m from ground level, these are not bonded into the walls of the fort. All these towers have in their tops a circular hole, 0.6 m in diameter and of similar depth. Excavation has located what was interpreted as the remains of an internal angle-tower at the north-east corner, though the evidence for this is of doubtful quality. Survey of the towers which project at the rounded corners has shown that in their present form they fail adequately to provide cover for the fort walls either side of the corner.

Excavations in 1958-61 examined parts of the fort defences and two principal areas within the fort walls. On the north wall, between the projecting tower and the north-west corner, in an area covered by a substantial probably medieval earthwork thrown up to strengthen this portion of the defences, a Roman postern gate was located. It was protected by the nearby tower, and was 1.52 m wide. Within the north-east corner of the fort excavations in 1958-61 by Charles Green examined two main areas within the fort walls. At the north-east corner, a series of trenches revealed insubstantial traces of mortar floors, possibly belonging to timber-framed Roman buildings with wattle-and-daub walls. These had burnt down, and were covered by layers of clay and debris which could have formed a platform for further timber buildings, all trace of which had been lost in the ploughsoil. One of these buildings lay right against the interior of the fort wall, and a series of indentations cut through the lowest courses of the wall in this corner are its only surviving trace. Pits and post-holes in the area gave some indication of later Middle Saxon (seventh or eighth century) occupation, though the nature of this was not entirely clear. The dating evidence recovered from the Roman buildings puts their destruction firmly in the middle years of the fourth century. A series of coin hoards, all

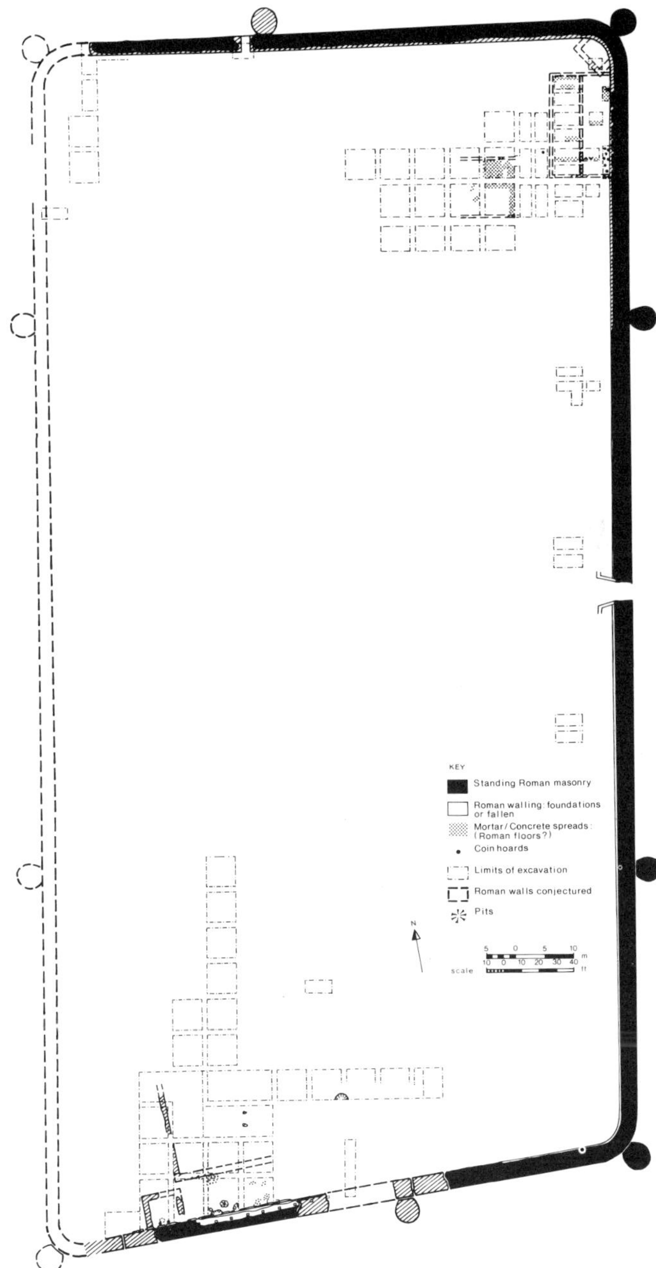

Fig. 43 Burgh Castle 1958-61.

of remarkably similar date around the decade AD 330-340 was found buried among these debris layers, which were also rich in pottery finds.

The other main area examined was the south-west corner, the site of a Norman motte, levelled in the mid-nineteenth century. Here a Roman masonry building was found lying next to the fort wall, and traces of an interval turret were also discovered. Above the rubble of this building, there were fragmentary traces of later floors, but the topmost portion of these deposits had been very much disturbed by the levelling of the Norman earthworks. To the north of this building lay an extensive cemetery, containing adults and children, very shallow under the present surface, and producing nothing with the bodies to ascertain its date.

In the Notitia Dignitatum, Burgh Castle appears to be named as *Gariannonum* from the Roman name *Gariennus* for the river Yare which was at its foot. It was garrisoned by *equites Stablesiani*.

Modern tradition has linked Burgh Castle with the site of *Cnobheresburg* mentioned by Bede, which was given by King Siehgbert of the East Angles to St Fursey for the foundation of his monastery in AD 630: the discovery of this cemetery has been thought to give substance to the identification, but in reality there is little hard evidence on which to support the link. The fort was converted in the early Norman period into a motte-and-bailey castle: the erection of the motte against the fort's south wall and the digging of a substantial ditch around it may have led to the collapse of parts of the fort's south wall.

Literature

Fox 1911, 279-323; Morris 1947; Morris & Hawkes 1949; Harrod 1859; Johnson 1980; Johnson 1983b.

STEPHEN JOHNSON

WALTON CASTLE

Documentary evidence suggests that at Walton, near Felixstowe, there once stood a fort of similar type to Burgh Castle. A series of sketches and a plan show the ruins of a number of walls, apparently with tile-courses, and round projecting towers, arranged in a narrow quadrilateral. Although there are severe discrepancies in written accounts of the site in the course of the eighteenth century, the consistency of the reports which indicate a walled and bastioned enclosure is sufficient to assume that a small fort of type similar to Burgh Castle existed here.

In the latter part of the 18th century, the fort, which originally stood some 100 m above sea level, appears to have tumbled into the sea. It lay within an area rich in Roman finds of all periods and may therefore have been a defended enclosure added to a coastal settlement.

Literature

Fox 1911, 287, 305.

STEPHEN JOHNSON

BRADWELL

The site lies very near the edge of marshy ground next to the sea at the north-east corner of the promontory south of the River Blackwater in Essex. Only the three inland sides of the fort now remain. The south wall is best preserved; on the site of the main west gate stands the Saxon Chapel of St Peter, dated to 652 and built predominantly of Roman material. Like Burgh Castle, the north and south walls of the fort are not parallel, and so the fort was not rectangular (Fig. 44). The surviving walls enclose 2 hectares.

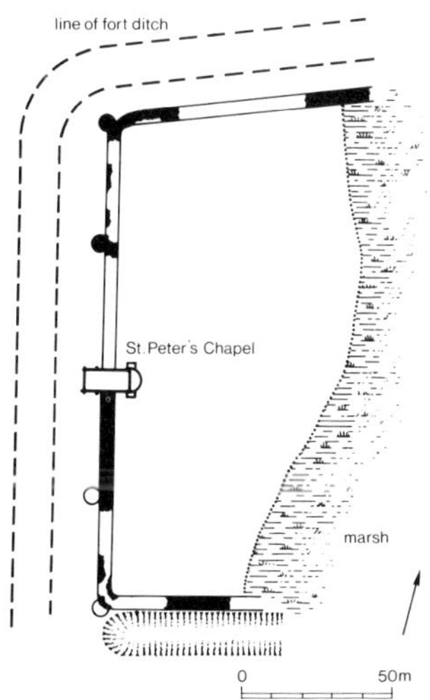

Fig. 44 Bradwell.

The remains were first discovered and examined in 1864. Because of the very acidic nature of the soil, little has survived, and the walls have been almost completely flattened, probably by cultivation. In 1865, the wall was reported to be 'upwards of 14 feet thick, and on the west side are foundations of two towers, one semicircular, one of horseshoe form'. Similar towers are presumed to have existed all round the circuit, but have not been located. The foundations of the wall are composed of boulders and rough stones and the core is of rubble concrete. The north-west angle bastion is 4.5 m in diameter, projecting 3.90 m from the wall. The interval tower is 38 m south of the north-west corner.

A section cut more recently across the defences 20 m north of the chapel showed that there was an offset course of tiles on the exterior of the fort wall at ground level. Both faces of the wall had a recess below ground level, as if the whole wall had been laid in wooden shuttering. No trace of any interior rampart was found, but 'a roll in the ground behind the north and west walls, and a mass of yellow clay behind the south wall indicate its existence'. The ditch was sectioned, but no precise outline of its shape was recoverable. A notable find from the bottom of the ditch was pottery of the pagan Saxon period.

Some interior buildings were found in the nineteenth century, near the south wall, but no pattern or sense was made of them. There also exist some fragments of what may be a Roman harbour connected with the site some distance out in the marshland, visible, according to local reports, as submerged masonry outlines.

In the Notitia Dignitatum, Bradwell, the Ythancaester of Bede, seems to be recorded by the name of Othona, with a garrison of the *numerus Fortensium*.

Literature
RCHM 1923, 13ff; Hull 1963.

STEPHEN JOHNSON

RECULVER

Reculver lies on a low mound on the northern coast of Kent, and is flanked to east and south by low ground that could have been marshland in the Roman period. It occupied a strategic point at the northern end of the Wantsum Channel which used to separate the Isle of Thanet from mainland Kent (Fig. 45). There is scant record at Reculver of Roman activity in the first or second centuries. Some mid-first century material has been discovered, and, west of the fort, the discovery of a number of pits and wells of predominantly second-century date suggest that there was a settlement at this point. The orientation of the later fort, facing northwards, and the records of the gradual encroachment of the sea coast as it moved south, suggest that the main settlement at Reculver of this period may have lain north of the later fort site, in an area now totally lost to the sea.

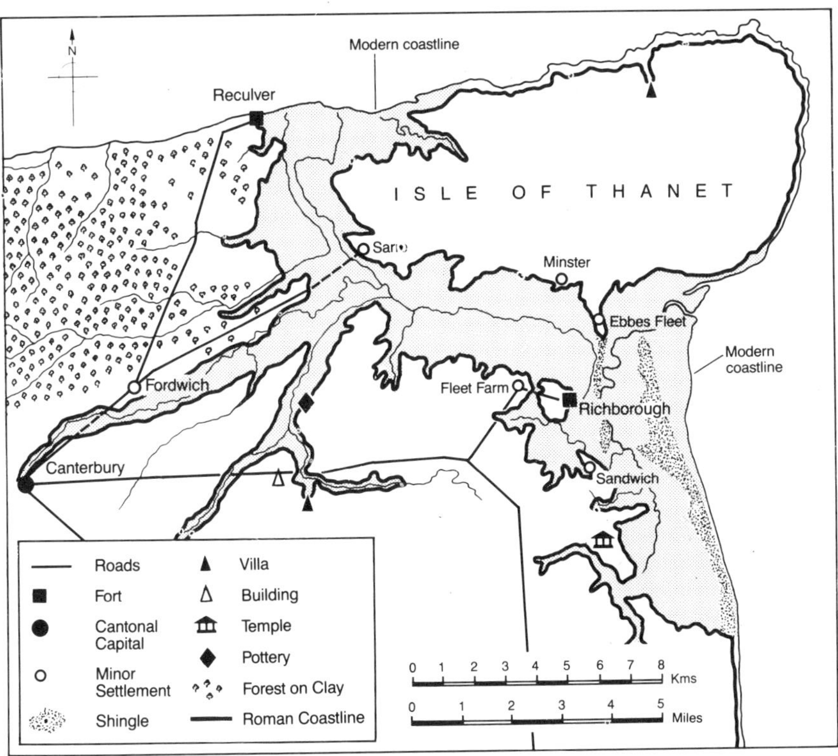

Fig. 45 North-east Kent in the Roman period.

The fort seems to have been planted, therefore, at the southern and eastern tip of the settlement, perhaps in an area close to an anchorage in the Wantsum Channel. It was nearly square, 170 x 180 m across the ramparts, with rounded angles, and masonry walls 3 m thick backed by an eastern rampart, 13.5 m wide. Only about half the fort now survives, for the northern wall and much of the north west quadrant has been lost in the sea (Fig. 46). Substantial portions of the east and south walls are now visible. Little of the facing can be seen: where this survives it appears to be in coursed small blockwork of greensand: the wall core is of rounded flint pebbles. The east gate is a single carriageway 2.7 m wide flanked by a single guard chamber to its north: the gate was blocked in the late third or fourth century. The south gate was similar in form to the east gate, a single portal with a chamber to the west. Outside the east wall of the fort excavations have located two circuits of ditches, one at 10 m, the other at 20 m from the walls.

Excavations within the fort took place from 1962 to 1974, and a number of internal buildings were identified. The headquarters lay south of the central road between the east and west gates. It measured 33 by 42 m, and at its rear was the usual range of five rooms, the central room of which contained an underground strong room. Within this

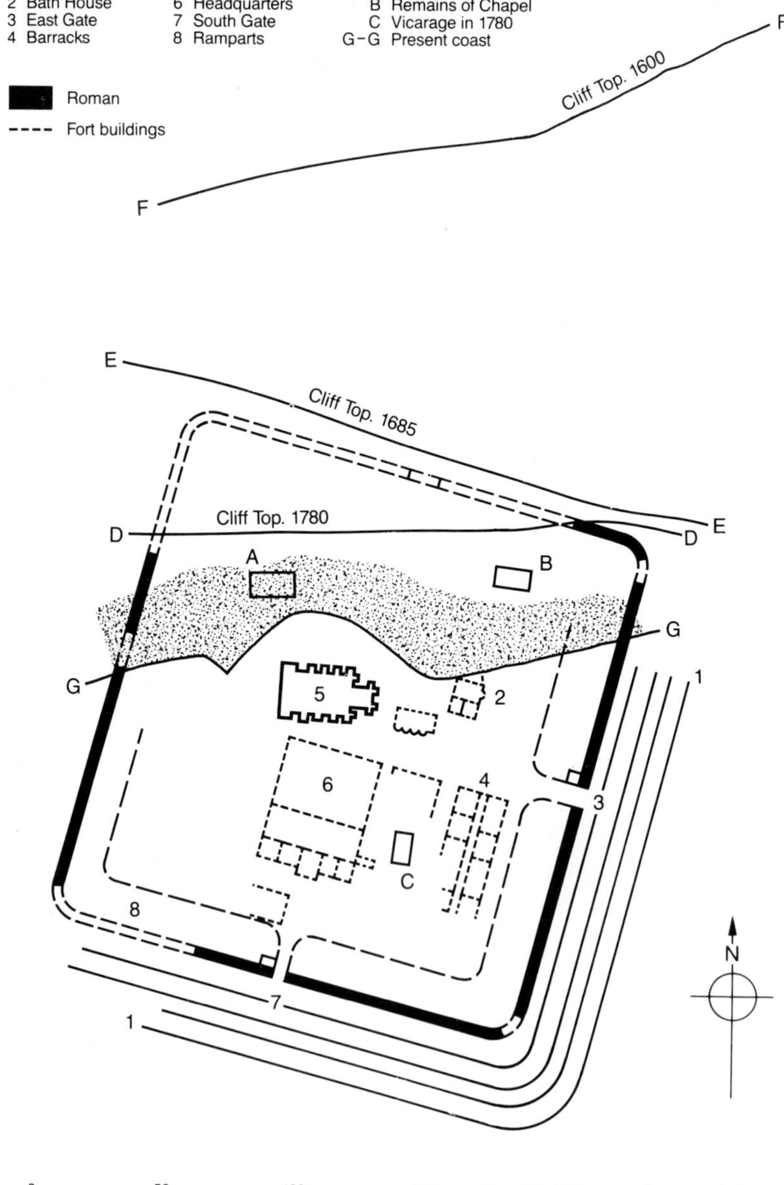

Fig. 46 Reculver.

room were found the fragments of the inscription which records the construction of the *principia*. Three buildings lay between the *principia* and the east rampart; two of them, long narrow buildings aligned north-south, were divided into separate rooms, some of which were decorated with plaster painted in several colours. North of the central road lay an internal bath-house.

The inscription, discovered in September 1960, reads *edem principiorum / cum basilica / sub ..r..io Rufino / Cos / ...] Fortunatus /...]t/*. When first published (Richmond 1961), it was suggested that the 'shrine of the headquarters with the basilica' refers to the main hub of the headquarters: the inscription therefore is the building record of the *principia*. It is more difficult to be precise about its date. Two men named Rufinus who were *consul ordinarius* are known in the fasti, and either (Q. Aradius Rufinus, and A. Triarius Rufinus) could be fitted with the fragmentary traces of the praenomen which exist on the inscription. Neither, however, is likely to have been the man who became a consular governor of Britannia Superior, for he is more likely to have been a suffect consul, and there are few records of suffect consuls after the second century. The Rufinus of the Reculver inscription may therefore have been consular governor of Britain at any time after the reign of Severus, or, less probably, in the late second century (Birley 1981, 173-6).

Reculver is listed in the Notitia Dignitatum as *Regulbium* where the *tribunus cohortis I Baetasiorum* was stationed. This cohort is known to have been at Maryport in Cumbria in the late second century, but was presumably transferred at the date of the fort's construction. Tiles stamped CIB have been found in excavations at Reculver. There is no other reference to the name of the fort in written sources

In AD 669, the site of 'Raculf' was given by Egbert, King of Kent, to Bassa, for the foundation of a minster. It grew in importance, but in AD 949 became one of the possessions of the Archbishopric of Canterbury, and by the later tenth century it had ceased to function as a monastic house. The present church, which lies roughly centrally within the Roman fort, retains much of the plan and outline of a seventh-century church. The east end was extended in the 13th century, and the twin towers, now a navigational aid, are of the late twelfth century. The church became the parish church for the local residents, but was abandoned in 1805 because of fears that the sea would overtake it.

Literature

Philp 1959; Philp 1969; Richmond 1961; Mann 1977.

STEPHEN JOHNSON

RICHBOROUGH

The topography around Richborough (*Rutupiae*) has changed greatly since the Roman period. What was then one of the main ports on Britain's south-east coast is now nearly 4 km from the sea. The Isle of Thanet, the north-easternmost part of Kent, was divided from the mainland by the Wantsum channel, which was probably partly marshland, partly open water (Fig. 45). It gave access to the mouth of the River Stour and to Canterbury; in the twelfth century the ships which carried the Caen stone for Canterbury Cathedral could still sail upstream as far as Fordwich to unload. The Roman forts at Reculver and Richborough guarded the northern and southern approaches to the Wantsum. Richborough's main advantage was its sheltered anchorage, a natural lagoon harbour protected to the seaward side by an offshore bank of shingle. The British placename *Rutupiae* may be translated as 'muddy waters'. The Roman town and fort was built on what originally was an island about 1.5 km long, now visible as a low hill rising above the flat surrounding area of drained former marshland. The exact line of the Roman shore and the position of any harbour installations is unknown; they are likely to be buried to a depth of several metres by silts deposited during the centuries of medieval marsh formation. It is thought that the Roman harbour buildings were probably on the eastern side of the site; if so, the changed course of the River Stour, which caused the erosion of the east side of the Saxon Shore fort, may have removed most of the evidence. By the seventh century the silting of the Wantsum had led to Richborough's replacement as a port by Sandwich, itself now equally cut off from the sea.

The visible remains at Richborough in the eleventh century were: the walls of the Saxon Shore fort, and within them, the cruciform foundation now known to be the passageways through the first century monumental arch: the medieval chapel of St. Augustine: 400 metres to the south-west there was the earthwork of the amphitheatre, already much eroded by ploughing.

In 1850 Charles Roach Smith published the first detailed archaeological account of the site (together with Reculver and Lympne), including finds made when the railway was constructed immediately east of the fort in 1846, and when the amphitheatre was excavated by Rolfe in 1849. Several tunnels and shafts were dug in the nineteenth century to investigate the foundations of the arch. Excavations by George Dowker in 1887 found metalled roads and masonry buildings west of the fort, where cropmarks had been noted in 1792. In 1900 John Garstang dug trenches to explore parts of the fort defences, including the west gate. Most of our knowledge of Richborough's archaeology, however, is the result of the large scale excavations from 1922 to 1938 financed by the Society of Antiquaries and directed by J.P. Bushe-Fox. They explored most of the area within the walls of the Saxon Shore fort, by a combination of area excavations, trenching and surface clearance, and uncovered remains of all periods of Richborough's occupation from the time of the Claudian conquest until the early fifth century. What is now displayed on the site is intended to be representative of its changing structural history during the whole Roman period (Fig. 47).

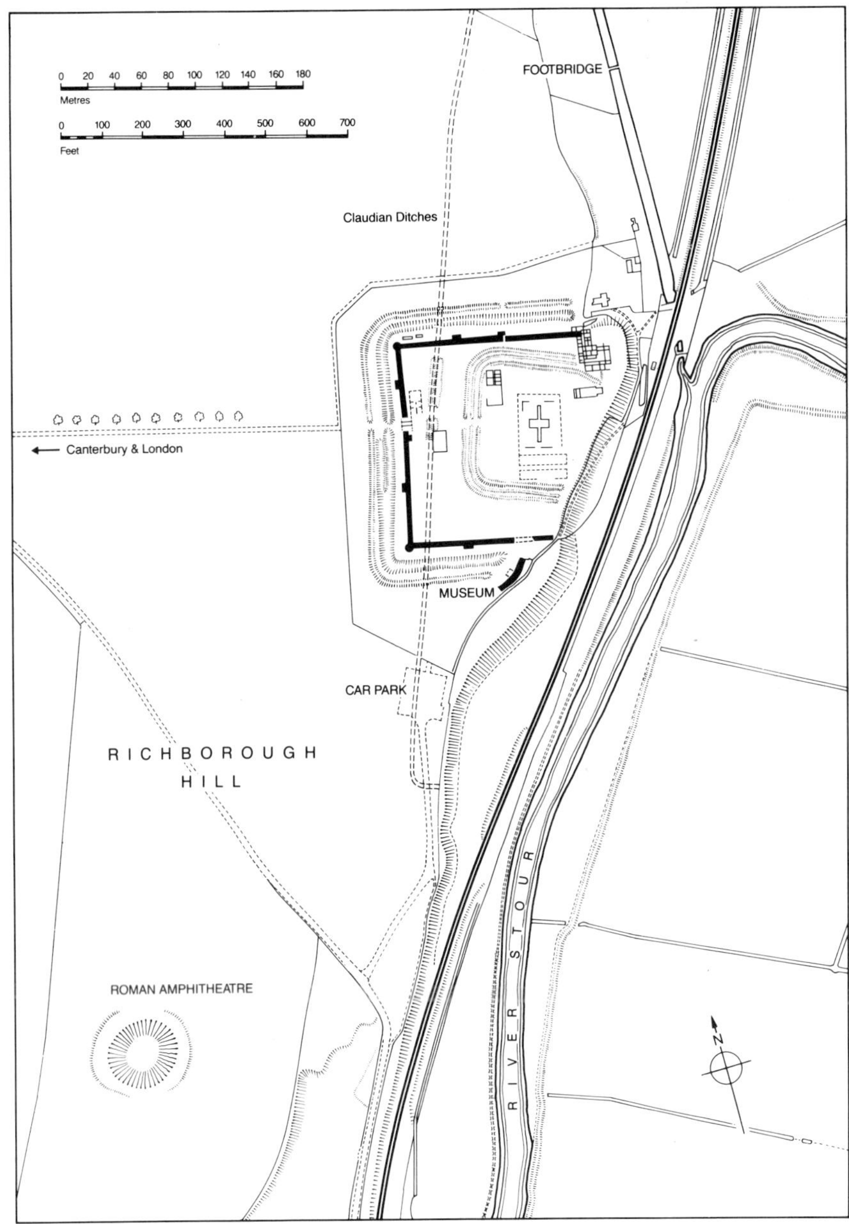

Fig. 47 Richborough: general plan of the site.

The Claudian beach-head fort

There is slight evidence of pre-Roman Iron Age occupation - pottery, ditches and a palisade trench - but nothing to indicate a site of importance. The earliest Roman structure is a double ditch, extending for a few hundred metres north and south of the third-century fort walls (630 metres overall). The finds from their primary fill suggest a Claudian date, and they are interpreted as the ditches of a beach-head fort built when the invasion forces landed in AD 43. A short length of the excavated ditches is displayed in the north-west corner of the fort.

Stores base

Immediately afterwards, a stores base was constructed with metalled roads and buildings of timber constructed with sill-beam foundations. Remains of about a dozen of these were found in the southern half of the later fort and in the north-east corner. The perimeter of some of them is now marked out in strips of concrete. The east-west street formed the beginning of Watling Street, leading westwards to Canterbury and London. A section dug across it west of the fort in 1958 showed that the channel which formerly isolated the site of Richborough had silted up by the time the road was built.

The monumental arch

Richborough subsequently developed as a main port of entry to Britain. About AD 80-90, a large monumental arch was built across the east-west street. It was a splendid landmark, the only Roman building in Britain known to have been covered externally in marble, and its size and grandeur indicate that it was an imperial project. The occasion for it was probably the effective completion, during Agricola's governorship (AD 78-84), of the process of conquest begun at Richborough by an army in which Vespasian had commanded a legion. This symbolic gateway to Britain was demolished when the Saxon Shore fort was built, and all that is now visible is the foundation of the two intersecting passageways above the massive supporting platform. That was of mortared flint, nearly 10 m deep, and carried the four great masonry piers of the Arch, which is estimated to have been over 25 m high. At least 40,000 tonnes of stone, chalk and flint would have been required.

The triple-ditched enclosure and urban structures

In the early third century the monument, by then in disrepair, was surrounded by three closely-spaced ditches, now re-excavated and displayed on all but the west side where erosion has removed them. Also displayed, cut through by the ditches, are the remains of what seems to have been a row of 2nd-century shops fronting the east-west street, with smaller rooms at the back. They had been demolished to below floor level. They were preceded by timber buildings and metal-working.

The other main excavated building in the town stood north-east of the Arch, and is identified as the *mansio*. There were three periods of construction, the first being of timber. That was replaced in the late 1st century by a building with stone foundations, including hypocaust-heated baths. The layout is now indicated in brown concrete. It was rebuilt again in the early 2nd century with masonry walls, now indicated in cream concrete. That structure was still standing when the triple ditches were dug round the Arch, since two of them stop short of it. It was demolished when the Saxon Shore fort was built, its site partly covered by the walls and by the fort bathhouse.

Another structure then demolished was a third-century barrow tomb; part of its wall is visible just within and south of the fort's west gate. Its presence suggests the limits of the urban area, and that if any buildings further west along Watling Street were then occupied, they were regarded as extra-mural. There has been little systematic excavation of buildings outside the fort walls. To the south-west, two Romano-Celtic temples were partly excavated when a new railway line was laid across them in 1926 and some walls and a late Roman inhumation cemetery were found when the car park and access road were laid out a few years later. Other buildings are known from aerial photography or from 19th century excavations. The amphitheatre excavated in 1849, had an arena surrounded by a wall of chalk and flint. The coins found were mainly of 3rd and 4th century date.

The Saxon Shore fort

In Ptolemy's *Geography* and the Antonine Itinerary *Rutupiae* is described respectively as a town and a port. In the third century it again acquired military significance. The triple ditches with an inner bank of earth surrounding the monumental Arch *c*.250 converted it in effect into a watchtower. Abundant finds from the ditches' infill, including marble veneer from the Arch, indicate the clearance or levelling of all structures on the site where the fort was to be built, *c.* AD 275. Significant evidence for this dating came from coins in a pit dug through footings laid across the *mansio* site for the fort's east wall, which in the event was built further east, where the river subsequently undermined it. The fort thus seems to have been built rather earlier than the period of Carausius, the date (AD 286-93) proposed in Cunliffe's Fifth Report on the excavations (1968). The fort was nearly square, measuring 145 metres internally north-south (Fig. 48). Externally there were two ditches, of which one on the west side was realigned. The main west gate had two rectangular towers, reusing ashlar masonry from a demolished monument in their foundations. On the north side is a small postern gate with a right-angled turn. Built into its north face is a funerary lion, its fore-parts missing. There were round towers at the outer corners, and rectangular external towers between the corner towers and the gates. These were built hollow, but the lower stages could only have been reached by ladders from above. The walls still stand up to a height of 8 metres, and are of coursed flint laid in lime mortar. The exterior is faced in a coursed rubble of small greensand blocks, with occasional use of ironstone and cream limestone for apparently decorative effect. Both inner and outer facings have double courses of tile at intervals of about one metre. The alignment of the west wall south of the gate diverges from that to the north, and there are several places on the north wall where vertical joins in the masonry indicate breaks between successive stages of the work. Little is known about internal buildings: the levelled platform of the Arch is thought to have been used as the foundation of the *principia*. Two rectangular buildings with porches, one facing east near the Arch foundation, the other facing north near the west gate, may have been *collegia* or temples. A small three-room bath-house was built over the site of the *mansio*. As is clear from these structures, the late Roman buildings stood at a higher level than their predecessors, and if there were also contemporary timber buildings as there were at Portchester, any evidence for this has now been removed along with the upper layers of deposits.

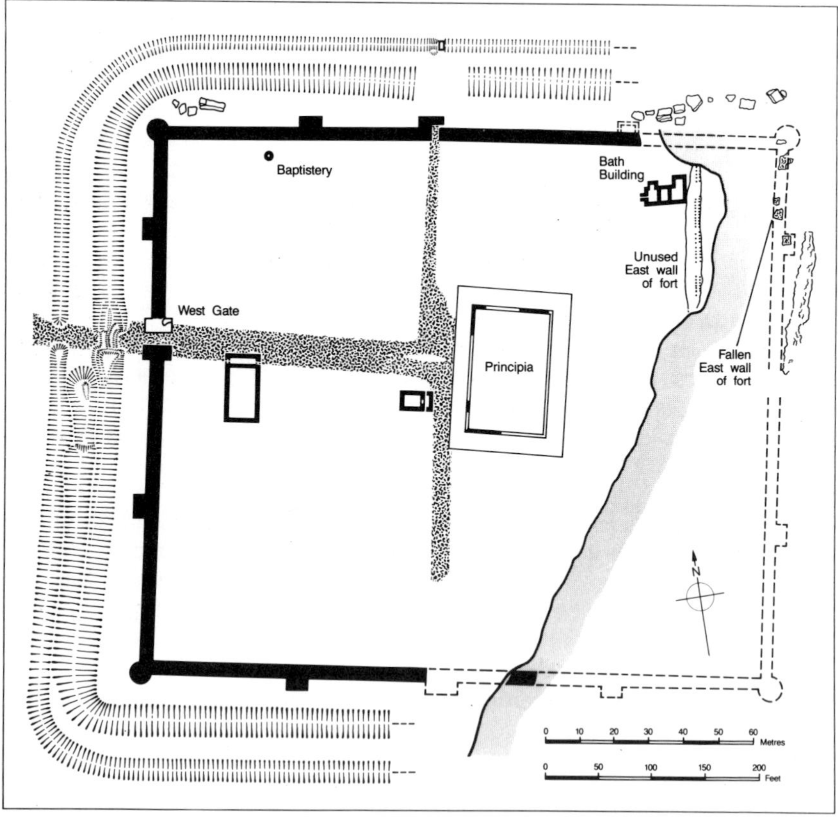

Fig. 48 Richborough: the Saxon Shore fort.

Richborough's military importance in the late Roman Period is shown by the landing there of Lupicinus in 360 and Count Theodosius in 368 with forces for their respective expeditions against barbarian raiders. It is listed in the Notitia Dignitatum as being garrisoned by troops of the Second legion Augusta, though the period of their presence is uncertain. The exceptionally numerous coins of the House of Theodosius, as well as other late Roman military metalwork, show that it was one of the last places in Britain to have been held in military strength, even as it had been the first. By the early 5th century there was a Christian community there, attested by the identification of a hexagonal masonry structure in the north-west corner as a font, and by the *chi-rho* monogram on artefacts. There was a medieval tradition that Saint Augustine, after landing on Thanet in AD 597, then came to Richborough. East of where the Arch had stood, the position is now marked out in concrete of a square-apsed late Saxon church, rebuilt with a curved apse in the 12th century. There is no indication of an earlier Saxon building. However, Richborough's harbour may have ceased to function as such by the 7th century, for when Saint Wilfrid came to Kent in AD 687, he disembarked at Sandwich. Nevertheless, the number of late 7th to 9th century Anglo-Saxon coins shows continued activity at Richborough until the time of the Viking attacks on the coast.

The site museum

The small site museum contains a selection of the finds made during the excavations. The pottery displayed includes good examples from among the finds of complete or restorable vessels from graves, pits and well; Gaullish terra sigillata, Rhenish barbotine-decorated beakers, and locally made mortaria and coarsewares are all represented. Since the site was occupied throughout the Roman period, the series of fibulae and coins is of particular importance; there are notable examples of late Roman metalwork. A recently made model of the monumental arch incorporates evidence from studies subsequent to the publication of the Fifth Richborough Report.

Literature

Roach Smith 1850; Bushe-Fox 1926, 1928, 1932, 1949; Cunliffe ed. 1968; Johnson 1979; Johnson 1981; Blagg 1984.

T.F.C. BLAGG

DOVER

In the Roman period, it appears that the River Dour, now a narrow stream running largely hidden through the town, flowed out to the sea through a broader estuary. Much of the central part of the valley in which the town lies will therefore have been the harbour, the higher ground to west and east affording space for settlement. Clearest traces of Roman occupation have been found on the west bank, where the nucleus of the

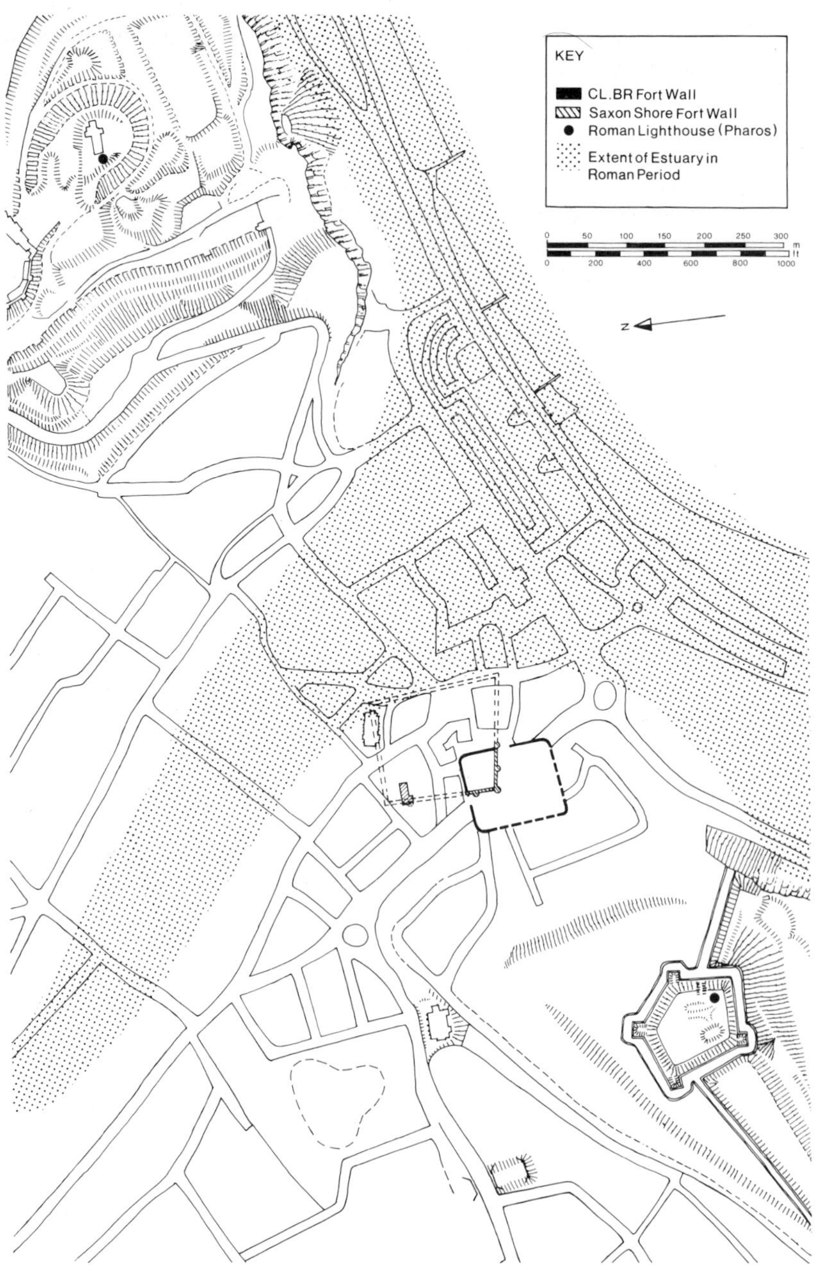

Fig. 49 Dover: general plan.

medieval town and port also lay. Three installations have been distinguished: an early, apparently unfinished, fort; a later *classis Britannica* fort; a Saxon Shore fort (Fig. 49).

The early unfinished fort

The traces of this fort which have been located lay wholly beneath the remains of the later *classis Britannica* installation. Traces of its north, east and south walls, only 1.40 m thick, have been found: these suggest that the layout was that of a parallelogram with rounded corners, measuring 89 m from north to south. Three internal buildings were identified, all of them long and narrow, separated into small compartments, and aligned on the fort's north-south axis. One of these buildings, identified as barracks, lay only 5 m from the fort wall, and it thus appears unlikely that the circuit walls of the fort were backed by a rampart of any size. All the structures belonging to this fort survived only as chalk rubble foundations beneath the later fort: the excavator considered therefore that it had not been completed.

Dating evidence for this fort was largely negative, though the general spread of pottery from the site and the suggestions that the fort was left unfinished and laid the blueprint for its successor led the excavator to propose a date in the late Trajanic period for its inception.

The Classis Britannica fort

This fort was a parallelogram with rounded corners, on the same orientation as the earlier fort (Fig. 50). It measured 93 m by 112 and occupied almost exactly one hectare. The walls, largely built of chalk, were narrow - only 1.20 m thick - and had no angle or internal towers, though there was a narrow berm and a shallow external ditch. Elements of two dual carriageway gates, that on the north with rectangular guard-chambers, and that on the east with U-shaped projecting guard chambers, were discovered.

Internally, the fort was closely packed with buildings, leaving little or no room for a rampart: on the west side, buildings lay within 1.90 m of the walls, while on the east the gap was 6 m. The north gate was set approximately two-thirds of the way along the north wall, and the fort was subdivided internally to reflect this arrangement, the eastern, larger, area apparently containing at least 9 long narrow chalk buildings subdivided into compartments, while the western part of the fort contained administrative and service buildings. Excavation, which concentrated on the line of a planned road across the site, exposed two store-buildings and part of another barrack-type building in the western portion, but little else.

Examination of the dating evidence suggested that for several of the buildings there were indications of up to three separate phases of use. Built perhaps around AD 130, period II may have begun around 155, the final period around the end of the second century, and abandonment and demolition of the fort by about AD 210. Finds of many tiles stamped with the letters CLBR clearly indicate the source of building materials for the fort and suggest a close link with the British Fleet.

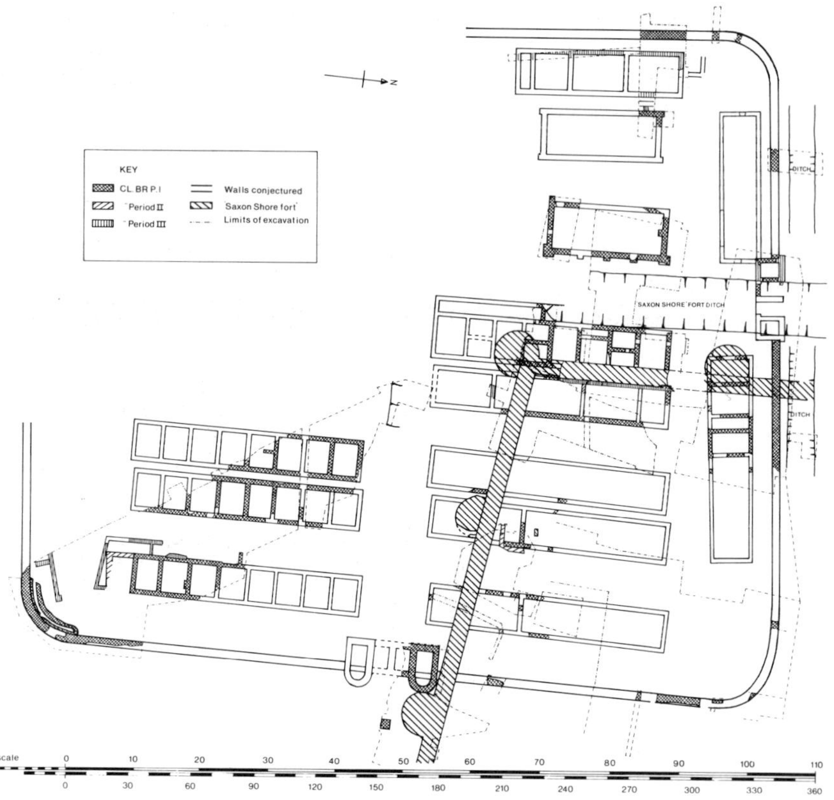

Fig. 50 Dover: the classis Britannica fort overlain by a corner of the Saxon Shore fort.

The Saxon Shore fort

The third fort on the site at Dover was an irregular polygon on the west bank of the River Dour. Its walls were 2.42 - 2.30 m thick, and have been located on the south and west sides of the enclosure: on both sides they were strengthened by externally projecting solid towers, some built as part of the original fortification, others added slightly later (Fig. 50). At the south-west angle of the circuit, the tower appears to have been a near circle, 6.75 m in diameter: intermediate towers were spaced between 23 and 30 metres apart, centre to centre. On the west side of the enclosure was a substantial ditch 7.3 m wide, with a berm of 5.5 m between it and the fort walls. The walls of the fort were built of tufa and chalk, and some of the towers, in particular those which are not bonded into the structure, stand on chamfered plinths and contain double tile courses.

Behind the fort wall was an earth rampart which helped to preserve earlier Roman structures close behind the newly constructed wall. The south-west corner of this later fort overlay the north-east corner of the earlier *classis Britannica* fort, but the major part of the newly enclosed area seems to have lain further to its north and east, closer to the Dour estuary, and it must have overlain buildings of the former settlement which lay around the earlier fort, and other buildings of which, including a substantial bathhouse, have been located in excavation.

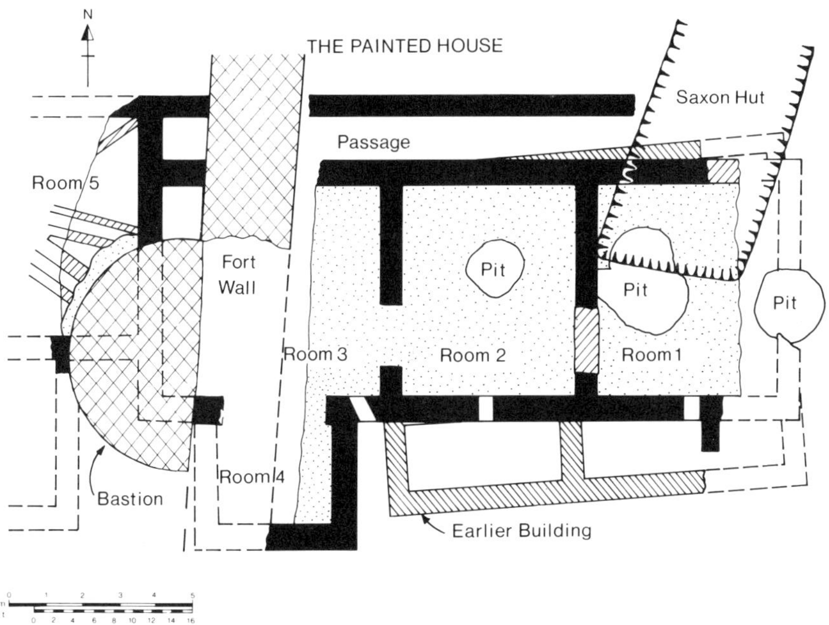

Fig. 51 Dover: the Painted House overlain by the west wall of the Saxon Shore fort.

One of the buildings of the settlement partially preserved beneath the rampart is the so-called 'painted house' (Fig. 51). These were the substantial remains of a number of rooms with *opus signinum* floors and walls bearing painted and decorated wall-plaster. Within the fort, away from the rampart areas, continual occupation and considerable medieval and later disturbance have made a coherent layout difficult to trace. In areas of the fort there have been finds of timber buildings and huts of Roman date, as well as a number of huts and possible grubenhäuser of Saxon date. A number of cemeteries have also been located in the Dover area: the closest to the forts lay about 80 m south of the *classis Britannica* fort, but it has not been adequately researched.

The excavators have assigned a late third century date to the construction of the Saxon Shore fort, but detailed evidence for this date has not yet been published.

Literature

Philp 1981; annual summaries of work in progress in *Britannia* 7(1976), 376: 8 (1977), 424: 9(1978), 471: 11 (1979), 401: 12 (1981), 366: 13 (1982), 393: 14 (1983), 334-5: 15 (1984), 330: 16 (1985), 315: 17 (1986), 426; for Saxon material, *Medieval Archaeology* 17 (1973), 145: 20 (1976), 164: 22 (1976), 147.

STEPHEN JOHNSON

DOVER LIGHTHOUSE

There are remains of two lighthouses either extant or recorded at Dover. One still stands within the castle, while the other stood on the western side of the Dour estuary, on the Western Heights, now all but obliterated by the Napoleonic fortification.

The lighthouse known as the 'pharos' stands to the west of the church of St Mary in Castro, within a part of the castle's defences which has been shown to be of Iron Age origin. In total, it stands almost 19 m high, the topmost 5.8 m of which was rebuilt between 1415-37. Externally it is octagonal at the base, with sides 4.6 m long, its diameter at the base nearly 12 m. Internally, there is a chamber 4.20 m square (Fig. 52). It is built of tufa and ragstone and flint, normally with double tile courses at regular intervals.

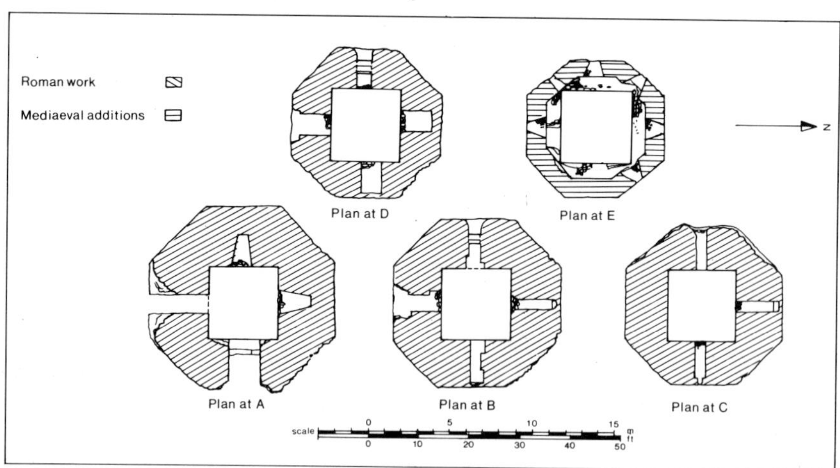

Fig. 52 Roman lighthouse at Dover Castle: plans.

Though much eroded, and in part re-faced, on its exterior, there are clear traces internally of large inverted U-shaped windows with voussoirs of stone or of alternating tile and stone. These large windows, of various widths, can be seen to lie at four separate definable floor levels, which are also marked by large beam holes for floor joists in the internal north and south walls (Fig. 53). Some of these openings have been blocked at later periods and only in one or two instances are they not present in all four directions at each level.

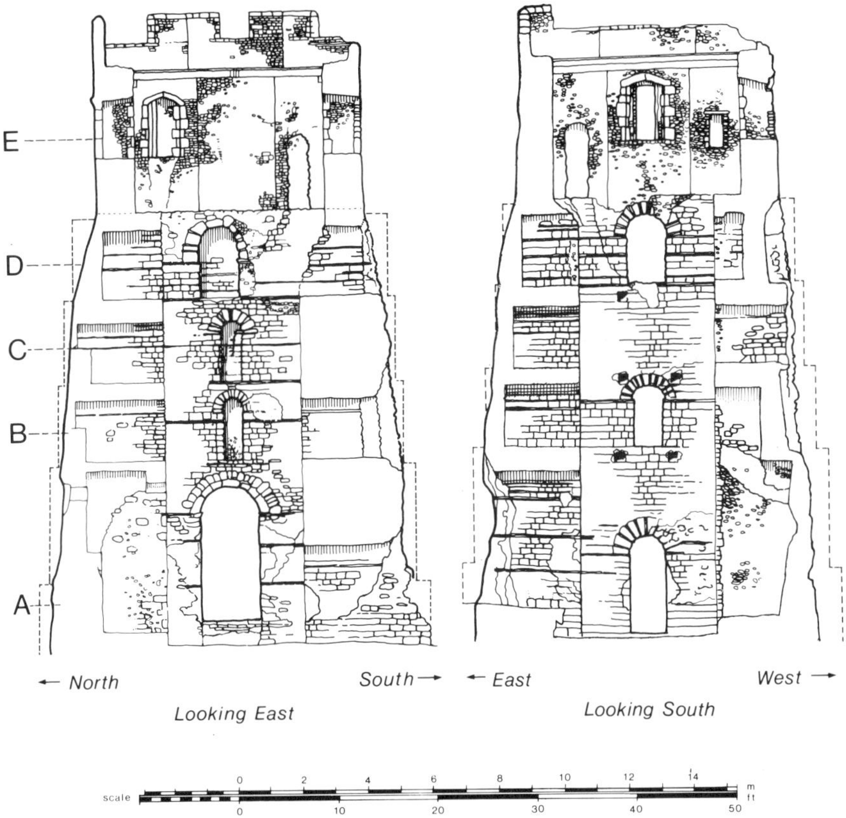

Fig. 53 Roman lighthouse at Dover Castle: sections.

The tower can be seen visibly to taper at present, although the size of the central chamber remains constant. It is likely therefore that the external octagonal face rose in a series of small steps, which perhaps coincided with the floor levels on the interior. If so, there were probably five such reductions in external dimensions in the present surviving height of the Roman masonry, in regular storeys of 2.6 m above the higher and larger ground floor openings. Reconstructions of the original size of the tower suggest that it could have had at least four more additional storeys above those which now survive, to stand originally to a height of around 24 m.

The remains of the other pharos, on the Western Heights, can now be traced only from documentary sources. Antiquarian accounts dating from the sixteenth century refer to the Roman lighthouse on the western hill, while ignoring the castle pharos, calling it the Bredenstone, and it seems to be shown in sixteenth and seventeenth century views of Dover Harbour. The tower appears to have suffered badly and was almost totally obliterated before 1805-6, when the threat of an invasion by Napoleon led to a rapid fortification of the Western Heights. A rudimentary description of a platform of solid Roman masonry, located when further work was carried out to the fortifications in 1861, suggests that it was hexagonal, and of similar size to the pharos in the castle. Some fragments of the foundations were erected above the site of this discovery.

It is not possible to date either of the two Dover lighthouses. In form, the stepped form of the pharos is similar to the recorded views of the lighthouse at Boulogne: it has been suggested that this could be the tower built by Caligula, referred to by Suetonius, and, by inference, that the Dover lighthouses were also of first century date.

Literature
Wheeler 1929.

STEPHEN JOHNSON

LYMPNE

The two points which most interest students of the Saxon Shore, and frontiers and their installations in general, are form and date: at Lympne both are to some extent uncertain. The position is excellent for a Shore Fort, provided the sea is brought some three kilometres nearer than the present coastline, for it consists of a south-facing slope looking out over a flat area which is virtually at sea level. Cunliffe's summary of recent study of the development of this flat marshy area - now Romney Marsh - strongly suggests that the Shore Fort of c.AD 300 stood just above the entrance of a large natural harbour (Cunliffe 1988). Deposition of silt from rivers and the movement of pebbles and sand by the sea have filled in the harbour, severing the Fort from the Shore (Fig. 54).

The hill-side position of the fort probably accounts for the present plan of remaining masonry, which is fragmentary and irregular (Fig. 55). Both features suggest that the stone-work has been moved from its original position by the slumping of the clay slope on which it is built. While this accounts for the present jumble it also removes any possibility of certainty over the original shape and position of the walls. The known remains include much of the west, north and east walls, investigated in the excavations of Roach Smith and Cunliffe. The south wall was explored by Horsley (Taylor 1944) and

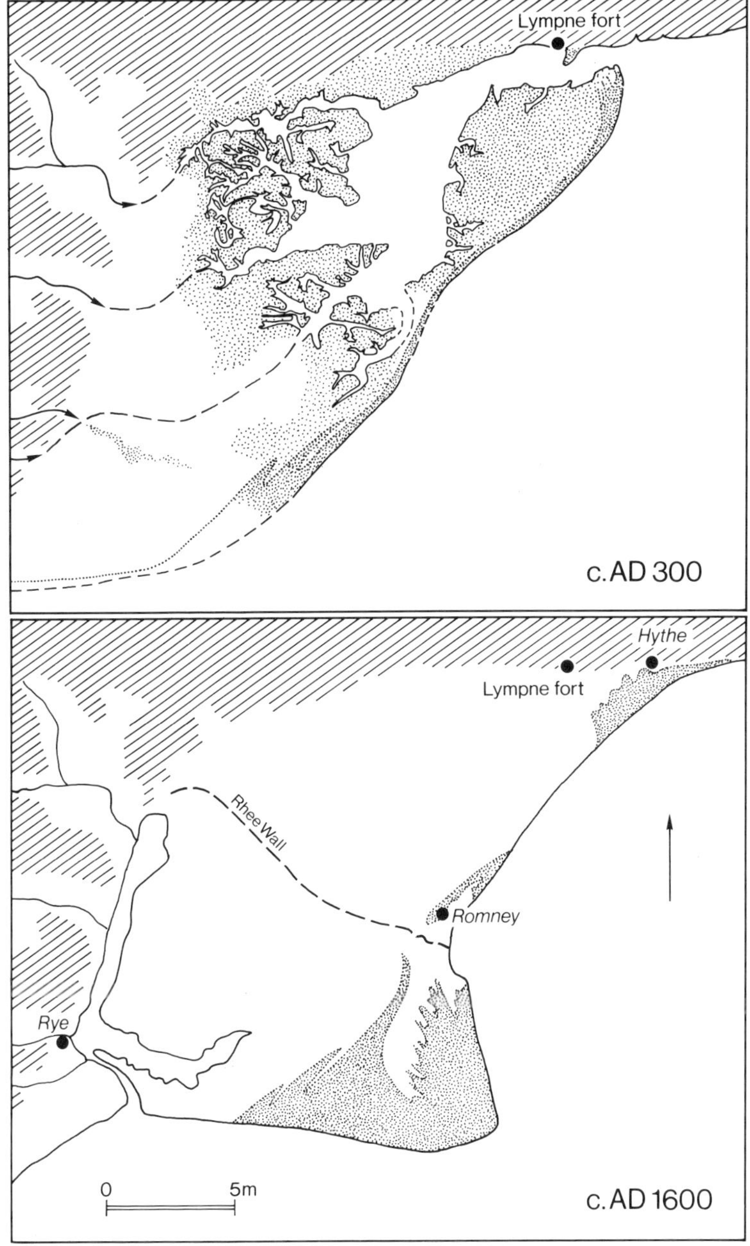

Fig. 54 The changing coastline in the area of Lympne (after Cunliffe).

published in more detail by Cunliffe. Internal buildings recorded are two - perhaps the *principia* and probably the bath-house - excavated by Roach Smith (summarized by Cunliffe 1980b, 256-8) together with parts of two more, too fragmentary for discussion. These buildings were not re-investigated by Cunliffe.

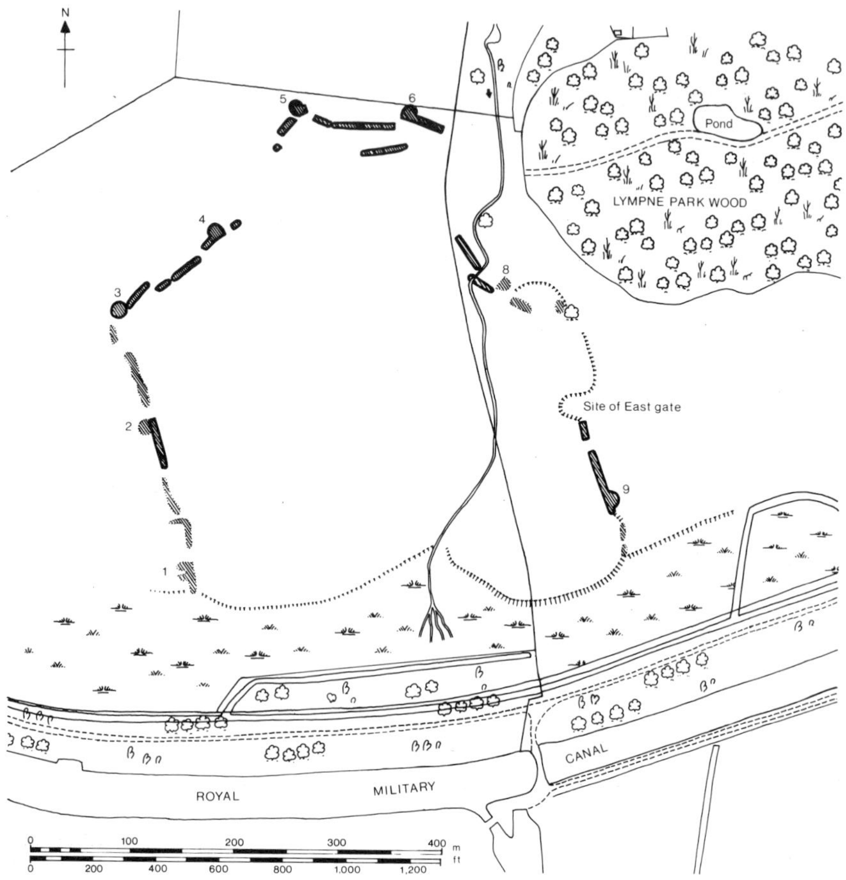

Fig. 55 Lympne: Stutfall Castle (after Cunliffe).

The gateways are certain in the east wall (fully excavated, and a full restoration suggested, by Cunliffe), and the west wall, a visible gap which was excavated by Roach Smith. In the north wall there is room for nothing more than a simple postern gate, and the remains are consistent with this. The south wall is too ruinous for any certainty.

The remains of eight towers (which Cunliffe terms 'bastions') have been established, of which at least four seem to project as stilted semicircles from a straight wall (Cunliffe

1980b, fig. 16, no. 9). At least one has a rounded surface which is more than a semicircle (*ibid.* fig.17 no.3). Cunliffe's restoration shows two walls joining this tower at 90° and on this basis it forms the north-west corner of a rectangular plan in which the fragments visible have been 'pulled' back into place up the hill (Fig. 56). All stonework seems to belong to one phase of construction which, typologically, might fit best at the end of the third century.

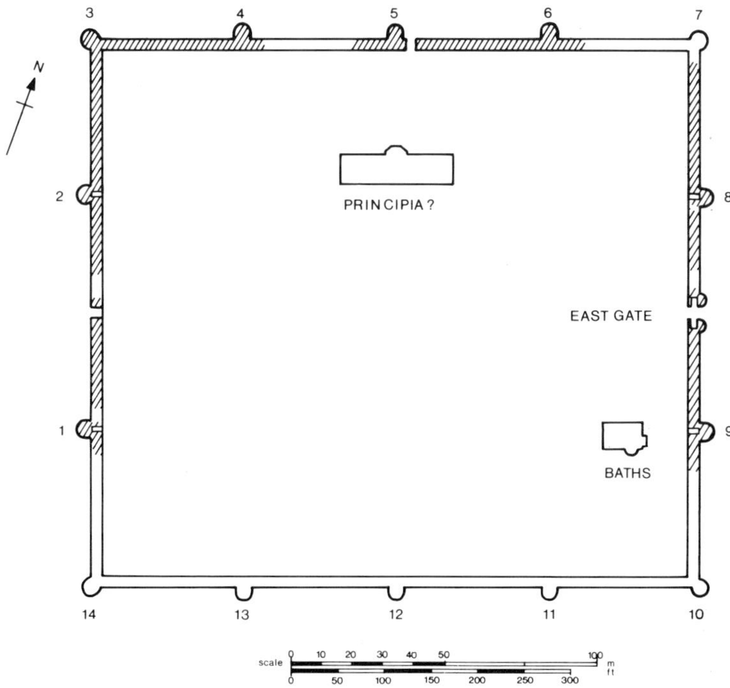

Fig. 56 Lympne: reconstructed plan of Saxon Shore fort (after Cunliffe).

There is some evidence on the site of an earlier date than this. This consists of an altar set up by Aufidius Pantera, prefect of the *classis Britannica*, to Neptune (RIB 66), a small amount of early pottery including less than 30 sherds of samian, some tiles with the stamp of the *classis Britannica*, and one coin. The altar was apparently re-used in the east gate and was encrusted with barnacles; it was therefore not only re-used, but had at some intermediate time been submerged in the sea. There is little or no evidence that tiles were being stamped by the fleet after about AD 200, and the Lympne examples could well have been brought from elsewhere for re-use. The early pottery is out of place on a site constructed in 270+, and the coin recorded in the nineteenth century as Antoninus Pius, could well be of Caracalla. That, like the samian, would be a most unusual loss after about 240-50.

There is therefore not enough evidence to suggest that the present remains occupy the same site as an earlier fort (of the *classis Britannica* ?) as at Dover, but the material which pre-dates 270 suggests at least an earlier site with military connections, in the neighbourhood. This fits well with the mention in the Antonine Itinerary (early third century) of *Portus Lemanis*, which at least suggests a harbour if not an accompanying fort. The partial super-imposition at Dover suggests a gap in time between the two forts, and, if a similar sequence applied at Lympne, it might well mean that the earlier site was no longer suitable. An obvious explanation would be the danger to a fort at the foot of the slope, of rising sea-level.

The end of occupation at Lympne is clearer than the beginning, but is still open to question. The weight of all the coins found lies in the period 260-348. No coins which I have examined are later than 348, and only 3 coins out of a total of 304 recorded can be dated after 348. It is enough to point out the sharp drop in coins lost after 348 and the contrast which this shows with sites such as Portchester and Richborough where later coins are common. The pottery, in so far as it is datable, is in complete agreement with the coins, for there are no pieces which need to be dated after 350, and there are several late fourth century types which would be expected in a site in this area, which are absent. The material evidence suggests abandonment around 350.

One historical source, the Notitia Dignitatum, peoples the fort (*Portus Lemanis*), around 395, with the *numerus Turnacensium.* I resolved this apparent conflict in the discussion of the coins in Cunliffe's excavation report (Cunliffe 1980b, 263) as follows: 'The conflict is more apparent than real. The coins, or physical structures or equipment could suggest the presence of a unit at Lympne; the entry in the Notitia is only evidence that one bureaucrat in the later fourth century Roman military machine had a reason for placing a number of troops in this fort of the Saxon Shore. The reason may be no more than incompetence or inertia, both military characteristics.'

Some adherents of written sources have, in desperation, suggested yet another site at Lympne, founded late in the fourth century when subsidence might have made the accepted site unsafe. A site on the hill-top has been found in field-walking (Cunliffe 1980b, 288 note 61) but the material remains seem to be continuous from the second century to the late fourth century.

A summary might be as follows:

i. In the general area of, possibly even beneath, the later fort, a fort of the *classis Britannica*, the *Portus Lemanis* of the Antonine Itinerary, the origin of the earlier material listed above.

ii. In the area of tumbled walls, a fort of the Saxon Shore, built about 270 of rectangular plan (an hypothesis which is consistent with the evidence, but is not certain): gates and towers known: abandoned about 350.

iii. In the Notitia Dignitatum, *c*. 395, a fort garrisoned by the *numerus Turnacensium*, which at present corresponds to nothing in reality.

Literature
Roach Smith 1850: 1852; Taylor 1944; Cunliffe 1980b.

RICHARD REECE

PEVENSEY

The late Roman walls of the fort at Pevensey form the main part of the enclosure walls of the bailey of the medieval castle, whose inner ward now occupies the south-eastern extremity of the Roman circuit (Fig. 57). The Roman walls have fallen on the south and on portions of the north side, and are interrupted by the Norman castle of *c*. 1100 on the south-east. Elsewhere they form a roughly oval circuit, closely fitted to a small promontory jutting into marshes which once will have been open sea.

The site is linked to the mainland by a road from the west which enters the fort at the main west gate. Smaller postern gates discovered on the north, east and south walls suggest either that there were other means of access to the fort across the marshes, or they gave access to a harbour, perhaps north of the promontory occupied by the fort. No trace of any such harbour has been found.

Excavation at the site has been limited. The earliest record is of excavation by C. Roach Smith in 1852, which traced elements of the line of the walls. Further work by L.F. Salzman in 1906-7 examined areas of the interior of the fort by a series of linked narrow trenches. Clearance work was undertaken as part of the consolidation work on the fort walls between then and 1936-9, when there were further excavations by F. Cotterill. These included the examination of layers at the foot of the interior of the north wall close to the postern gate site, clearance of the east gateway, and complete excavation of the west gateway. Since 1939 there has been no further excavation at the site.

The walls enclose around 3.67 ha within a rough oval of 290 by 170 m at its maximum extent. The walls are generally 3.67 m thick, with the ground level higher within the circuit than outside it: this is a result of dumping of material from the Norman castle ditch to cover the interior of the Roman walls. Work at various points on the circuit has established that the walls' foundations are a layer of stiff clay set in a trench, and pinned to the ground with vertical wooden stakes. Above this was laid a chalk and flint foundation, on which was set a framework of timber beams, extending in a criss-cross pattern encountered at several points in the wall-circuit, under the bastions, and encountered also at the excavation of the west gate. The space around the beams was

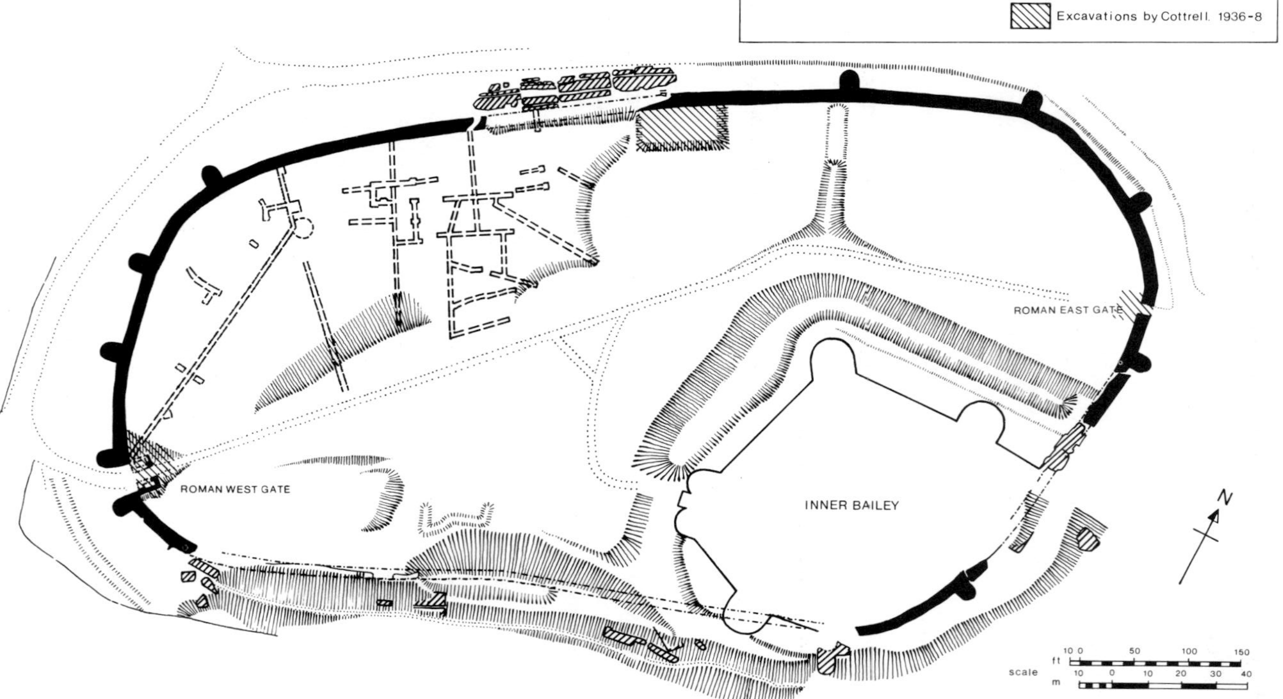

Fig. 57 Pevensey Castle.

filled with crushed chalk, and the whole foundation capped by a thick layer of mortar to bring it up to ground level.

The wall superstructure was laid on this base: first one or two courses of large coarse stone, which in places form a roughly laid external plinth course, then the wall of small blockwork round a rubble core. Externally this facing is interspersed either with courses of double tiles for bonding, or with larger, flatter sandstone courses which have the same function. Internally, there seem to have been no tile-courses, and the wall was stepped back at least twice. Much of the circuit of walls has a consistent height of about 8.3 m, and there is little sign of repair later than the Roman period. In places there are traces of a string course and a parapet wall above that height, but these may be a medieval addition. There is no indication of how access may have been gained to the tops of the walls.

At irregular intervals round the wall, external bastions of solid masonry were built. They are U-shaped, and project between 5.10 and 5.60 m from the wall face. All seem to be of one build with the wall; only one now stands above rampart walk level (D); before its conversion into a machine-gun post in 1941, this tower retained a large U-shaped window, probably of Roman origin. At the west gate, flanked by two U-shaped towers, there are fragmentary traces of a chamber at wall-walk level.

The main gate, to the west, was a single-portalled narrow passage between two rectangular towers recessed at the back of the flanking towers in the main wall. These formed an enfiladed courtyard similar to those exposed in excavation at Portchester. The foundations on which these gate towers stood seem to be the same build as the remainder of the fort walls, with evidence for timber beams in their foundations very clearly exposed on excavation in 1936-9. The towers were 3.7 x 5.8 m, and the passageway between them 2.4 m wide. The other three gates were single entrances: that on the north wall was a postern 2 m wide, which is described as a curved passage through the wall: it was located by Roach Smith and Salzman, but is not visible today. The south postern gate was located by Roach Smith and described as a very narrow postern entrance, its situation almost directly opposite the postern in the north wall. The east gate was rebuilt in medieval times, but was on the site of a Roman gateway. It is 2.8 m wide.

No interior buildings of the Roman period are currently visible. Salzman's excavations, however, located a series of hearths, spaced around 6 m apart, which he interpreted as part of a series of regularly spaced barrack accommodation close to the north wall. His excavations also found a timber-lined well.

Dating of the site is hampered by the lack of well-published work on the interior of the site. Although excavations by Cotterill in 1936-9 reportedly recovered large amounts of pottery and 'late third century' occupation material (including coins) from the fort's initial occupation layers, the fort is usually considered to be dated by the *terminus post quem* provided by a single Constantinian coin of AD 330-335 found within one of the empty beam-holes, some 0.9 - 1.2 m underneath one of the towers. The exact circumstances of this find, published by Bushe Fox (1932b) have never been revealed, and it may not be possible to investigate them. If the coin was stratified in the position from which it was recovered, the construction of the fort must date from the 330s at the earliest. But there must be doubts over the value of this evidence.

The fort is generally regarded to be *Anderitum*, mentioned in the Notitia Dignitatum (*Not. Dig. Oc.* 28.10) as the location for the *praepositus numeri Abulcorum*. The name, however, is missing from the text of the Notitia, and has to be supplied from the *pictura* (frontispiece). Units bearing the fort's name, both troops and a naval unit, are also found stationed elsewhere in the Notitia text - at *Vico Julio*, in the field army in Gaul and based at Paris (*Not. Dig. Oc.* 41.17; 7.100; 42.22, 23 respectively). It is assumed therefore that the original fort garrison, both naval and infantry, was removed from their home and replaced by the *numerus Abulcorum*.

The name *Anderitum* survived into the Saxon period. In the year AD 477 the Anglo-Saxon Chronicle records that a Saxon expedition into Britain drove some Saxons in flight into the forest called *Andreadsleag*. In AD 491, the fort itself seems to be mentioned. In this year Aelle and Cissa 'besieged *Andredadsceaster* and slew everyone who lived there'. The forest of *Abdred* seems to have stretched from the mouth of the Lympne over 200 km to Hampshire.

Literature

Roach Smith 1858; Salzman 1907; Salzman 1908; Bushe-Fox 1932.

STEPHEN JOHNSON

PORTCHESTER

Portchester Castle stands at the head of Portsmouth Harbour, on the end of a promontory extending into the tidal mudflats. To the north, on Portsdown Hill, is a chalk outcrop which was a source of lime (burnt from the chalk) and flints for building. At the present time a navigable creek passes not far from the east side of the castle, but tidal erosion has brought the sea right up to the walls. The site chosen for the Roman fort was retained as a stronghold for much of the medieval period, and both a castle and a priory were built within it. From the sixteenth century the defensive emphasis was on Portsmouth itself at the mouth of the harbour, though subsequently a ring of fortifications was built round the whole area, so that sites in and near Portsmouth now represent the entire history of coastal fortification from the third to the twentieth century.

A few small areas of the castle were investigated by the Ministry of Works earlier this century, and the ditches were cleared. An extensive programme of excavation, directed by Barry Cunliffe, from 1961 to 1979, investigated an area of some 3772 square metres (40,600 square feet) on the southern side of the outer bailey to the west of the medieval churchyard, together with other areas by the gates, inside the inner bailey of the castle and across the earthworks.

A small amount of mid-first century pottery was retrieved, probably from a temporary settlement, but no other evidence has been found for any activity on the site until the late third century, when the fort was constructed. On the evidence of coin finds, it has been suggested that this may have taken place in the reign of Carausius, perhaps between AD 286 and 290. Most probably the fort on the harbour was intended as a fleet base for clearing the Channel of pirates, in conjunction with a base on the Gallic shore; it is possibly the *Portus Adurni* of the Notitia Dignitatum.

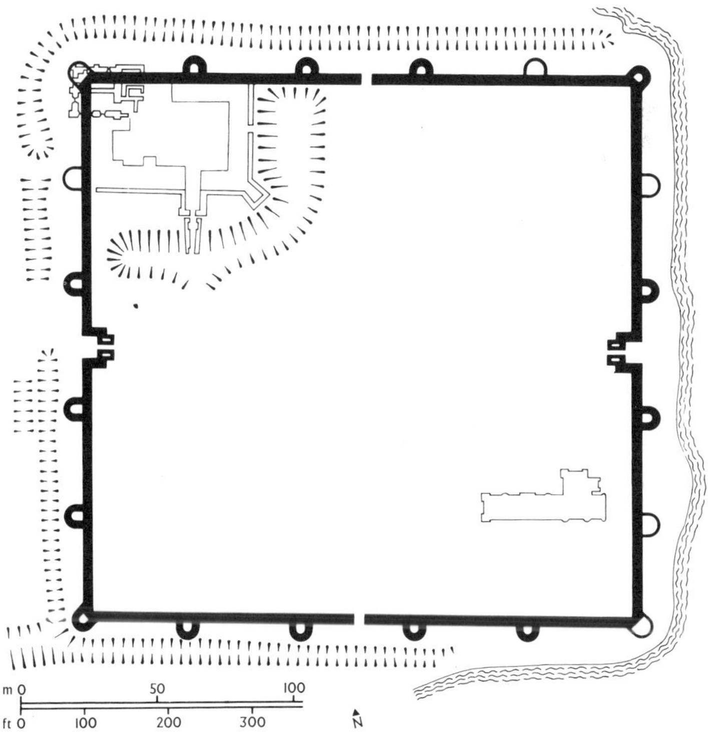

Fig. 58 Portchester Castle: Roman fort (in solid black) with medieval castle and church.

The defences

The fort (Fig. 58) measures 183 by 187.1 m, enclosing 3.43 hectares (8.48 acres), and is surrounded by a double ditch. The principal gates are in the centre of the east and west walls, and there were posterns (blocked in the Norman period) in the north and south walls. In addition to corner bastions, there were originally four projecting towers on each side of the fort: twelve survive. These are D-shaped and hollow, unlike those at Lympne and Pevensey. The walls were laid on a base raft of timber and flint, the timbers with cross-bracing as has also been found at Pevensey. They were 3.1 m (10 ft) wide above ground, constructed of flint and chalk in chalky mortar, with bonding courses of tile or limestone. The main gates were set back from the wall, in a courtyard formed by an inward turn of the fort walls, whilst the postern gates were simple arched openings.

Internal buildings and occupation
In the excavated area, traces of most buildings had been largely destroyed by later ploughing; there was, however, evidence for timber buildings laid out within a regular grid of streets. After the initial phase, there is little evidence for occupation in the last decade of the third century, though the fort was used in the first quarter of the fourth century, and more heavily down to 350, with some rebuilding of timber structures. This occupation continued to the end of the century, becoming less orderly after 365. Evidence of occupation takes the form of some 350 kg of pottery, 603 coins, numerous small objects and some 36,000 bone fragments. The army presence is clearly attested, as is the existence of civilian life, particularly from the burial of some 27 infants inside the fort, and finds of jewellery and women's shoes. Industrial activity is indicated by metal- and antler-working, along with weaving and spinning. Beef was important in the meat diet, to which peacocks, fowling and fishing added variety. Dogs and cats were living in the fort.

It is difficult to say whether a civilian population took over an abandoned fort, or whether a militia together with their families formed a continuing military garrison. Certainly the fort was occupied up to the end of Roman Britain and beyond.

Literature
Cunliffe 1975.

JULIAN MUNBY

BEAUPORT PARK

The role of the *classis Britannica* in the iron industry of the Weald of south-eastern Britain in the second and third centuries AD has been discussed in several papers (Cleere 1975; 1977; 1983). It is incontrovertible that it was intimately involved with the large-scale operations at a number of sites in the eastern part of the Weald, as evidenced by the large numbers of tiles bearing the CL BR stamp of the fleet (Brodribb 1969), although the precise nature of that involvement is uncertain.

Beauport Park is the largest of the sites known to have been associated with the fleet (Fig. 59). It was first investigated when a slag bank covering nearly 1 ha was quarried away in the nineteenth century for road metalling. Extensive fieldwork in the 1960s indicated that the whole establishment, which was undefended, extended over at least 5 ha, and it is conceivable, on the basis of a fragmentary inscription, that it may have been the headquarters of the *vilicus* responsible to the imperial procurator in charge of this mining region (Wright & Hassall 1971, 289).

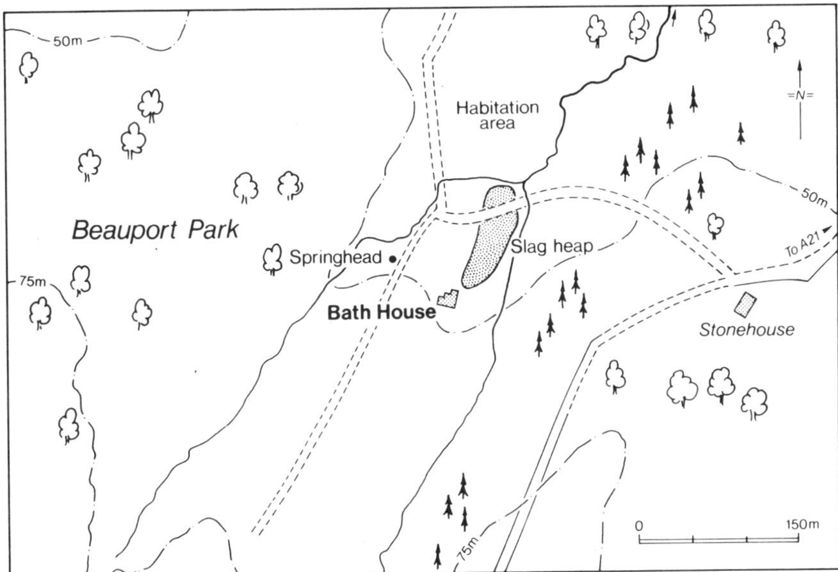

Fig. 59 Beauport Park: general plan of the bath-house area.

The only systematic excavation that has been carried out on the site was in the early 1970s when a well-built bath-house of military type was discovered when part of the site was being landscaped for a municipal golf-course. It was remarkably well preserved, with walls standing to over 2 m in several places. This was due to the fact that the bath-house had been built into part of the slag bank. A decade or so after the site was abandoned there was a catastrophic collapse of that part of the slag bank overlooking the bath-house, which was buried under two to three metres of debris.

Analysis of the structure (Fig. 60) shows that it comprised, in its initial phase (phase A), four rooms (a *frigidarium*, a *tepidarium*, and two *caldaria*) plus a cold plunge bath. After a short period of abandonment it was reconstructed with the addition of a second *caldarium* (or possibly *sudatorium*), an *apodyterium*, a second cold bath and a semicircular hot bath, and one of the original *caldaria* was converted into a second *tepidarium* (phase B.i). Following the collapse of the wall between the *praefurnium* and the *sudatorium*, a new *praefurnium* was built beyond the second cold bath, which was converted into a hot bath (phase B.ii).

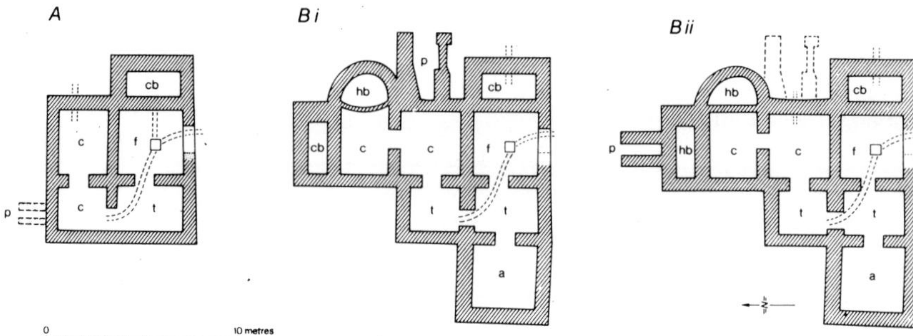

Fig. 60 Beauport Park: phasing of the bath-house.

The dating evidence suggests that the bath-house was built in the second quarter of the second century. The short period of abandonment seems to date from the closing years of that century, and phase B lasted until around the middle of the third century, on the basis of a coin of Decius.

Apart from a short 'squatter' episode, the site was never reoccupied. When the fleet pulled out of the Beauport Park establishment, reusable material, such as window-glass, lead pipe, the bronze *testudo* etc., was removed and the bath-house slowly disintegrated. The circumstances of its burial meant that it was not used as a source of building material in later periods, with the result that it has been possible, by careful measurement and analysis of all the building debris, to calculate its original dimensions with great accuracy - to carry out what the late Sir Ian Richmond once described as 'a quantity survey in reverse'. Meticulous scrutiny of the 12.8 tonnes of tile fragments revealed over 1600 CL BR stamps of the *classis Britannica*.

It is regrettable that this exceptionally well preserved Roman building is not accessible at the present time. The remains are protected by a substantial wooden cover and deep layers of clean sand, provided by the excavating group at their own expense. Negotiations have been in progress for over a decade with central and local government authorities, in the hope that the bath-house can be properly conserved, presented, and managed so that it can be visited by the general public, but no satisfactory solution has so far been devised.

Literature

Brodribb & Cleere 1988

HENRY CLEERE

Abbreviations

AE	*Année Épigraphique* (Paris).
CIL	ed. T. Mommsen *et al.*, *Corpus Inscriptionum Latinarum* (Berlin 1866 cont.).
ILS	ed. H. Dessau, *Inscriptiones Latinae Selectae* (Berlin 1892-1916).
P. Dura	C.B. Welles, R.O. Fink & J.F. Gilliam, *The Excavations at Dura Europos, Final Report V, part I: The Parchments and Papyri* (New Haven 1959).
RIB	R.G. Collingwood and R.P. Wright, *The Roman Inscriptions of Britain. Vol. I: Inscriptions on Stone* (Oxford 1965).
RIC	ed. H. Mattingly, E.A. Sydenham *et al.*, *Roman Imperial Coinage* (London 1923 cont.).

Bibliography

Ager, B. 1987 Late Roman Belt-fittings from Canterbury, *Archaeologia Cantiana* 104, 25-31.

Akeroyd, A.V. 1966 *Changes in relative land- and sea-level during the Postglacial in southern Britain with particular reference to the post-Mesolithic period*. Unpublished M.A. thesis, Institute of Archaeology, University of London.

Akeroyd, A.V. 1972 Archaeological and historical evidence for subsidence in southern Britain, *Philosophical Transactions of the Royal Society of London* A. 272, 151-69.

Alcock, L. 1971 *Arthur's Britain* (London).

Alcock, L. 1972 *'By South Cadbury is that Camelot...':the excavations of Cadbury Castle 1966-70* (London).

Aldsworth, F. 1978 The Droxford Anglo-Saxon cemetery, Soberton, Hampshire, *Proc. Hampshire Field Club* 35, 93-182.

Allen, R.H., Fordham, S.J., Hazelden, J., Moffat, A.J. & Sturdy, R.G. 1983 *Soils of England and Wales. Sheet 6. South-East England.* Scale 1:250,000. Soil Survey of England and Wales (Harpenden, Herts).

Applebaum, S. 1972 Roman Britain, in Finberg, H.P.R. ed., *The Agrarian History of England and Wales*, Vol. I, part II, 3-282.

Atkinson, D. 1933 Classis Britannica, in *Historical Essays in Honour of James Tait*. (Manchester), 1-11.

Aubrey, J. 1980 *Monumenta Britannica* (ed. Fowles, J. & Legg, R.).

Bakka, E. 1958 *On the Beginnings of Salin's Style I in England*. Universitet i Bergen Arbok.

Bakka, E. 1973 Goldbrakteatern in Norwegischen Grabfunden: Datierungsfragen, *Frühmittelalterliche Studien* 7, 35-87.

Bakka, E. 1981 Scandinavian-type gold bracteates in Kentish and continental grave finds, in Evison, V. ed. *Angles, Saxon and Jutes*, 11-38.

Bartholomew, P. 1984 Fourth-Century Saxons, *Britannia* 15, 168-86.

Battely, J. 1711 *Antiquitates Rutupinae* (Oxford).

Belot, E. & Vanbrugghe, N. 1981 Les enduits peints des casernes de la Classis Britannica à Boulogne-sur-Mer, *Septentrion* 11, 29-31

Bennett, P. 1978 Moat House, Rough Common, in 'Some Minor Excavations by the Canterbury Archaeological Trust in 1977-78', *Archaeologia Cantiana* 94, 158-64.

Bennett, P. 1980 Excavations at 68-69A Stour Street, *Archaeologia Cantiana* 96, 406-10.

Bennett, P. 1981 Excavations at Nos 68-69A Stour Street, *Archaeologia Cantiana* 97, 279-80.

Bennett, P. 1984 The Topography of Roman Canterbury, *Archaeologia Cantiana* 100, 52-3.

Bennett, P. forthcoming a Evaluation trenching and watching recording brief works undertaken in advance of construction in the grounds of Christ Church College, Canterbury.

Bennett, P. forthcoming b *Excavations in the Castle Street and Stour Street Areas*. The Archaeology of Canterbury vol. vi.

Bennett, P. forthcoming c Salvage Excavations at Linden Grove, *Archaeologia Cantiana* 105 for 1988.

Bennett, P., Frere, S.S. & Stow, S. 1982 *Excavations at Canterbury Castle*. The Archaeology of Canterbury, vol. i (Maidstone).

Bennett, P. & Houliston, M. forthcoming Excavations at Burgate, *Archaeologia Cantiana* 105.

Biddle, M. 1972 Winchester: the development of an early capital, in Jahnkuhn, H. *et al.* eds, *Vor-und Frühformen der Europäischen Stadt im Mittelalter*, 229-261.

Birley, A. 1981 *The Fasti of Roman Britain* (Oxford).

Blagg, T.F.C. 1984 Roman architectural ornament in Kent, *Archaeologia Cantiana* 100, 65-80.

Blockley, K. & Day, M. 1978 Excavations at 16 Watling Street, *Archaeologia Cantiana* 94, 273.

Blockley, P. 1986 Excavations at Ridingate, *Archaeologia Cantiana* 103, 205-9.

Blockley, P. 1987a Excavations at St John's Lane, Canterbury, *Archaeologia Cantiana* 104, 293-5.

Blockley, P. 1987b Excavations at St Mildred's Tannery, *Archaeologia Cantiana* 104, 314.

Blockley, P. *et al.* forthcoming *Excavations in the Marlowe Car Park and Surrounding Areas*. The Archaeology of Canterbury, vol. v.

Bloemers, J.H.F. & de Weerd, M.D. 1983 Het Romeinse Kampdorf van de Brittenburg, *Het Leidse Jaarboekje*, 245-51

Bloemers, J.H.F. & de Weerd, M.D. 1984 Van Brittenburg naar Lugdunum. Opgravingen in de bouwput van de nieuwe uitwateringssluis in Katwijk 1982, *De uitwateringssluizen van Katwijk 1404-1984*, 41-51 (Leiden).

Böhme, H.W. 1974 *Germanische Grabfunde des 4. bis 5. Jahrhunderts zwischen unterer Elbe und Loire*. Münchner Beiträge zur Vor- und Frühgeschichte 19.

Böhme, H.W. 1976 Das Land zwischen Elbe- und Wesermündung vom 4. bis 6. Jh, *Führer zu Vor- und Frühgeschichtlichen Denkmälern* 29, 205-225.

Böhme, H.W. 1986 Das Ende der Römerherrschaft in Britannien und die angelsächsische Besiedlung Englands im 5. Jahrhundert, *Jahrbuch des Römisch-Germanischen Zentralmuseums* 33, 469-574.

Brenot, C. 1974 Les monnaies romaines des fouilles d'Alet, *Les Dossiers du Centre Régionale d'Archéologie d'Alet* 2, 131-42.

Brodribb, G. 1969 Stamped tiles of the Classis Britannica, *Sussex Archaeological Collections* 107, 102-25.

Brodribb, G. & Cleere, H. 1988 The Classis Britannica bath-house at Beauport Park, East Sussex, *Britannia* 19, 217-74.

Brooks, D. 1988 The Case for Continuity in Fifth-century Canterbury Re-examined', *Oxford Journal of Archaeology* 7.1 (March 1988), 99-114.

Brulet, R. 1989 *La Gaule septentrionale au Bas-Empire. Occupation du sol et défense du territoire dans l'arrière-pays du Limes aux IVe et Ve siècles.* (Trier).

Burrin, P.J. 1981 Loess in the Weald, *Proceedings of the Geologists' Association* 92, 87-92.

Burrin, P.J. 1988 The Holocene floodplain and alluvial fill deposits of the Rother Valley and their bearing on the evolution of Romney Marsh, in Eddison, J. & Green, C. eds 1988, 31-52.

Bushe-Fox, J.P. 1926 *First report on the excavations of the Roman fort at Richborough, Kent*. Society of Antiquaries Research Report No. 6 (London).

Bushe-Fox, J.P. 1928 *Second report on the excavations of the Roman fort at Richborough, Kent*. Society of Antiquaries Research Report No. 7 (London).

Bushe-Fox, J.P. 1932a *Third report on the excavations of the Roman fort at Richborough, Kent*. Society of Antiquaries Research Report No. 10 (London).

Bushe-Fox, J.P. 1932b Some notes on Roman coast defences, *Journal of Roman Studies* 22, 60-71.

Bushe-Fox, J.P. 1949 *Fourth report on the excavations of the Roman fort at Richborough, Kent*. Society of Antiquaries Research Report No. 16 (London).

Camden, W. 1610 *Britannia* trans. P. Holland

Camden, W. 1695 *Britannia* ed. E. Gibson.

Catt, J.A. 1978 The contribution of loess to soils in lowland Britain, in Limbrey, S. & Evans, J. eds, *The effects of man on the landscape: the lowland zone* Council for British Archaeology Research Report No. 21 (London), 12-20.

Chadwick, S. 1958 The Anglo-Saxon cemetery at Finglesham, Kent:a reconsideration, *Medieval Archaeology* 2, 1-71.

Clayton, K.M. & Straw, A. 1979 *The geomorphology of the British Isles: eastern and central England* (London).

Cleere, H. 1970 *The Romano-British industrial site at Bardown, Wadhurst*. SussexArchaeological Society Occasional Paper No. 1.

Cleere, H. 1975 The Roman iron industry of the Weald and its connexions with the Classis Britannica, *Archaeological Journal* 131 for 1974, 171-99.

Cleere, H. 1976 Some operating parameters for Roman ironworks, *Institute of Archaeology Bulletin* 13, 233-46.

Cleere, H. 1977 The Classis Britannica, in Johnston, D. ed. 1977, 16-19.

Cleere, H. 1983 The organisation of the iron industry in the western Roman provinces in the Early Empire, with special reference to Britain, *Offa* 40, 103-14.

Cleere, H. & Crossley, D. 1985 *The iron industry of the Weald* (Leicester).

Coleman, A. 1952 Some aspects of the development of the Lower Stour, Kent, *Proceedings of the Geologists' Association* 63, 63-86.

Cook, A.M. & Dacre, M.W. 1985 *Excavations at Portway Andover 1973-1975*. Oxford University Committee for Archaeology Monograph 4 (Oxford).

Crummy, P. 1981 *Aspects of Anglo-Saxon and Norman Colchester*. Council for British Archaeology Research Report 39 (London).

Cunliffe, B.W. 1968 The British Fleet, in Cunliffe, B.W. ed. 1968, 255-71.

Cunliffe, B.W. 1975 *Excavations at Portchester Castle. Vol. I: Roman*. Society of Antiquaries Research Report No. 32 (London).

Cunliffe, B.W. 1976 *Excavations at Portchester Castle, II: Saxon*. Society of Antiquaries Research Report No. 33 (London).

Cunliffe, B.W. 1980a The evolution of Romney Marsh: a preliminary statement, in Thompson, F.H. ed. 1980, 37-54.

Cunliffe, B.W. 1980b Excavations at the Roman Fort at Lympne, Kent 1976-78, *Britannia* 11, 227-88.

Cunliffe, B.W. 1988 Romney Marsh in the Roman period, in Eddison, J. & Green, C. eds 1988, 83-89.

Cunliffe, B.W. ed. 1968 *Fifth report on the excavations of the Roman fort at Richborough, Kent*. Society of Antiquaries Research Report No. 23 (London).

D'Olier, B. 1972 Subsidence and sea-level rise in the Thames estuary, *Philosophical Transactions of the Royal Society of London*, A. 272, 121-30.

Day, M. 1979 Research and Discoveries, 35 St Margaret's Street, *Archaeologia Cantiana* 95, 275-76.

de Melker, B.R. 1987 *De ontwikkeling van de stad Aardenburg en haar bestuurlikje instellingen in de Middeleeuwen* (Middelburg).

de Vries, D. 1968 The early history of Aardenburg to 1200, *Berichten van de Rijksdienst voor het Oudheidkundig Bodemonderzoek* 18, 227-9.

de Weerd, M.D. 1986 Recent Excavations near the Brittenburg: a rearrangement of old evidence, in Unz, C. ed., *Studien zu den Militärgrenzen Roms III* (Stuttgart), 284-91.

Degrassi, A. 1951 *I fasti consolari dell'impero romano dal 30 a.C. al 613 d.C.* (Rome).

Delmaire, R. 1978 Une nouvelle inscription latine à Boulogne-sur-Mer, *Septentrion* 8, 25-8.

Detsicas, A. 1983 *The Cantiaci* (Gloucester).

Devoy, R.J. 1979 Flandrian sea-level changes and vegetational history of the Lower Thames Estuary, *Philosophical Transactions of the Royal Society of London*, B.285, 355-407.

Devoy, R.J. 1980 Post-glacial environmental change and Man in the Thames Estuary: a synopsis, in Thompson, F.H. ed. 1980, 134-48.

Domaszewski, A.v. 1908 *Die Rangordnung des römischen Heeres*. 2nd ed. B. Dobson (Cologne 1967).

Dore, J.N. & Gillam, J.P. 1979 *The Roman Fort at South Shields. Excavations 1875-1975* (Newcastle).

Driver, J. & Rady, J. forthcoming *Excavations in the Cathedral Precincts II: Meister Omer's, Linacre Garden and St Gabriel's Chapel*. The Archaeology of Canterbury, vol. iv.

Dumville, D.N. 1974 Some aspects of the chronology of the *Historia Britonnum*, *Bulletin of the Board of Celtic Studies* 25, 439-445.

Dumville, D.N. 1977 Sub-Roman Britain: history and legend, *History* 62, 173-192.

Dumville, D.N. 1984 The chronology of the *De Excidio Britanniae*, Book I, in Lapidge, M. & Dumville, D. eds, *Gildas: New Approaches*, 61-84.

Eddison, J. & Green, C. eds 1988 *Romney Marsh: evolution, occupation, reclamation*. Oxford University Committee for Archaeology Monograph 24 (Oxford).

Edwards, D.A. & Green, C.J.S. 1977 The Saxon Shore fort and settlement at Brancaster, Norfolk, in Johnston, D.E. ed. 1977, 21-29.

Ennever, C.C. & Tebbutt, C.F. 1977 An aid to Ashburnham navigation, *Wealden Iron* 11, 14.

Everard, C.E. 1980 On sea-level changes, in Thompson, F.H. ed. 1980, 1-23.

Evison, V.I. 1965 *The Fifth Century Invasions South of the Thames* (London).

Evison, V.I. 1968 Quoit Brooch Style buckles, *Antiquaries Journal* 48, 231-248.

Evison, V.I. 1977 Supporting-arm brooches and Equal-arm brooches in England, in Hässler, H.J. ed., *Studien zur Sachsenforschung* , 127- 47.

Evison, V.I. 1981 Distribution maps and England in the first two phases, in Evison, V.I. ed., *Angles, Saxons and Jutes*, 126-167.

Evison, V.I. 1988 *An Anglo-Saxon Cemetery at Alton, Hampshire.* Hampshire Field Club Monograph 4.

Fox, G.E. 1911 Romano-British Suffolk, in Page, W. ed., *The Victoria History of the County of Suffolk* (London), Vol. I, 279-323.

Frere, S.S. 1966 The end of towns in Roman Britain, in Wacher, J.S. ed., *Civitas Capitals of Roman Britain*, 87-100.

Frere, S.S. 1970 The Roman Theatre at Canterbury, *Britannia* 1, 83-112.

Frere, S.S. 1984 Canterbury: The Post-war Excavations, *Archaeologia Cantiana* 100, 29-46.

Frere, S.S., Bennett, P., Rady, J. & Stow, S. 1987 *Canterbury Excavations: Intra- and Extra-Mural sites, 1949-55 and 1980-84*, The Archaeology of Canterbury, vol. viii (Maidstone).

Frere, S.S. & Stow, S. 1983 *Excavations in the St George's Street and Burgate Street Areas*. The Archaeology of Canterbury, vol. vii (Maidstone).

Frere, S.S., Stow, S. & Bennett, P. 1982 *Excavations on the Roman and Medieval Defences of Canterbury*, The Archaeology of Canterbury, vol. ii (Maidstone).

Funnell, B.M. & Pearson, I. 1984 A guide to the Holocene geology of north Norfolk, *Bulletin of the Geological Society of Norfolk* 34, 123-40.

Galliou, P. 1980 Le défense de l'Armorique au Bas-Empire, *Mémoires de la Société d'Histoire et d'Archéologie de Bretagne* 57, 235-85.

Gibson, M. & Wright, S.M. 1988 *Joseph Mayer of Liverpool 1803-1886*. Society of Antiquaries Occasional Paper 11 (London).

Gilliam, J.F. 1941 The Dux Ripae at Dura, *Transactions and Proceedings of the American Philological Association* 72, 157-175 (= *Mavors II. Roman Army Papers* (Amsterdam 1986), 23-41.

Goodburn, R. & Bartholomew, P. eds 1976 *Aspects of the Notitia Dignitatum*. British Archaeological Reports S-15 (Oxford).

Goodsall, R.H. 1981 *The Kentish Stour* (Rochester).

Gosselin, J.-Y. & Seillier, Cl. 1978 Fouilles de la rue de Lille à Boulogne-sur-Mer. Vestiges gallo-romaines et médiévaux, *Septentrion* 8, 50-57.

Gosselin, J.-Y. & Seillier, Cl. 1981 Fouilles de Boulogne-sur-Mer. Campagnes 1980-1982, *Septentrion* 11, 19-20.

Gosselin, J.-Y., Seillier, Cl., Florin, B. & Leduc, M. 1978 Fouilles de sauvetage du camp de la flotte de Bretagne à Boulogne-sur-Mer (Pas-de-Calais), *Septentrion* 8, 18-22.

Gosselin, J.-Y., Seillier, Cl. & Leclercq, P. 1976 Boulogne antique. Essai de topographie urbaine, *Septentrion* 6, 5-15.

Green, C. 1961 East Anglian coastline level since Roman times, *Antiquity* 35, 21-28.

Green, C. & Hutchinson, J. 1965 Relative land and sea levels at Great Yarmouth, Norfolk, *Geographical Journal* 131, 86-90.

Green, R.D. 1968 *Soils of Romney Marsh. Bulletin 4, Soil Survey of Great Britain* (Harpenden, Herts).

Grimes, W.F. 1968 *The excavation of Roman and Medieval London* (London)
Groenman-van Waateringe, W. 1986 The Horrea of Valkenburg ZH, in Unz, C. ed., *Studien zu den Militärgrenzen Roms III* (Stuttgart), 159-68.

Hall, J. & Merrifield, R. 1986 *Roman London* (London).
Hardman, F.W. & Stebbing, W.P.D. 1940 Stonar and the Wantsum Channel, *Archaeologia Cantiana* 53, 62-80.
Harrison, K. 1976 *The Framework of Anglo-Saxon History to AD 900* (Cambridge).
Harrod, H. 1859 Notice of excavations made at Burgh Castle, Suffolk, in the years 1850 and 1855, *Norfolk Archaeology* 5, 146-60.
Haseloff, G. 1974 Salin's Style I, *Medieval Archaeology* 18, 1-15.
Haseloff, G. 1981 *Die germanische Tierornamentik der Völkerwanderungszeit.*
Haverfield, F. 1924 Roman Britain, a retrospect, in Macdonald, G. ed., *The Roman Occupation of Britain* (Oxford), 59-88.
Hawkes, C.F.C. 1956 The Jutes of Kent, *Dark Age Britain: Studies presented to E.T. Leeds*, 91-111.
Hawkes, S.C. 1968 The physical geography of Richborough, in Cunliffe, B.W. ed. 1968, 224-30.
Hawkes, S.C. 1969 Early Anglo-Saxon Kent, *Archaeological Journal* 126, 186-192.
Hawkes, S.C. 1973 A Late Roman Buckle from Tripontium, *Transactions of the Birmingham and Warwickshire Archaeological Society* 85, 145-189.
Hawkes, S.C. 1974a Some recent finds of Late Roman buckles, *Britannia* 5, 386-93.
Hawkes, S.C. 1974b British Antiquity 1973-4: Post-Roman and pagan Anglo-Saxon, *Archaeological Journal* 131, 408-423.
Hawkes, S.C. 1982 Anglo-Saxon Kent *c.* 425-725', *Archaeology in Kent to AD 1500.* Council for British Archaeology Research Report 48, 64-78.
Hawkes, S.C. 1986 The early Saxon Period, in Briggs, G. et al eds, *The Archaeology of the Oxford Region*, 64-108.
Hawkes, S.C. & Dunning, G.C. 1961 Soldiers and settlers in Britain, fourth to fifth century, *Medieval Archaeology* 5, 1-70.
Hawkes, S.C. & Dunning, G.C. 1962-3 Krieger und Siedler in Britannien während des 4. und 5. Jahrhunderts, *43-44 Bericht der Römisch-Germanischen Kommission*, 155-231.
Hawkes, S.C. & Pollard, M. 1981 The gold bracteates from sixth- century graves in Kent, *Frühmittelalterliche Studien* 15, 316-70.
Heliot, P. 1958 Sur la topographie antique et les origines chrétiennes de Boulogne-sur-Mer, *Revue Archéologique* I, II.
Heurgon, J. 1948 Les problèmes de Boulogne, *Revue des Études Anciennes* 50.
Heurgon, J. 1949 *De Gesoriacum à Bononia.* Collection Latomus II.
Hill, C., Millett, M. & Blagg, T. 1980 *The Roman riverside wall and monumental arch in London.* London and Middlesex Archaeological Society Special Paper No. 3 (London).
Hinchliffe, J. & Green, C.J.S. 1985 *Excavations at Brancaster 1974 and 1977.* East Anglian Archaeology 23 (Dereham).

Hines, J. 1984 *The Scandinavian Character of Anglian England in the pre-Viking Period.* British Archaeological Reports 124 (Oxford).

Horsley, J. 1732 *Britannia Romana* (London).

Hull, M.R. 1963 Bradwell, in Powell, W.R. ed., *The Victoria History of the County of Essex* (London) Vol. 3, 52-55.

Hutchinson, J.N. 1988 Recent geotechnical, geomorphological and archaeological investigations of the abandoned cliff backing Romney Marsh at Lympne, Kent, in Eddison, J. & Green, C. eds 1988, 88-89.

Jackson, K. 1958 The site of Mount Badon, *Journal of Celtic Studies* 2, 152-5.

Jarrett, M.G. 1976 *Maryport, Cumbria: a Roman fort and its garrison*. Cumberland and Westmorland Antiquarian and Archaeological Society Extra Series 23 (Kendal).

Jelgersma, S. 1961 *Holocene sea-level changes in the Netherlands.* Mededeelingen Geologische Stichting Serie C-VI, no.7.

Jenkins, F. 1958 *Archaeological Newsletter* 6, no. 5 (1958), 126-7.

Jenkins, F. 1960 Two Pottery Kilns and a Tilery of the Roman Period at Canterbury (*Durovernum Cantiacorum*), *Archaeologia Cantiana* 74, 151-61.

Jenkins, F. & Boyle, J. 1951 *Archaeological Newsletter* 3, no. 9 (March 1951), 145-147.

Jenkins, F. & Boyle, J. 1952 *Archaeological Newsletter* 4, no. 10 (August-December, 1952), 157-159.

Johns, C.M. & Potter, T.W. 1985 The Canterbury Late Roman Treasure, *Antiquaries Journal* 65, 312-52.

Johnson, S. 1970 The construction date of the Saxon Shore fort at Richborough, *Britannia* 1, 240-8.

Johnson, S. 1976 *The Roman Forts of the Saxon Shore* (London).

Johnson, S. 1980 A later Roman helmet from Burgh Castle, *Britannia* 11, 303-12.

Johnson, S. 1981 The construction of the Saxon Shore fort at Richborough, in Detsicas, A. ed., *Collectanea Historica*: Essays in memory of Stuart Rigold (Maidstone).

Johnson, S. 1983a *Late Roman Fortifications* (London).

Johnson, S. 1983b *Burgh Castle: excavations by Charles Green, 1958-61*. East Anglian Archaeology 20 (Dereham).

Johnston, D.E. ed. 1977 *The Saxon Shore*. Council for British Archaeology Research Report No. 18 (London).

Jones, A.H.M. 1964 *The Later Roman Empire 284-602* (Oxford).

Jones, D.K.C. 1981 *The geomorphology of the British Isles: southeast and southern England* (London).

Jones, M.E. & Casey, P.J. 1988 The Gallic Chronicle restored: a chronology for the Anglo-Saxon invasion and the end of Roman Britain, *Britannia* 19, 367-98.

Kent, J.P.C., Tatton-Brown, T. & Welch, M. 1983 A Visigothic gold tremissis and a fifth-century firesteel from the Marlowe Theatre site, Canterbury, *Antiquaries Journal* 63, 371-3.

Kerlouégan, F. 1968 Le Latin du *De Excidio Britanniae* de Gildas, in Barley, M.W. & Hanson, R.P.C. eds, *Christianity in Britain 300-700*, 151-176.

Kidd, D. 1976 Review of Myres & Southern 1973, *Medieval Archaeology* 20, 202-204.

Kienast, D. 1966 *Untersuchungen zu den Kriegsflotten des römischen Kaiserzeit* (Bonn).

Kirk, J.R. & Leeds, E.T. 1954 Three early Saxon graves from Dorchester, Oxon, *Oxoniensia* 17-18, 63-76.

Lambert, J.M. & Jennings, J.N. 1960 *The making of the Broads: a reconsideration of their origin in the light of new evidence*. Royal Geographical Society Research Series 3 (London).

Langouët, L. 1974 L'histoire d'Alet à la lumière des récentes fouilles, *Les Dossiers du Centre Régional d'Archéologie d'Alet* 2, 3-5.

Langouët, L. 1976 Alet. Ville ancienne, *Les Dossiers du Centre Régional d'Archéologie d'Alet* 4, 57-81.

Langouët, L. 1977 The 4th century Gallo-Roman site at Alet (Saint-Malo), in Johnston, D. ed. 1977, 38-45.

Langouët, L. 1983 Les fouilles archéologiques du bastion de Solidor, Saint-Malo, *Les Dossiers du Centre Régional d'Archéologie d'Alet.*

Langouët, L. 1987 Les fouilles archéologiques de la zone des cathédrales d'Alet (Saint-Malo), *Les Dossiers du Centre Régional d'Archéologie d'Alet.*

Langouët, L. 1988 Les Coriosolites. Un peuple armoricain, *Supplément aux Dossiers du Centre Régional d'Alet.*

Langouët, L. & Josseaume, G. 1979 Où se situait le castellum de Constantia mentionné dans la Notitia Dignitatum ?, *Les Dossiers du Centre Régional d'Archéologie d'Alet* 7, 3-9.

Le Bourdelles, H. 1988 Boulogne antique: Gesoriacum et Bononia, *Revue du Nord* 70, No. 276, 77-82.

Lebon, C. 1984 The Roman Ford at Iden Green, Benenden, *Archaeologia Cantiana* 101, 69-81.

Leland, J. 1907 *The Itinerary of John Leland in or about the Years 1535-1543*, Vol. IV, ed. Lucy Toulmin Smith (London).

Leman, P. 1981 Contribution à la localisation de Quentovic ou la relance d'un vieux débat, *Revue du Nord* 63, No. 251, 935-45.

Lemmon, C.H. & Hill, J.D. 1966 The Romano-British site at Bodiam, *Sussex Archaeological Collections* 104, 88-102.

Levalet, D. 1982 Un élément du Litus Saxonicum dans la région d'Avranches, *Recueil d'études offert en hommage au doyen Michel de Boüard II* (Caen), 361-75.

Mann, J.C. 1976 What was the Notitia Dignitatum for ?, in Goodburn, R. & Bartholomew, P. eds, 1-10.

Mann, J.C. 1977a Duces and comites in the 4th century, in Johnston, D.E. ed. 1977, 11-15.

Mann, J.C. 1977b The Reculver inscription - a note, in Johnston, D.E. ed. 1977, 15.

Mann, J.C. 1979 Power, force and the frontiers of the Empire. A review article of E.N. Luttwak, The Grand Strategy of the Roman Empire from the first century AD to the third, *Journal of Roman Studies* 69, 175-83.

Marsden, P. 1980 *Roman London* (London).

May, V.J. 1966 A preliminary study of recent coastal change and sea defences in South East England, *Southampton Research Series in Geography* 3, 3-24.

Mazo-Karras, R. 1985 Seventh-century jewellery from Frisia: a re-examination, *Anglo-Saxon Studies in Archaeology and History* 4, 159-177.

Merrifield, R. 1965 *The Roman City of London* (London).

Merrifield, R. 1983 *London: City of the Romans* (London).

Mertens, J. 1962 Oudenburg et le Litus Saxonicum en Belgique, *Helinium* 2, 51-62.

Mertens, J. 1978 Het Laat-Romeins castellum te Oudenburg, *Archaeologia Belgica* 206, 73-6.

Mertens, J. 1987 Oudenburg Romeinse Legerbasis aan de Nordzeekust, *Archaeologicum Belgii Speculum* 4.

Mertens, J. & van Impe, L. 1971 Het Laat-Romeins grafveld van Oudenburg, *Archaeologia Belgica* 135.

Miller, M. 1975a Relative and absolute publication dates of Gildas's De Excidio in Medieval scholarship, *Bulletin of the Board of Celtic Studies* 26, 169-174.

Miller, M. 1975b Bede's use of Gildas, *English Historical Review* 355, 241-61.

Mitard, P.H. 1974 Le céramique du IVe siècle ornée à la molette d'Alet (Saint-Malo, Ille et Vilaine), *Les Dossiers du Centre Régional d'Archéologie d'Alet* 2, 42-8.

Morris, A.J. 1947 The Roman Saxon Shore fort at Burgh Castle, *Proceedings of the Suffolk Institute of Archaeology* 24, 100-20.

Morris, A.J. & Hawkes, C.F.C. 1949 The fort of the Saxon Shore at Burgh Castle, Suffolk, *Archaeological Journal* 106, 66-69.

Morris, J. 1965 Dark Age Dates', in Jarrett, M.G. & Dobson, B. eds, *Britain and Rome: Essays presented to E. Birley*, 145-85.

Munby, J.T. 1977 Art, archaeology and antiquaries, in Munby, J. & Henig, M. eds, *Roman Life and Art in Britain*. British Archaeological Report 41 (Oxford).

Myres, J.N.L. 1946 The coming of the Saxons, *New English Review* 13, 271-282.

Myres, J.N.L. 1951 The Adventus Saxonum, in Grimes, W.F. ed., *Aspects of Archaeology in Britain and Beyond: Essays presented to O.G.S. Crawford*, 221-41.

Myres, J.N.L. 1960 Pelagius and the end of Roman rule in Britain, *Journal of Roman Studies* 50, 21- 36.

Myres, J.N.L. 1969 *Anglo-Saxon Pottery and the Settlement of England* (Oxford).

Myres, J.N.L. 1970 The Angles, the Saxons and the Jutes, *Proceedings of the British Academy* 56, 3-32.

Myres, J.N.L. 1986 *The English Settlements* (Oxford).

Myres, J.N.L. & Green, B. 1973 *The Anglo-Saxon Cemeteries of Caistor-by-Norwich and Markshall, Norfolk*. Society of Antiquaries Research Report No. 30 (London).

Myres, J.N.L. & Southern, W.H. 1973 *The Anglo-Saxon Cremation Cemetery at Sancton, East Yorkshire*. Hull Museum Publication 218.

Ordnance Survey 1983 *Londinium. A descriptive map and guide to Roman London* (2nd ed.).

Painter, K.S. 1965 A Roman silver treasure from Canterbury, *Journal of the British Archaeological Association* 28 (1965), 1-14.

Pape, L. 1978 *La civitas des Osismes à l'époque gallo-romaine* (Paris).

Peacock, D.P.S. 1973 Forged brick-stamps from Pevensey, *Antiquity* xlvii, no. 186, June 1973, 138-40.

Pflaum, H.-G. 1960-1 *Les carrières procuratoriennes équestres sous le Haut-Empire romaine* (Paris).

Philp, B. 1959 Reculver: excavations on the Roman fort in 1957, *Archaeologia Cantiana* 73, 96-115.

Philp, B. 1969 *The Roman fort at Reculver* (West Wickham).

Philp, B. 1981 *The excavations of the Roman forts of the Classis Britannica at Dover, 1970-1977.* Kent Monograph Series 3 (Dover).

Piggott, S. 1976 *Ruins in a Landscape* (Edinburgh).

Piggott, S. 1985 *William Stukeley, an Eighteenth-century Antiquary* (2nd ed. London).

Piton, D. 1985 La céramique sigillée découverte à Etaples, *Les Cahiers de Quentovic* 10.

Plettke, A. 1921 *Ursprung und Ausbreitung der Angeln und Sachsen.* Die Urnenfriedhöfe in Niedersachsen Band 3.

Rady, J. 1987 Excavations at Nos 36-7 Stour Street, *Archaeologia Cantiana* 104 (1987), 300-3.

Rahtz, P.A. 1958 Dover: Stembrook and St Martin-le-Grand 1956, *Archaeologia Cantiana* 72, 111-37.

RCHM 1923 Bradwell, in *Essex IV (South East)*, 13-14.

Reddé, M. 1986 *Mare Nostrum*. Mélanges de l'École français de Rome No. 260 (Paris).

Reichstein, J. 1975 *Die Kreuzförmige Fibel: Zur Chronologie der späten römischen Kaiserzeit und der Völkerwanderungszeit in Skandinavien, auf dem Kontinent und in England*. Offa-Bücher Band 15.

Richmond, I.A. 1961 A new building inscription from the Saxon Shore fort at Reculver, Kent, *Antiquaries Journal* 41, 224-28.

Rigold, S.E. 1972 Roman Folkestone reconsidered, *Archaeologia Cantiana* 87, 31-42.

Roach Smith, C. 1850 *The Antiquities of Richborough, Reculver and Lympne in Kent* (London).

Roach Smith, C. 1852 *Report on Excavations made on the site of the Roman Castrum at Lympne in Kent in 1850* (London).

Roach Smith, C. 1858 *Report on excavations made upon the site of the Roman castrum at Pevensey in Sussex in 1852* (London).

Robinson, A.H.W. & Cloet, R.L. 1953 Coastal evolution at Sandwich Bay, *Proceedings of the Geologists' Association* 64, 69-82.

Robinson, D.A. & Williams, R.B.G. 1983 The Sussex coast past and present, in The Geography Editorial Committee, University of Sussex, *Sussex: environment, landscape and society* Chap 3, 50-66.

Rodwell, W. & Rowley, T. 1975 *Small Towns of Roman Britain*. British Archaeological Reports British Series 15 (Oxford).

Roe, D. 1981 *The Lower and Middle Palaeolithic in Britain* (London).

Romeinen 1987 *De Romeinen langs de Vlaamse Kust: Catalogue d'exposition.*

Salzmann, L.F. 1907 Excavations at Pevensey, 1906-7, *Sussex Archaeological Collections* 51, 99-114.

Salzmann, L.F. 1908 Excavations at Pevensey 1908-9, *Sussex Archaeological Collections* 52, 83-95.

Sanquer, R. 1972 Chronique d'archéologie antique et médiévale, *Bulletin de la Société Archéologique Française* 98, 43-53.

Sanquer, R. 1977 The castellum at Brest, in Johnston, D. ed. 1977, 45-50.

Sanquer, R. 1978 Nantes antique, *Archéologie en Bretagne* 17, 1-44.

Schmid, P. 1976 Review of Myres and Green 1973, *Germania* 54, 523-527.

Schmid, P. 1977 Zur chronologischen Auswertung von Siedlungsfunden des 4. bis 5. Jahrhunderts n. Chr. zwischen Elbe und Weser, in Kossack, G. & Reichstein, J. eds, *Archäologische Beiträge zur Chronologie der Völkerwanderungszeit*. Antiquitas III, Band 20.

Seillier, C. 1977 The Gallic evidence, Boulogne and coastal defences in the 4th and 5th centuries, in Johnston, D. ed. 1977, 35-38.

Seillier, C. 1984 Les enceintes romaines de Boulogne-sur-Mer, *Revue du Nord* 66, No. 260, 169-80.

Seillier, C. 1986 Boulogne, base navale romaine, *Revue du Nord*, No. 1 spécial hors série - collection Histoire, 163-78.

Seillier, C. 1987 Les cimitières romains tardifs du Pas-de-Calais, *Mémoires de la Commission départementale d'histoire et d'archéologie du Pas-de-Calais* 25, 15-26.

Seillier, C. & Gosselin, J.-Y. 1969 Nouvelles estampilles de la Flotte de Bretagne en provenance de Boulogne-sur-Mer, *Revue du Nord* 202, 363-72.

Seillier, C. & Gosselin, J.-Y. 1973 La flotte de Bretagne à Boulogne-sur-Mer, *Septentrion* 3, 55-6.

Seillier, C. & Gosselin, J.-Y. 1975 Les substructions antiques du château des comtes à Boulogne, *Septentrion* 5, 71.

Seillier, C., Gosselin, J.-Y., Leclercq, P. & Piton, D. 1971 Fouille de Boulogne-sur-Mer (Bononia). Rapport préliminaire, *Revue du Nord* 211, 669-79.

Sennequier, G. & Tuffreau-Libre, M. 1977 Le cimitière gallo-romain à inhumations (Bas-Empire) du château d'Etaples (Pas-de-Calais), *Latomus* 36, 933-41.

So, C.L. 1965 Coastal platforms of the Isle of Thanet, Kent, *Transactions of the Institute of British Geographers* 37, 147-56.

So, C.L. 1966 Some coastal changes between Whitstable and Reculver, Kent, *Proceedings of the Geologists' Association* 77, 475-90.

So, L.C. 1971 Early coastal recession around Reculver, *Archaeologia Cantiana* 86, 93-97.

Somner, W. 1693 *The Ports and Forts of Kent*, ed. E. Gibson (Oxford).

Souquet, G. 1865 Rapport sur les fouilles faites au château d'Etaples en 1864, *Bulletin Commission Départmentale des Antiquités Historiques* 2, 270-4.

St Joseph, J.K. 1936 The Roman fort at Brancaster, *Antiquaries Journal* 16, 444-60.

Starr, C.G. 1960 *The Roman Imperial navy, 31 BC - AD 324* (New York).

Steers, J.A. 1964 *The coastline of England and Wales* 2nd ed. (Cambridge).

Stevens, C.E. 1941a The British sections of the Notitia Dignitatum, *Archaeological Journal* 97 for 1940, 125-54.

Stevens, C.E. 1941b Gildas Sapiens, *English Historical Review* 223, 353-373.

Stukeley, W. 1776 *Itinerarium Curiosum* 2nd ed. (London).

Swanton, M.J. 1973 *The Spearheads of the Anglo-Saxon Settlements* (London).

Tatton-Brown, T. 1984 The Towns of Kent, in Haslam, J. ed., *Anglo-Saxon Towns in Southern England*, 1-36.

Taylor, M.V. 1944 Roman Britain in 1943. I. Sites explored, *Journal of Roman Studies* 34, 76-85.

Thompson, E.A. 1979 Gildas and the history of Britain, *Britannia* 10, 203-26.

Thompson, F.H. ed. 1980 *Archaeology and Coastal Change*. Society of Antiquaries of London Occasional Paper (New Series) 1 (London).

Tooley, M.J. & Switsur, R. 1988 Water level changes and sedimentation during the Flandrian Age in the Romney Marsh area, in Eddison, J. & Green, C. eds 1988, 53-71.

Trimpe-Burger, J.A. 1985 Aardenburg-Rodanburg-Burg aan de Rudannâ, *Naamkunde* 17, 335-46.

Wacher, J. 1969 *Excavations at Brough-on-Humber, 1958-61*. Society of Antiquaries Research Report No. 25 (London).

Wacher, J. 1975 *The towns of Roman Britain* (London).

Welch, M.G. 1971 Romans and Saxons in Sussex, *Britannia* 2, 232-7.

Welch, M.G. 1975 Mitcham grave 205 and the chronology of applied brooches with floriate cross decoration, *Antiquaries Journal* 55, 86-93.

Welch, M.G. 1976 *Highdown and its Saxon Cemetery*. Worthing Museum and Art Gallery Publication 11.

Welch, M.G. 1983 *Early Anglo-Saxon Sussex*. British Archaeological Reports 112 (Oxford 2 vols).

West, R.G. 1972 Relative land-sea-level changes in southeastern England during the Pleistocene, *Philosophical Transactions of the Royal Society of London*, A.272, 87-98.

West, S. 1985 *West Stow. The Anglo-Saxon Village*. East Anglian Archaeology Report 24.

Wheeler, R.E.M. 1929 The Roman lighthouses of Dover, *Archaeological Journal* 86, 47-58.

White, D.A. 1961 *Litus Saxonicum* (Wisconsin).

White, H.O. 1928 *The geology of the country near Ramsgate and Dover*. Memoir of the Geological Survey of England and Wales (London).

Wilkes, J.J. 1969 *Dalmatia* (London)

Will, E. 1960 Les remparts romains de Boulogne-sur-Mer, *Revue du Nord* 42, No. 168.

Williams, A. & Frere, S.S. 1948 Canterbury Excavations, Christmas 1945 and Easter 1946, *Archaeologia Cantiana* 61, 1-45.

Winterbottom, M. 1974-5 The Preface of Gildas's *De Excidio*, *Transactions of the Honourable Society of Cymmrodorion*, 277-287.

Wood, I. 1987 The fall of the Western Empire and the end of Roman Britain, *Britannia* 18, 251-62.

Wright, R.P. & Hassall, M.W.C. 1971 Roman Britain in 1970: II. Inscriptions, *Britannia* 2, 289-304.

Wright, T. 1845 *The Archaeological Album* (London).

Youngs, S.M., Clark, J. & Barry, T. 1985 Medieval Britain and Ireland in 1984, *Medieval Archaeology* 29, 158-230.

Ypey, J. 1969 Zur tragweise frühfränkischer Gürtelgarnituren auf Grund niederländischer Befunde, *Rijksdienst voor het Oudheidkundig Bodemonderzoek* 19, 89-127.